THE SURROGA

FLESH

TES
AND BONE

CREATED AND WRITTEN BY
ROBERT VENDITTI

ILLUSTRATED AND COLORED BY
BRETT WELDELE

EDITED BY
CHRIS STAROS

BOOK DESIGN BY
JIM TITUS

The Surrogates:
Flesh and Bone © and ™
2009 Robert Venditti.

Editorial Cartoon on page 33
© Mike Luckovich (used with permission).

Published by Top Shelf Productions,
PO Box 1282, Marietta, GA 30061-1282, USA.

Publishers: Chris Staros and Brett Warnock.
Top Shelf Productions®
and the Top Shelf logo are registered
trademarks of Top Shelf Productions, Inc.
All Rights Reserved. No part of this publication
may be reproduced without permission,
except for small excerpts for purposes of review.

First Printing, July 2009.
Printed in China.

Visit our online catalog at
www.topshelfcomix.com.

ISBN 978-1-60309-018-6
1. Graphic Novels
2. Science Fiction

chapter
ONE

Fuel

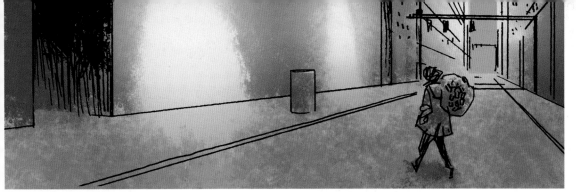

MAN, THAT'S THE *SICKEST* THING I'VE EVER SEEN--

--EVEN FOR A *BONER*.

DUDE, HOW DO PEOPLE *LIVE* LIKE THAT?

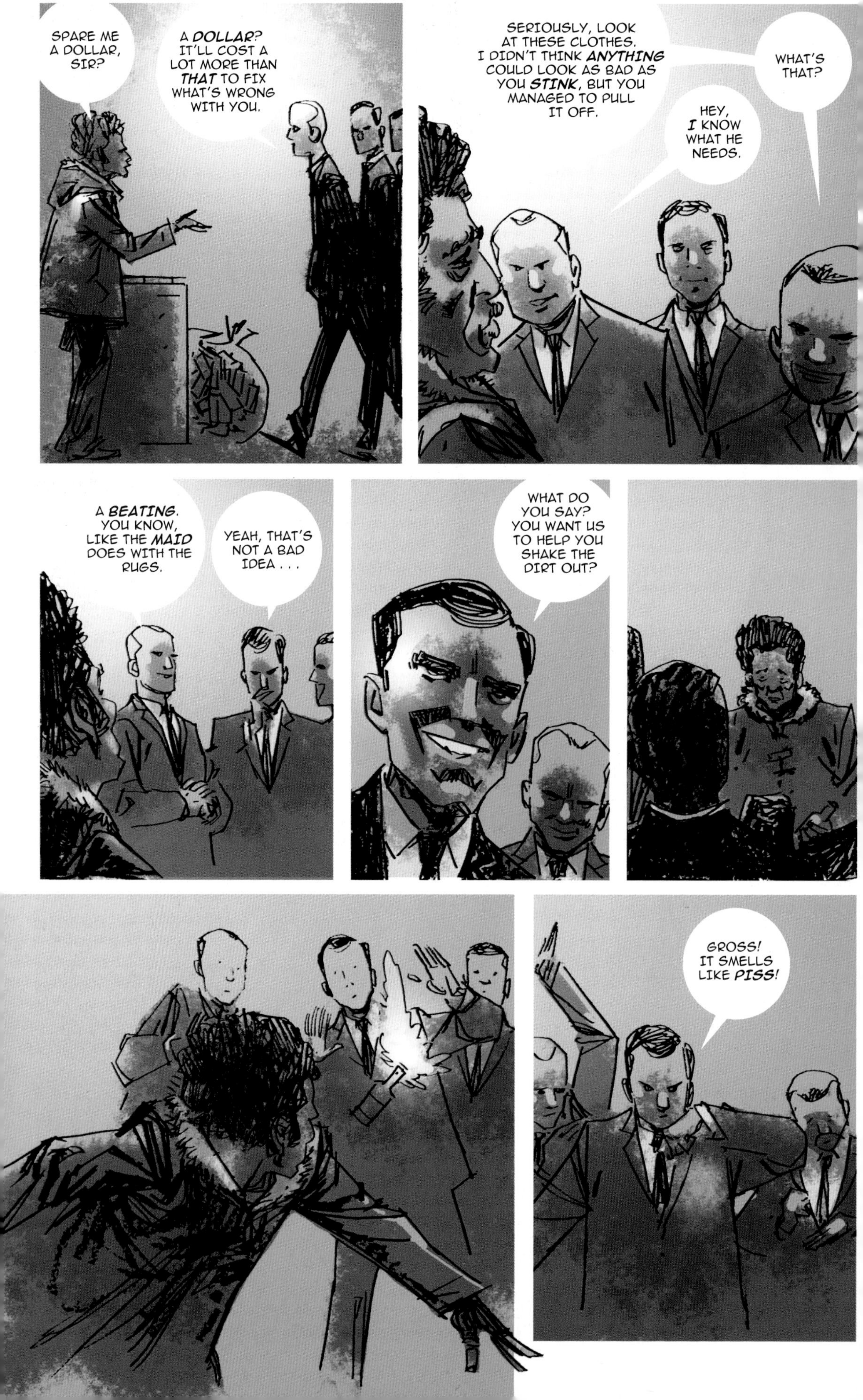
SPARE ME A DOLLAR, SIR?
A DOLLAR? IT'LL COST A LOT MORE THAN THAT TO FIX WHAT'S WRONG WITH YOU.
SERIOUSLY, LOOK AT THESE CLOTHES. I DIDN'T THINK ANYTHING COULD LOOK AS BAD AS YOU STINK, BUT YOU MANAGED TO PULL IT OFF.
WHAT'S THAT?
HEY, I KNOW WHAT HE NEEDS.
A BEATING. YOU KNOW, LIKE THE MAID DOES WITH THE RUGS.
YEAH, THAT'S NOT A BAD IDEA . . .
WHAT DO YOU SAY? YOU WANT US TO HELP YOU SHAKE THE DIRT OUT?
GROSS! IT SMELLS LIKE PISS!

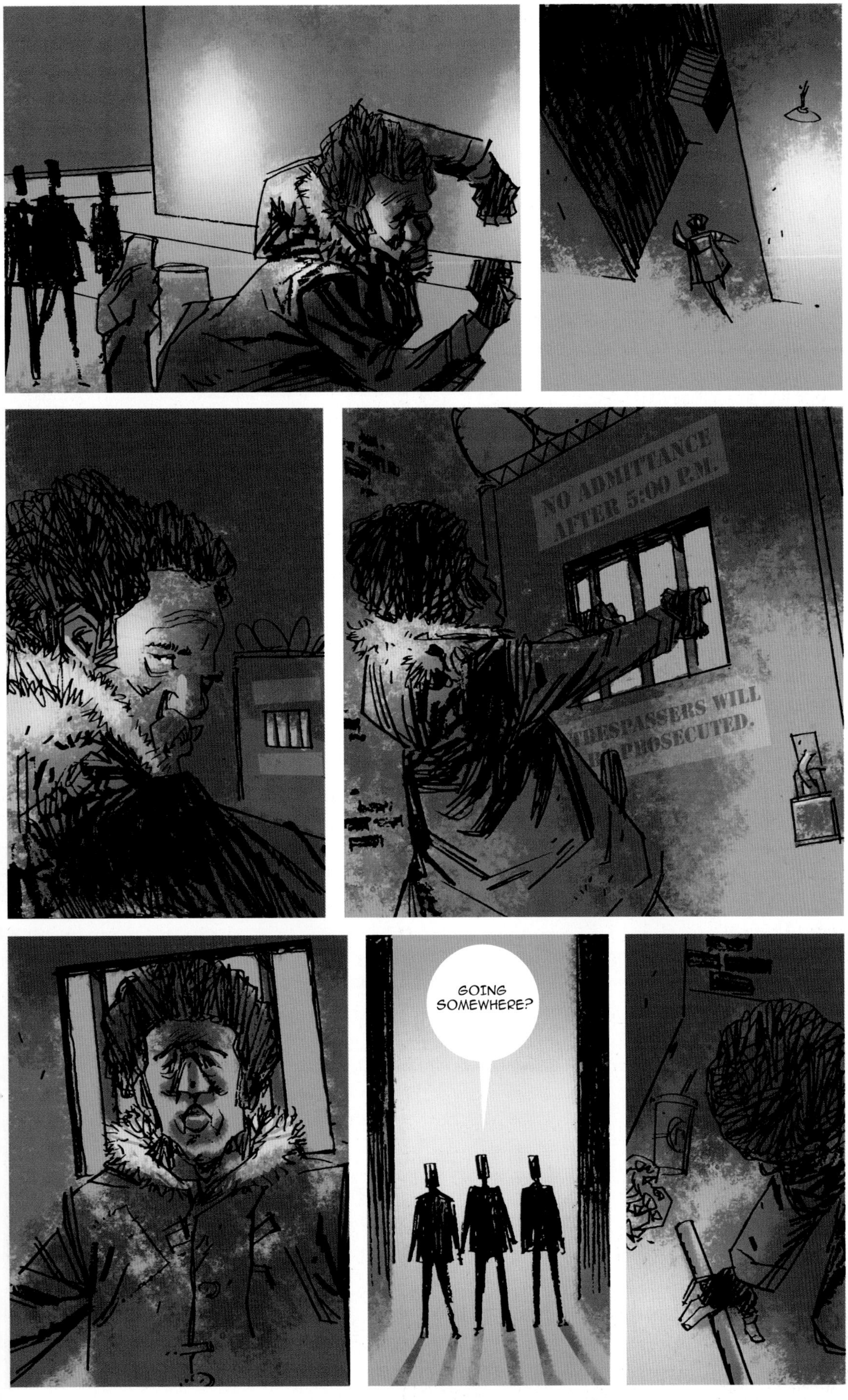
NO ADMITTANCE AFTER 5:00 P.M.
TRESPASSERS WILL
PROSECUTED.
GOING SOMEWHERE?

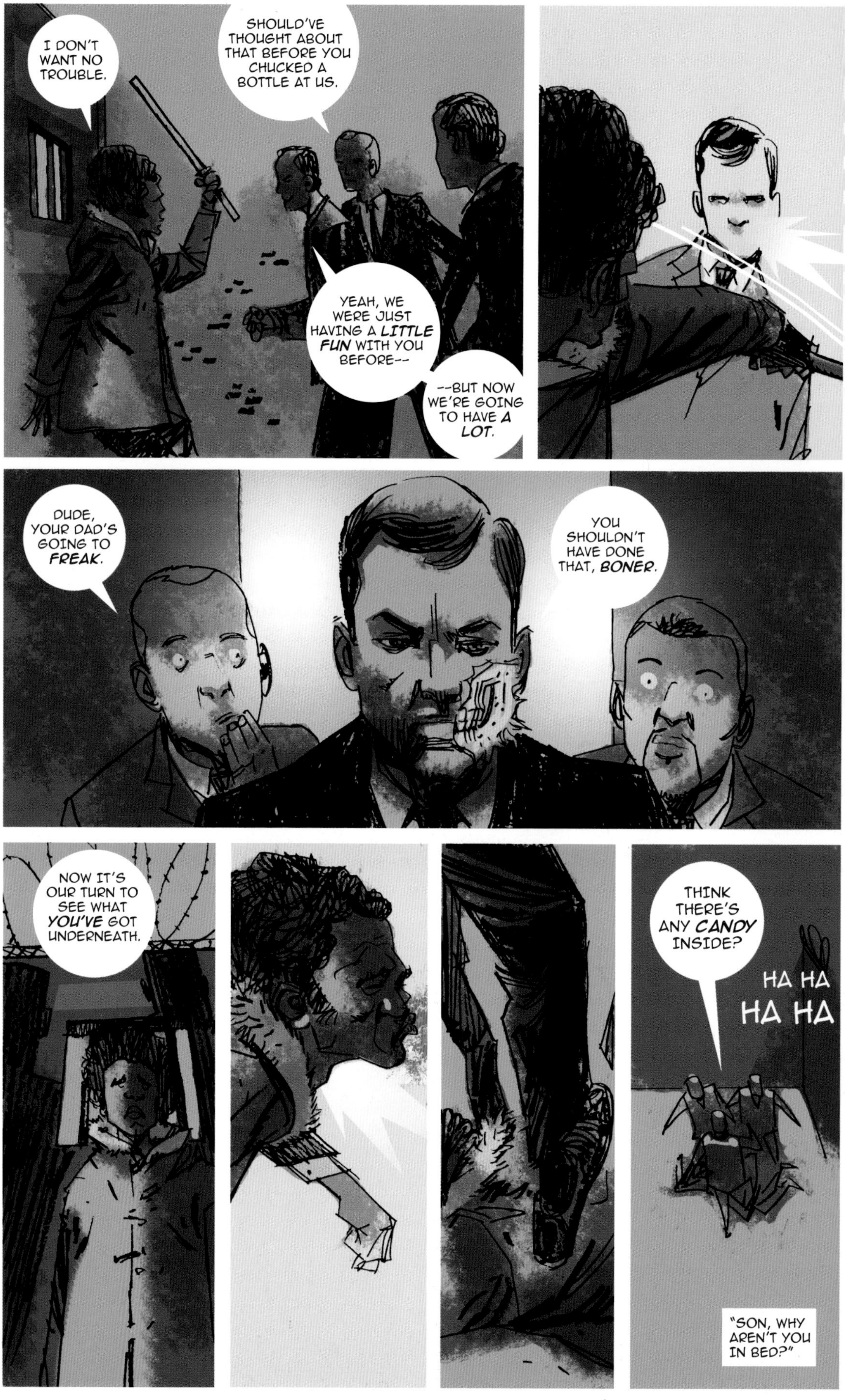
I DON'T WANT NO TROUBLE.
SHOULD'VE THOUGHT ABOUT THAT BEFORE YOU CHUCKED A BOTTLE AT US.
YEAH, WE WERE JUST HAVING A LITTLE FUN WITH YOU BEFORE--
--BUT NOW WE'RE GOING TO HAVE A LOT.
DUDE, YOUR DAD'S GOING TO FREAK.
YOU SHOULDN'T HAVE DONE THAT, BONER.
NOW IT'S OUR TURN TO SEE WHAT YOU'VE GOT UNDERNEATH.
THINK THERE'S ANY CANDY INSIDE?
HA HA
HA HA
"SON, WHY AREN'T YOU IN BED?"

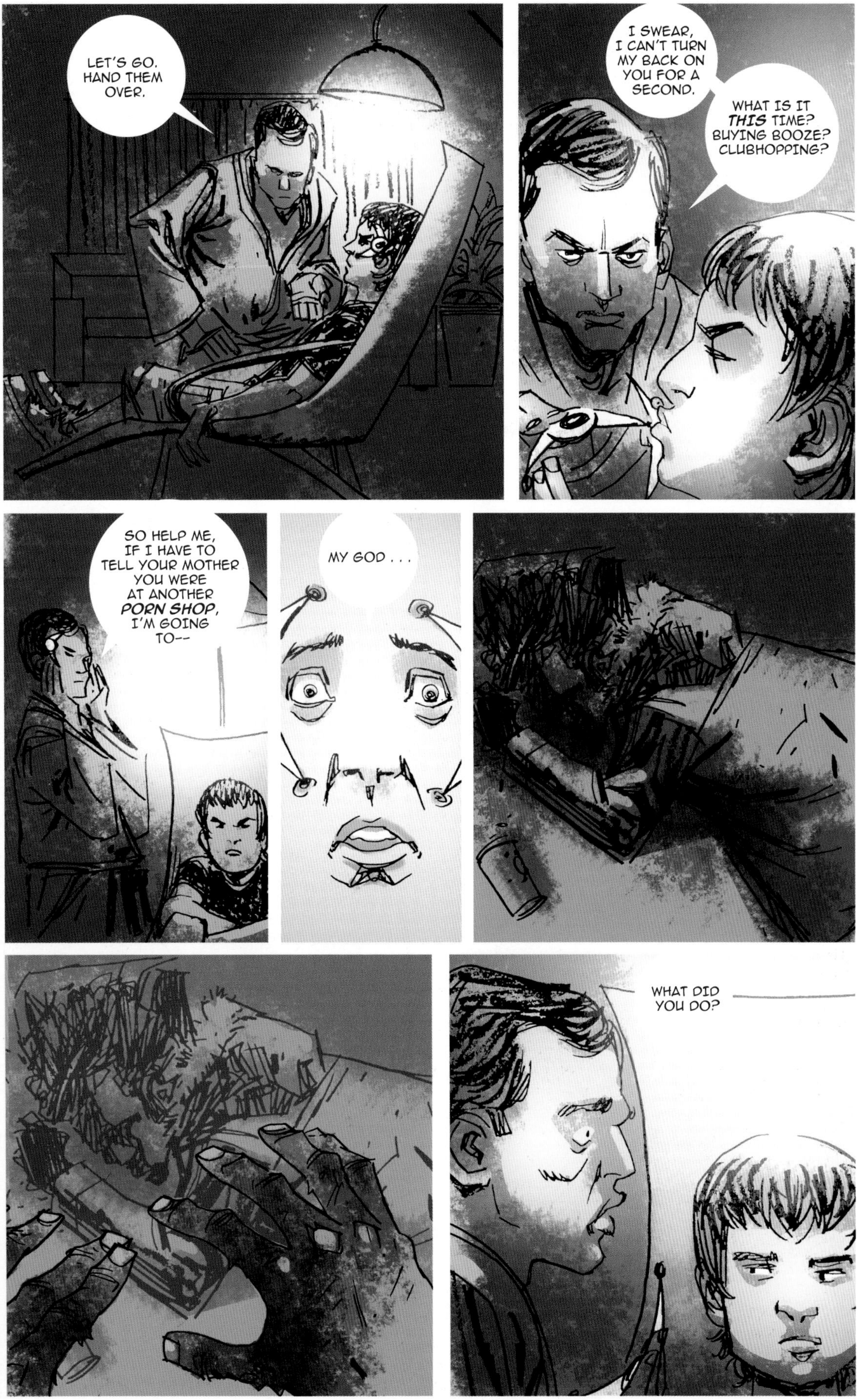
LET'S GO. HAND THEM OVER.
I SWEAR, I CAN'T TURN MY BACK ON YOU FOR A SECOND.
WHAT IS IT *THIS* TIME? BUYING BOOZE? CLUBHOPPING?
SO HELP ME, IF I HAVE TO TELL YOUR MOTHER YOU WERE AT ANOTHER ***PORN SHOP***, I'M GOING TO--
MY GOD . . .
WHAT DID YOU DO?

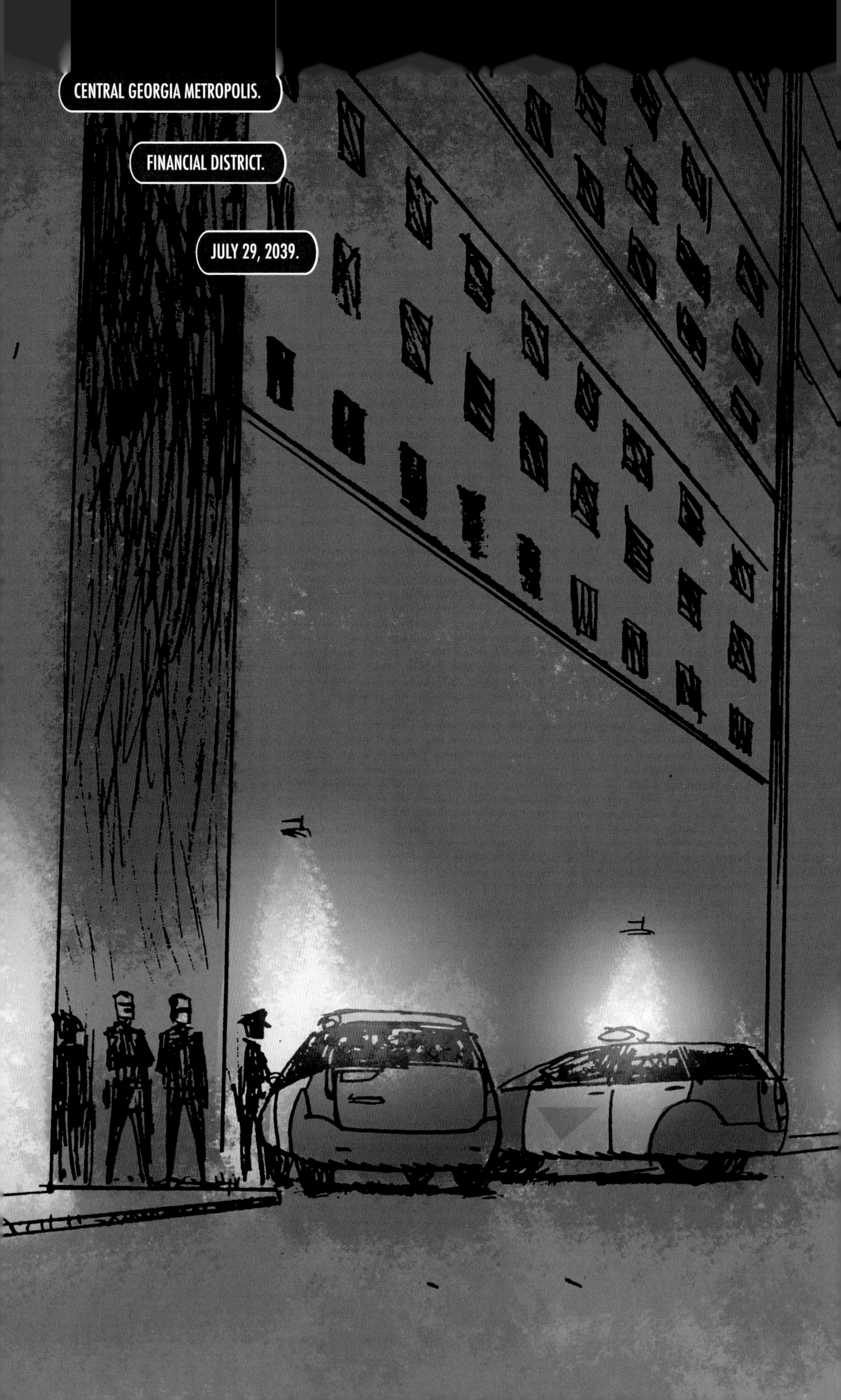
CENTRAL GEORGIA METROPOLIS.
FINANCIAL DISTRICT.
JULY 29, 2039.

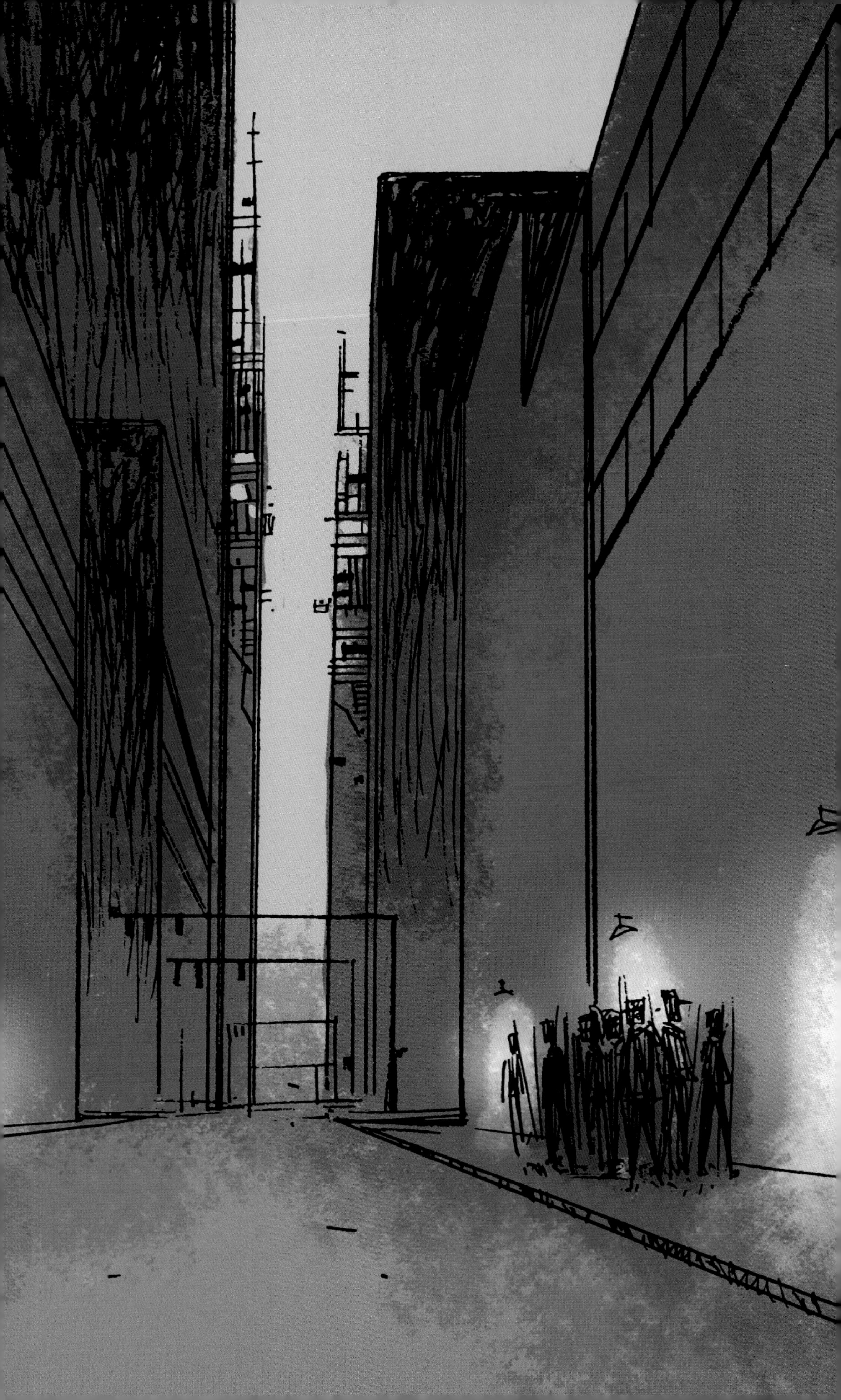

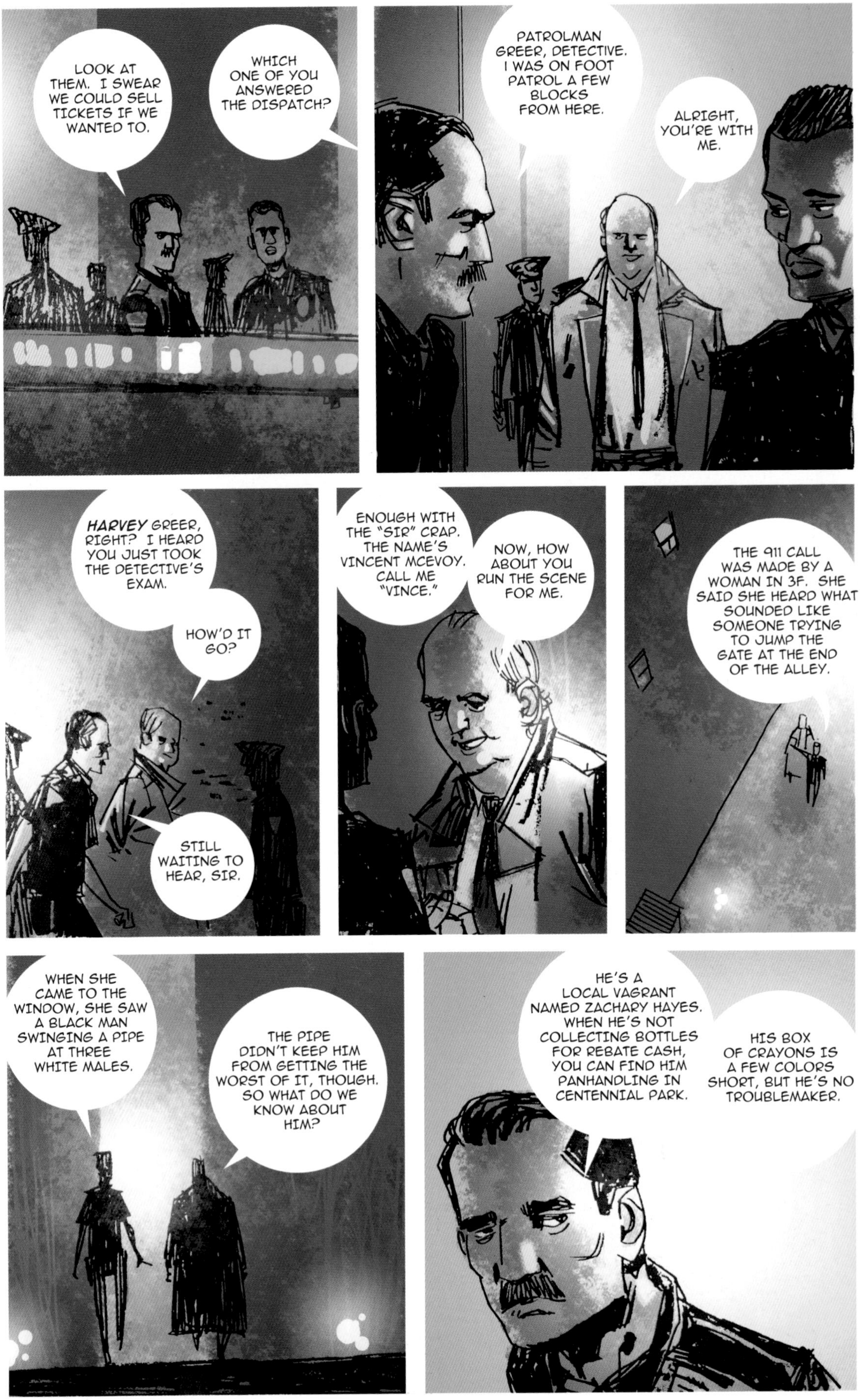

LOOK AT THEM. I SWEAR WE COULD SELL TICKETS IF WE WANTED TO.
WHICH ONE OF YOU ANSWERED THE DISPATCH?
PATROLMAN GREER, DETECTIVE. I WAS ON FOOT PATROL A FEW BLOCKS FROM HERE.
ALRIGHT, YOU'RE WITH ME.
HARVEY GREER, RIGHT? I HEARD YOU JUST TOOK THE DETECTIVE'S EXAM.
HOW'D IT GO?
STILL WAITING TO HEAR, SIR.
ENOUGH WITH THE "SIR" CRAP. THE NAME'S VINCENT MCEVOY. CALL ME "VINCE."
NOW, HOW ABOUT YOU RUN THE SCENE FOR ME.
THE 911 CALL WAS MADE BY A WOMAN IN 3F. SHE SAID SHE HEARD WHAT SOUNDED LIKE SOMEONE TRYING TO JUMP THE GATE AT THE END OF THE ALLEY.
WHEN SHE CAME TO THE WINDOW, SHE SAW A BLACK MAN SWINGING A PIPE AT THREE WHITE MALES.
THE PIPE DIDN'T KEEP HIM FROM GETTING THE WORST OF IT, THOUGH. SO WHAT DO WE KNOW ABOUT HIM?
HE'S A LOCAL VAGRANT NAMED ZACHARY HAYES. WHEN HE'S NOT COLLECTING BOTTLES FOR REBATE CASH, YOU CAN FIND HIM PANHANDLING IN CENTENNIAL PARK.
HIS BOX OF CRAYONS IS A FEW COLORS SHORT, BUT HE'S NO TROUBLEMAKER.

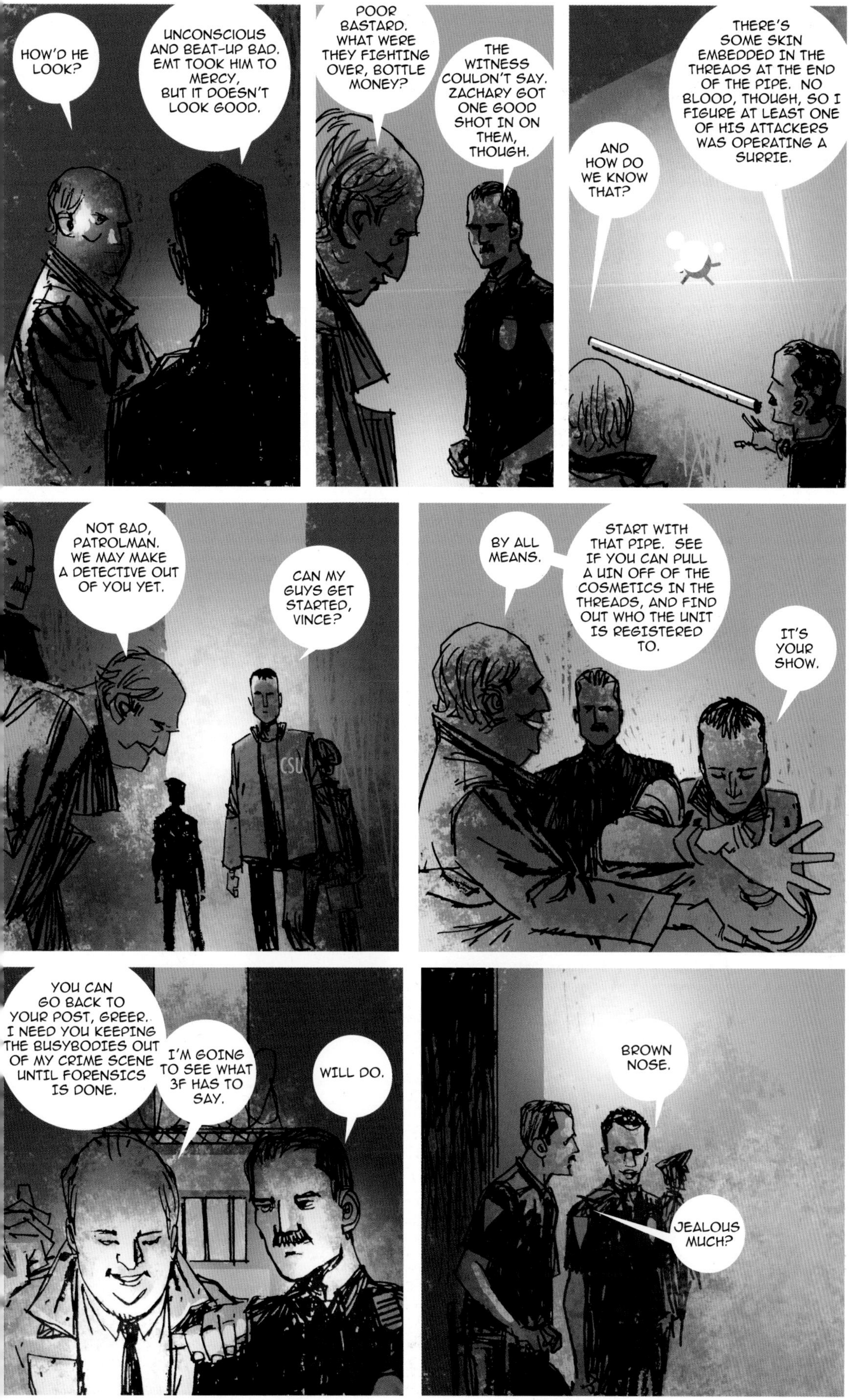
HOW'D HE LOOK?
UNCONSCIOUS AND BEAT-UP BAD. EMT TOOK HIM TO MERCY, BUT IT DOESN'T LOOK GOOD.
POOR BASTARD. WHAT WERE THEY FIGHTING OVER, BOTTLE MONEY?
THE WITNESS COULDN'T SAY. ZACHARY GOT ONE GOOD SHOT IN ON THEM, THOUGH.
THERE'S SOME SKIN EMBEDDED IN THE THREADS AT THE END OF THE PIPE. NO BLOOD, THOUGH, SO I FIGURE AT LEAST ONE OF HIS ATTACKERS WAS OPERATING A SURRIE.
AND HOW DO WE KNOW THAT?
NOT BAD, PATROLMAN. WE MAY MAKE A DETECTIVE OUT OF YOU YET.
CAN MY GUYS GET STARTED, VINCE?
CSU
BY ALL MEANS.
START WITH THAT PIPE. SEE IF YOU CAN PULL A UIN OFF OF THE COSMETICS IN THE THREADS, AND FIND OUT WHO THE UNIT IS REGISTERED TO.
IT'S YOUR SHOW.
YOU CAN GO BACK TO YOUR POST, GREER. I NEED YOU KEEPING THE BUSYBODIES OUT OF MY CRIME SCENE UNTIL FORENSICS IS DONE.
I'M GOING TO SEE WHAT 3F HAS TO SAY.
WILL DO.
BROWN NOSE.
JEALOUS MUCH?

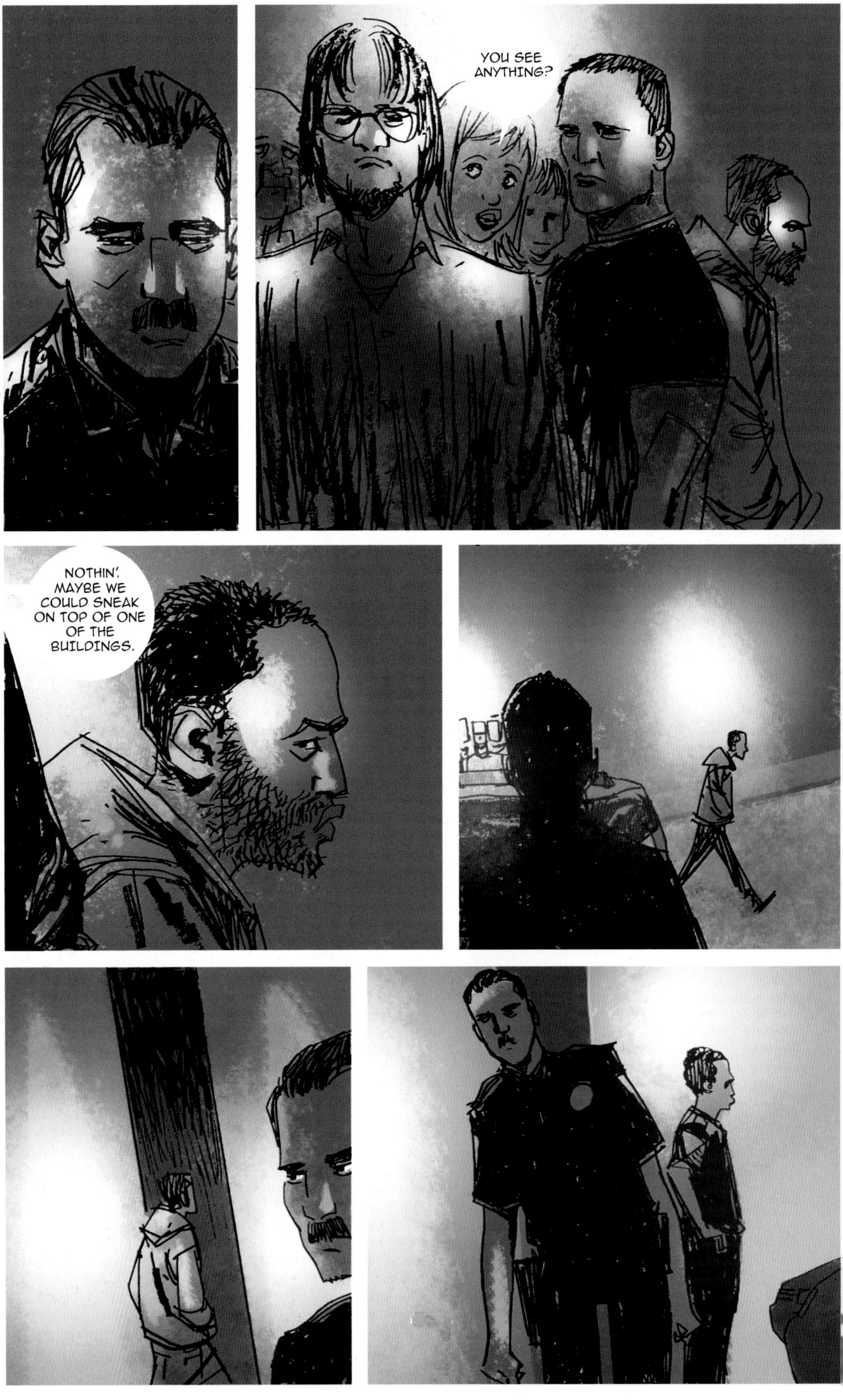
YOU SEE ANYTHING?
NOTHIN'. MAYBE WE COULD SNEAK ON TOP OF ONE OF THE BUILDINGS.

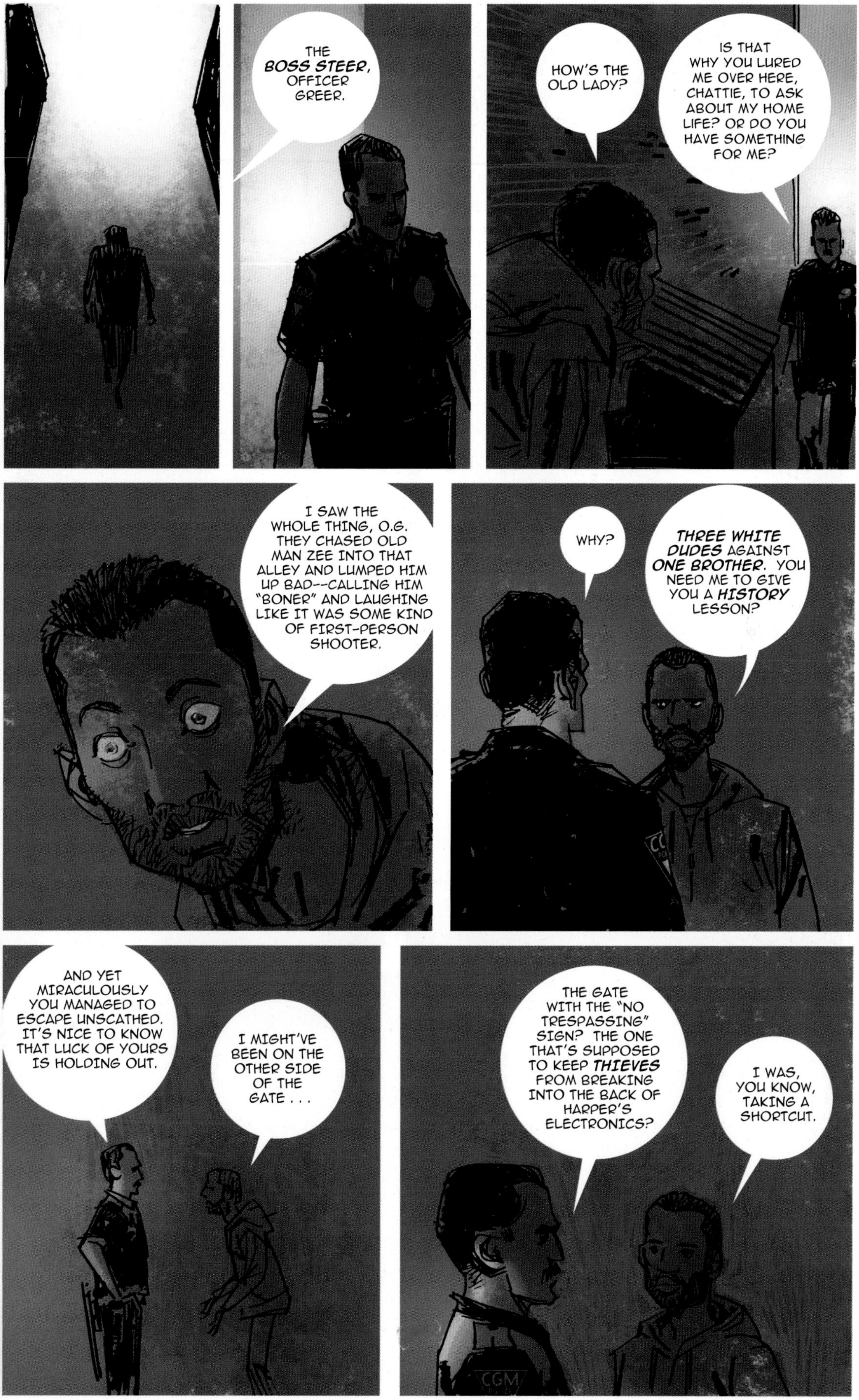
THE BOSS STEER, OFFICER GREER.
HOW'S THE OLD LADY?
IS THAT WHY YOU LURED ME OVER HERE, CHATTIE, TO ASK ABOUT MY HOME LIFE? OR DO YOU HAVE SOMETHING FOR ME?
I SAW THE WHOLE THING, O.G. THEY CHASED OLD MAN ZEE INTO THAT ALLEY AND LUMPED HIM UP BAD--CALLING HIM "BONER" AND LAUGHING LIKE IT WAS SOME KIND OF FIRST-PERSON SHOOTER.
WHY?
THREE WHITE DUDES AGAINST ONE BROTHER. YOU NEED ME TO GIVE YOU A HISTORY LESSON?
AND YET MIRACULOUSLY YOU MANAGED TO ESCAPE UNSCATHED. IT'S NICE TO KNOW THAT LUCK OF YOURS IS HOLDING OUT.
I MIGHT'VE BEEN ON THE OTHER SIDE OF THE GATE . . .
THE GATE WITH THE "NO TRESPASSING" SIGN? THE ONE THAT'S SUPPOSED TO KEEP THIEVES FROM BREAKING INTO THE BACK OF HARPER'S ELECTRONICS?
I WAS, YOU KNOW, TAKING A SHORTCUT.

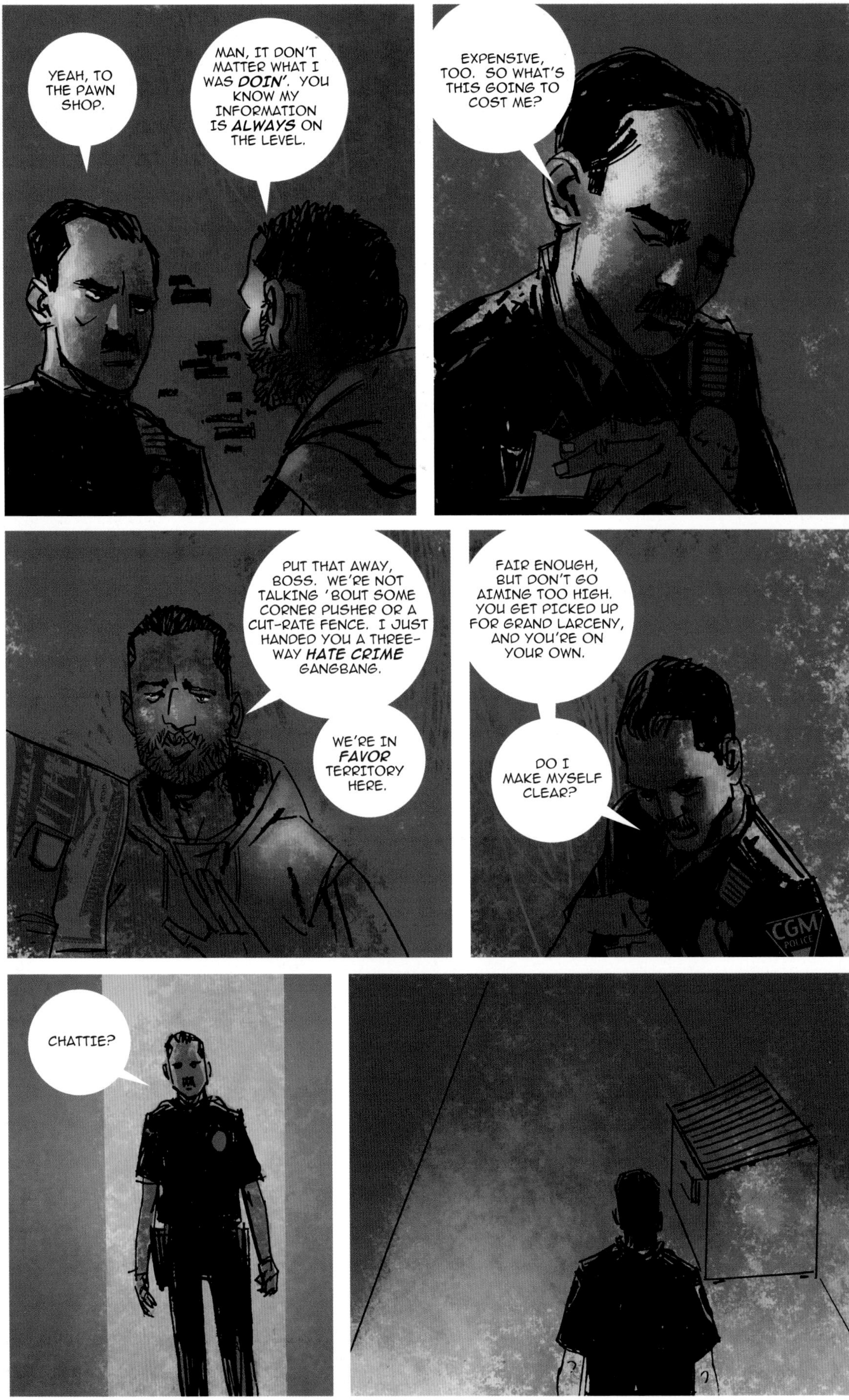
YEAH, TO THE PAWN SHOP.
MAN, IT DON'T MATTER WHAT I WAS DOIN'. YOU KNOW MY INFORMATION IS ALWAYS ON THE LEVEL.
EXPENSIVE, TOO. SO WHAT'S THIS GOING TO COST ME?
PUT THAT AWAY, BOSS. WE'RE NOT TALKING 'BOUT SOME CORNER PUSHER OR A CUT-RATE FENCE. I JUST HANDED YOU A THREE-WAY HATE CRIME GANGBANG.
WE'RE IN FAVOR TERRITORY HERE.
FAIR ENOUGH, BUT DON'T GO AIMING TOO HIGH. YOU GET PICKED UP FOR GRAND LARCENY, AND YOU'RE ON YOUR OWN.
DO I MAKE MYSELF CLEAR?
CGM POLICE
CHATTIE?

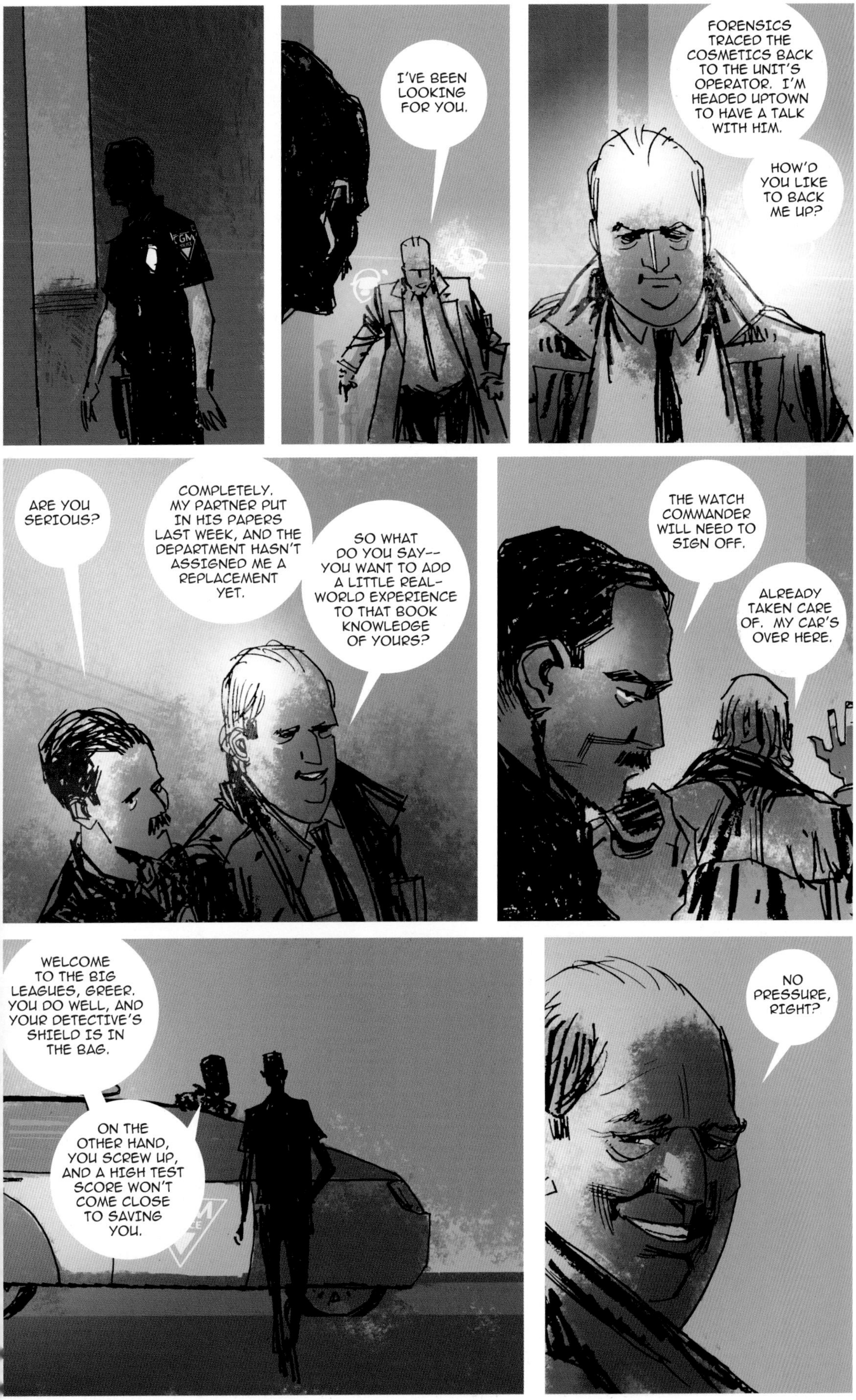
I'VE BEEN LOOKING FOR YOU.
FORENSICS TRACED THE COSMETICS BACK TO THE UNIT'S OPERATOR. I'M HEADED UPTOWN TO HAVE A TALK WITH HIM.
HOW'D YOU LIKE TO BACK ME UP?
ARE YOU SERIOUS?
COMPLETELY. MY PARTNER PUT IN HIS PAPERS LAST WEEK, AND THE DEPARTMENT HASN'T ASSIGNED ME A REPLACEMENT YET.
SO WHAT DO YOU SAY-- YOU WANT TO ADD A LITTLE REAL-WORLD EXPERIENCE TO THAT BOOK KNOWLEDGE OF YOURS?
THE WATCH COMMANDER WILL NEED TO SIGN OFF.
ALREADY TAKEN CARE OF. MY CAR'S OVER HERE.
WELCOME TO THE BIG LEAGUES, GREER. YOU DO WELL, AND YOUR DETECTIVE'S SHIELD IS IN THE BAG.
ON THE OTHER HAND, YOU SCREW UP, AND A HIGH TEST SCORE WON'T COME CLOSE TO SAVING YOU.
NO PRESSURE, RIGHT?

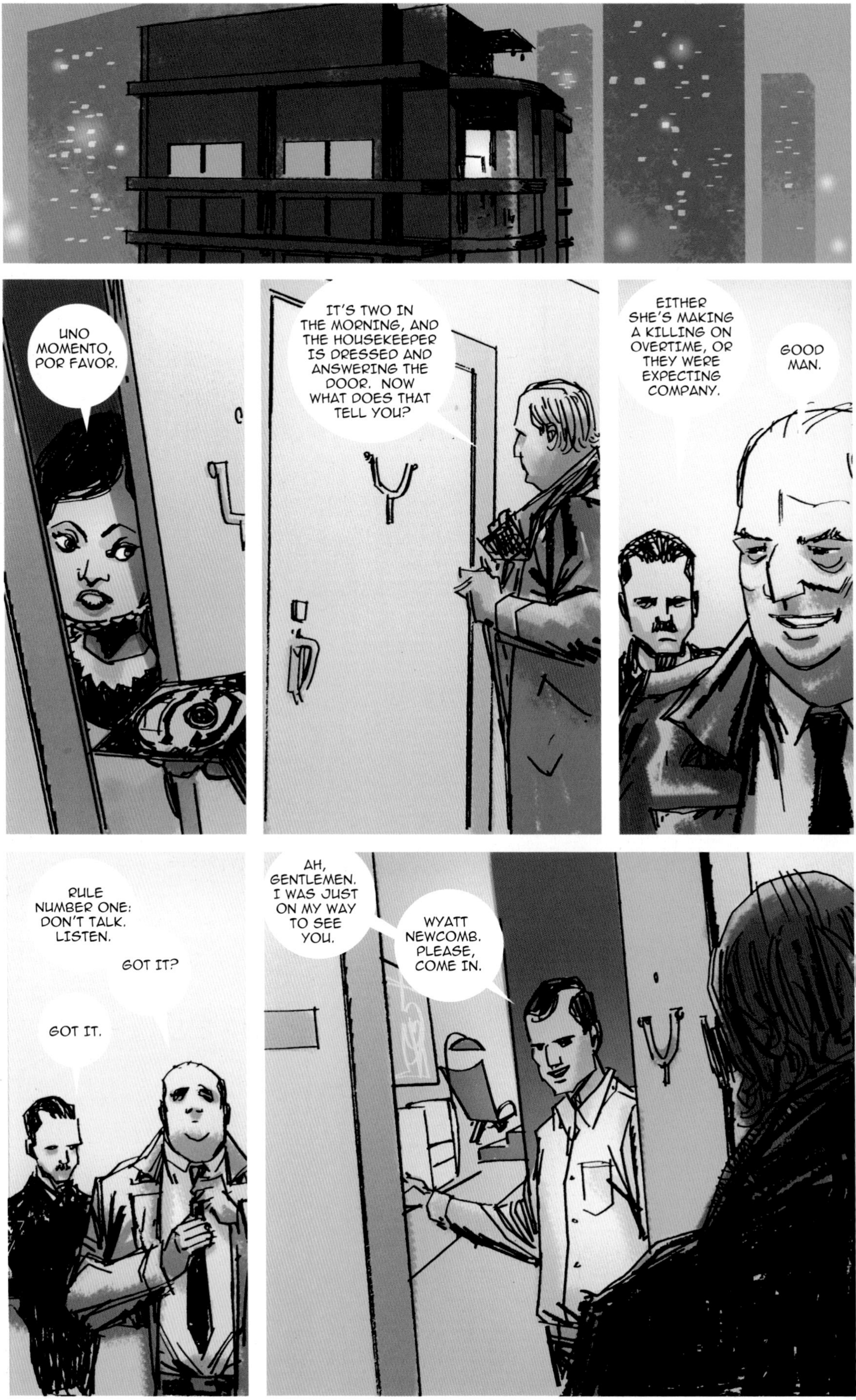
UNO MOMENTO, POR FAVOR.
IT'S TWO IN THE MORNING, AND THE HOUSEKEEPER IS DRESSED AND ANSWERING THE DOOR. NOW WHAT DOES THAT TELL YOU?
EITHER SHE'S MAKING A KILLING ON OVERTIME, OR THEY WERE EXPECTING COMPANY.
GOOD MAN.
RULE NUMBER ONE: DON'T TALK. LISTEN.
GOT IT?
GOT IT.
AH, GENTLEMEN. I WAS JUST ON MY WAY TO SEE YOU.
WYATT NEWCOMB. PLEASE, COME IN.

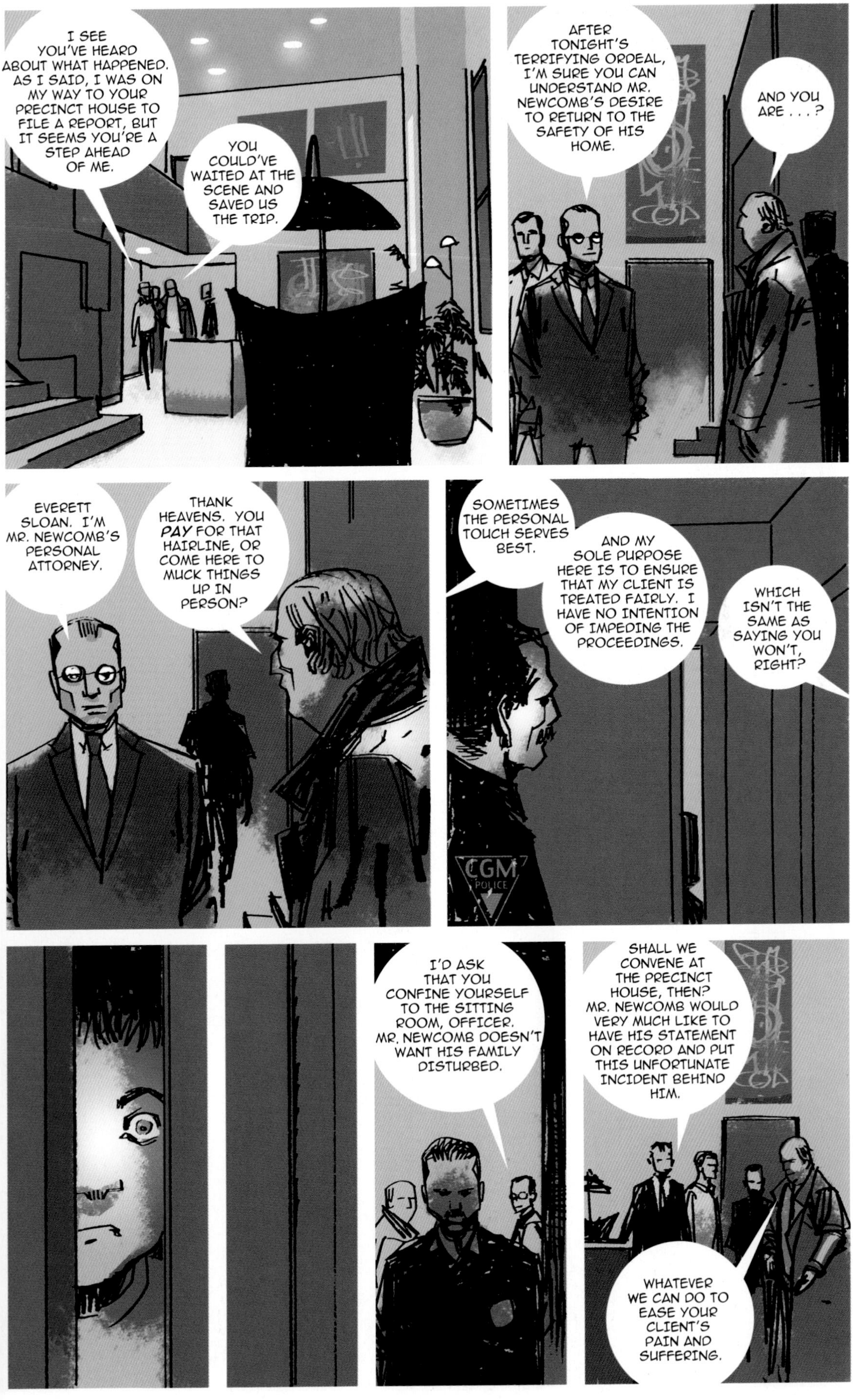
I SEE YOU'VE HEARD ABOUT WHAT HAPPENED. AS I SAID, I WAS ON MY WAY TO YOUR PRECINCT HOUSE TO FILE A REPORT, BUT IT SEEMS YOU'RE A STEP AHEAD OF ME.
YOU COULD'VE WAITED AT THE SCENE AND SAVED US THE TRIP.
AFTER TONIGHT'S TERRIFYING ORDEAL, I'M SURE YOU CAN UNDERSTAND MR. NEWCOMB'S DESIRE TO RETURN TO THE SAFETY OF HIS HOME.
AND YOU ARE . . . ?
EVERETT SLOAN. I'M MR. NEWCOMB'S PERSONAL ATTORNEY.
THANK HEAVENS. YOU *PAY* FOR THAT HAIRLINE, OR COME HERE TO MUCK THINGS UP IN PERSON?
SOMETIMES THE PERSONAL TOUCH SERVES BEST.
AND MY SOLE PURPOSE HERE IS TO ENSURE THAT MY CLIENT IS TREATED FAIRLY. I HAVE NO INTENTION OF IMPEDING THE PROCEEDINGS.
WHICH ISN'T THE SAME AS SAYING YOU WON'T, RIGHT?
CGM POLICE
I'D ASK THAT YOU CONFINE YOURSELF TO THE SITTING ROOM, OFFICER. MR. NEWCOMB DOESN'T WANT HIS FAMILY DISTURBED.
SHALL WE CONVENE AT THE PRECINCT HOUSE, THEN? MR. NEWCOMB WOULD VERY MUCH LIKE TO HAVE HIS STATEMENT ON RECORD AND PUT THIS UNFORTUNATE INCIDENT BEHIND HIM.
WHATEVER WE CAN DO TO EASE YOUR CLIENT'S PAIN AND SUFFERING.

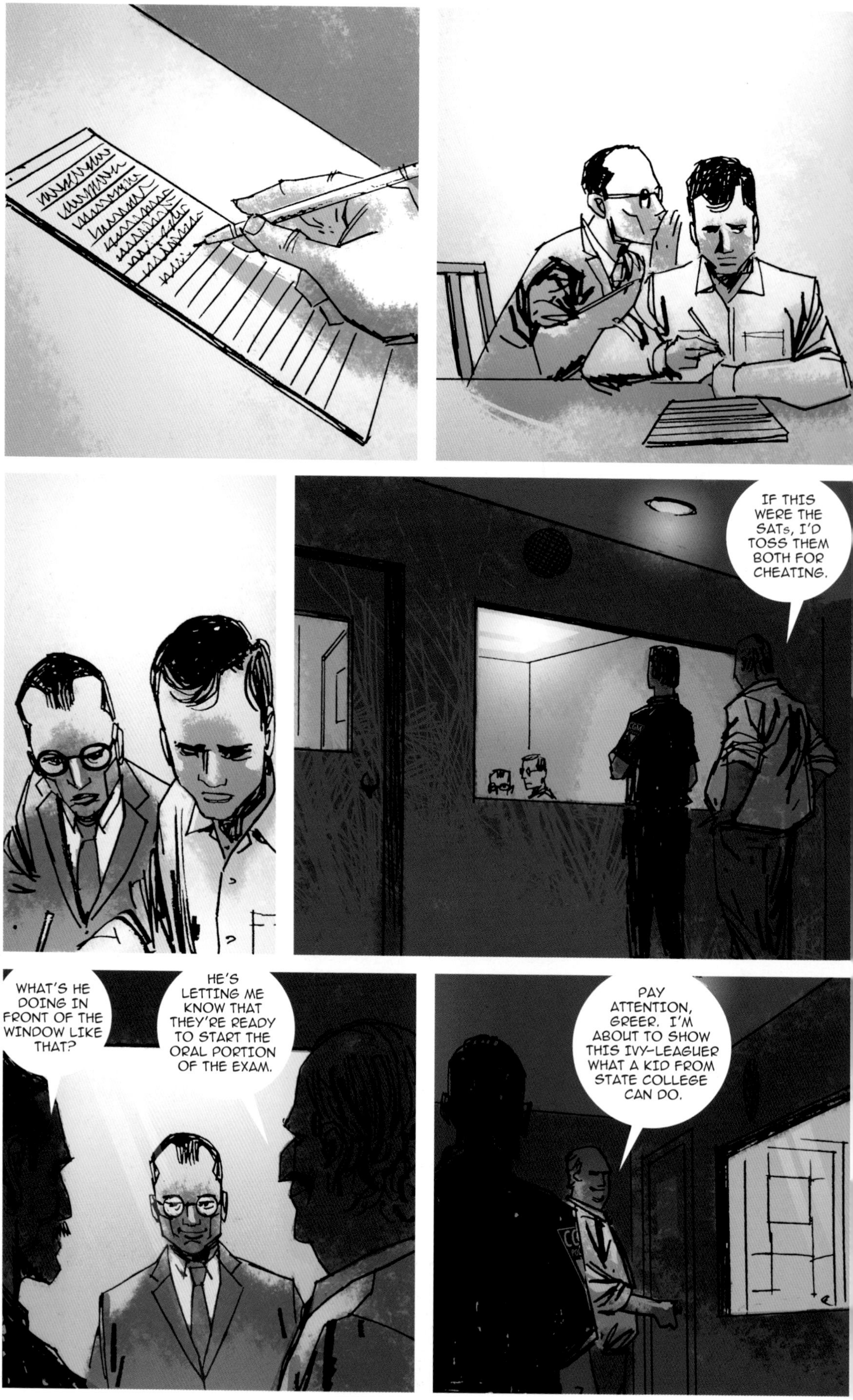
IF THIS WERE THE SATs, I'D TOSS THEM BOTH FOR CHEATING.
CGM
WHAT'S HE DOING IN FRONT OF THE WINDOW LIKE THAT?
HE'S LETTING ME KNOW THAT THEY'RE READY TO START THE ORAL PORTION OF THE EXAM.
PAY ATTENTION, GREER. I'M ABOUT TO SHOW THIS IVY-LEAGUER WHAT A KID FROM STATE COLLEGE CAN DO.

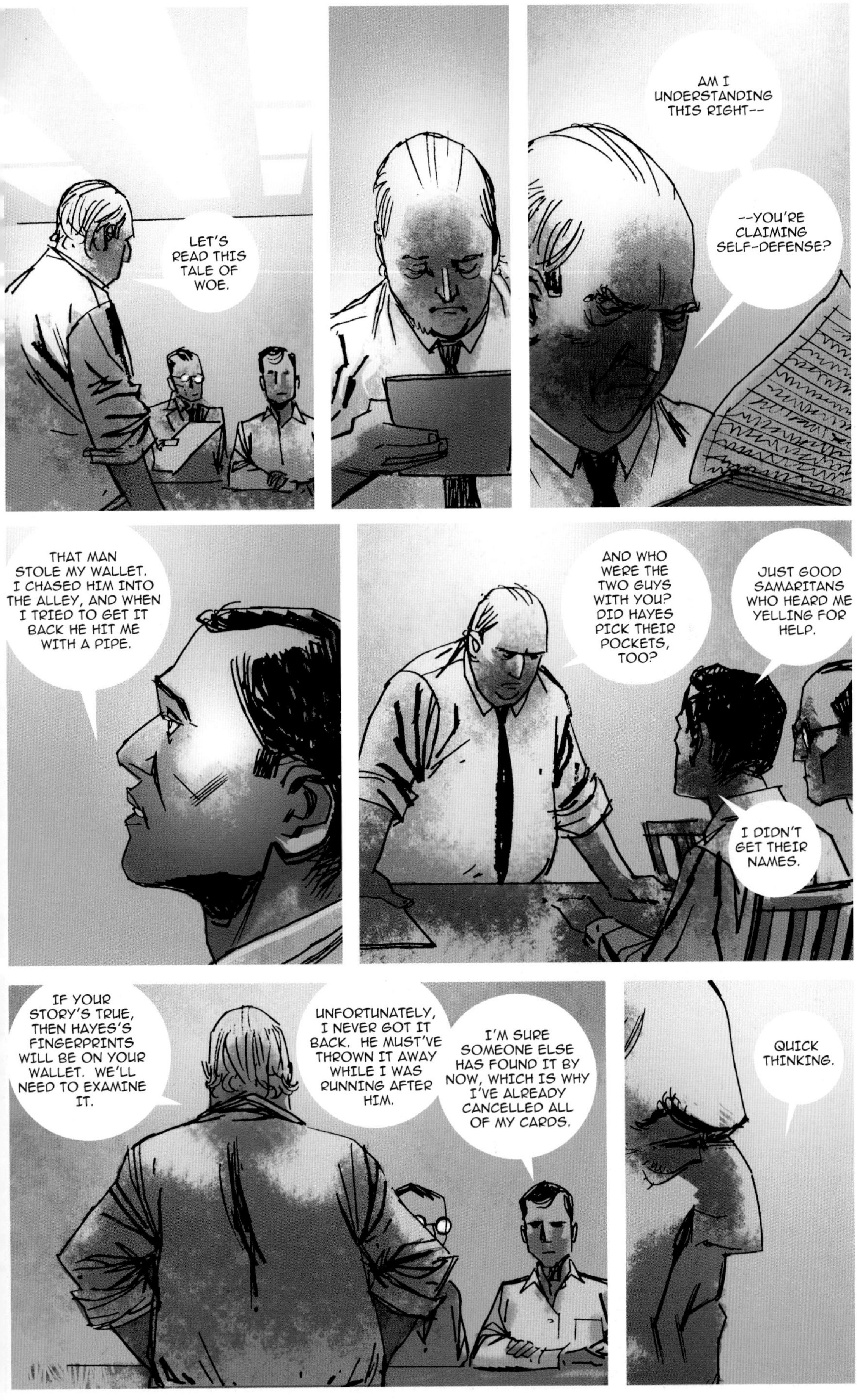
LET'S READ THIS TALE OF WOE.
AM I UNDERSTANDING THIS RIGHT--
--YOU'RE CLAIMING SELF-DEFENSE?
THAT MAN STOLE MY WALLET. I CHASED HIM INTO THE ALLEY, AND WHEN I TRIED TO GET IT BACK HE HIT ME WITH A PIPE.
AND WHO WERE THE TWO GUYS WITH YOU? DID HAYES PICK THEIR POCKETS, TOO?
JUST GOOD SAMARITANS WHO HEARD ME YELLING FOR HELP.
I DIDN'T GET THEIR NAMES.
IF YOUR STORY'S TRUE, THEN HAYES'S FINGERPRINTS WILL BE ON YOUR WALLET. WE'LL NEED TO EXAMINE IT.
UNFORTUNATELY, I NEVER GOT IT BACK. HE MUST'VE THROWN IT AWAY WHILE I WAS RUNNING AFTER HIM.
I'M SURE SOMEONE ELSE HAS FOUND IT BY NOW, WHICH IS WHY I'VE ALREADY CANCELLED ALL OF MY CARDS.
QUICK THINKING.

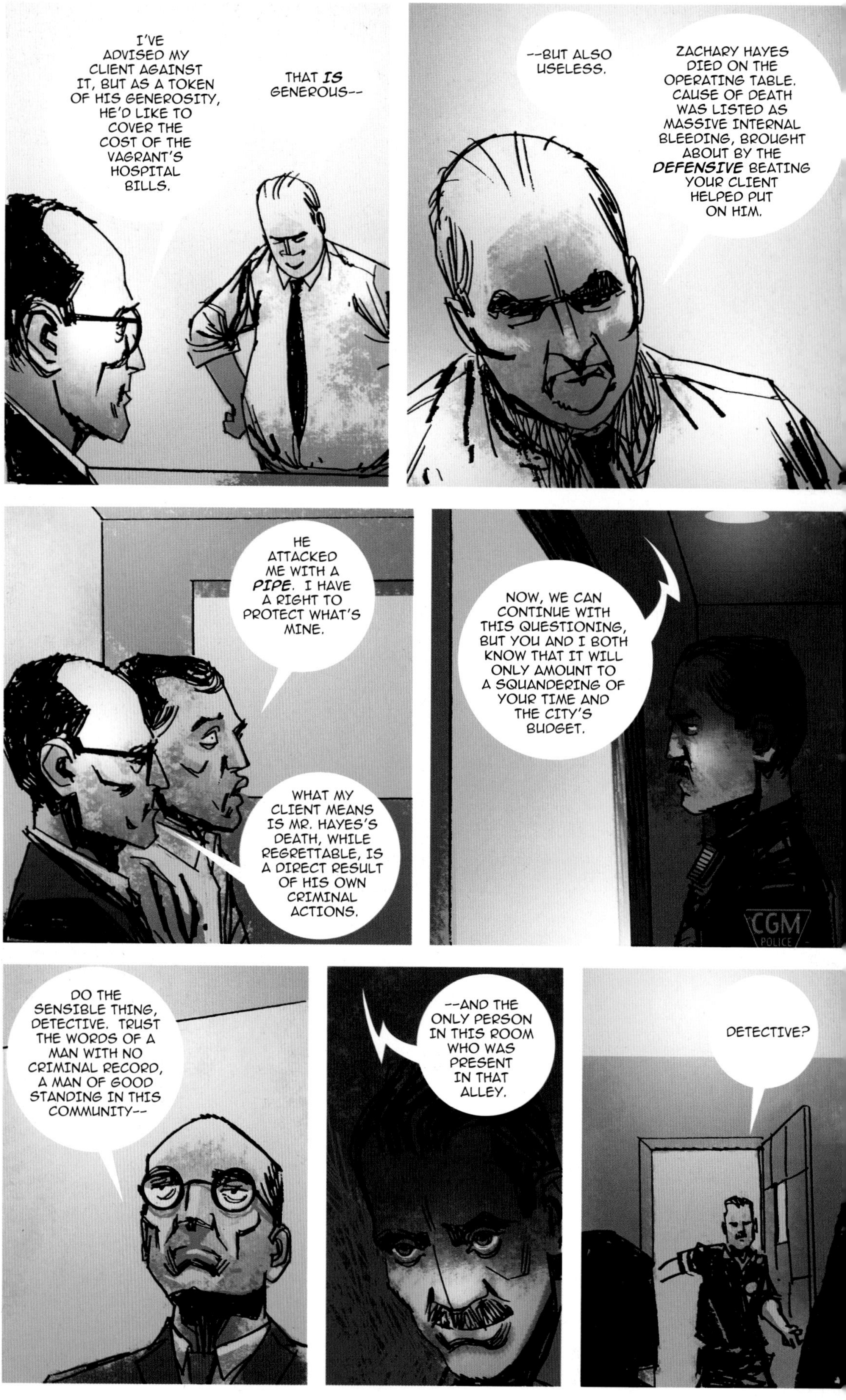
I'VE ADVISED MY CLIENT AGAINST IT, BUT AS A TOKEN OF HIS GENEROSITY, HE'D LIKE TO COVER THE COST OF THE VAGRANT'S HOSPITAL BILLS.
THAT *IS* GENEROUS--
--BUT ALSO USELESS.
ZACHARY HAYES DIED ON THE OPERATING TABLE. CAUSE OF DEATH WAS LISTED AS MASSIVE INTERNAL BLEEDING, BROUGHT ABOUT BY THE *DEFENSIVE* BEATING YOUR CLIENT HELPED PUT ON HIM.
HE ATTACKED ME WITH A *PIPE*. I HAVE A RIGHT TO PROTECT WHAT'S MINE.
WHAT MY CLIENT MEANS IS MR. HAYES'S DEATH, WHILE REGRETTABLE, IS A DIRECT RESULT OF HIS OWN CRIMINAL ACTIONS.
NOW, WE CAN CONTINUE WITH THIS QUESTIONING, BUT YOU AND I BOTH KNOW THAT IT WILL ONLY AMOUNT TO A SQUANDERING OF YOUR TIME AND THE CITY'S BUDGET.
CGM
POLICE
DO THE SENSIBLE THING, DETECTIVE. TRUST THE WORDS OF A MAN WITH NO CRIMINAL RECORD, A MAN OF GOOD STANDING IN THIS COMMUNITY--
--AND THE ONLY PERSON IN THIS ROOM WHO WAS PRESENT IN THAT ALLEY.
DETECTIVE?

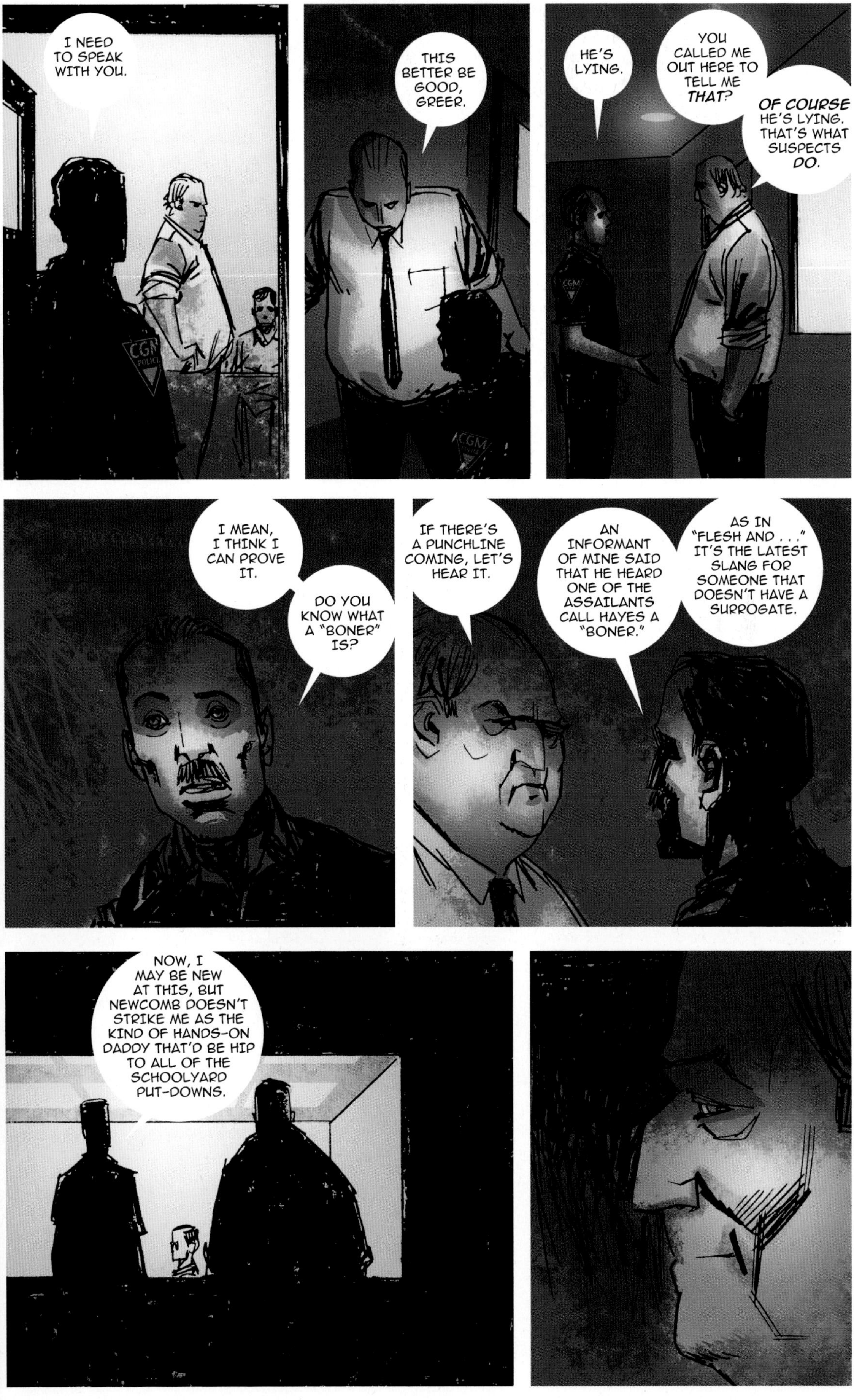

I NEED TO SPEAK WITH YOU.
THIS BETTER BE GOOD, GREER.
HE'S LYING.
YOU CALLED ME OUT HERE TO TELL ME *THAT?*
OF COURSE HE'S LYING. THAT'S WHAT SUSPECTS ***DO.***
I MEAN, I THINK I CAN PROVE IT.
DO YOU KNOW WHAT A "BONER" IS?
IF THERE'S A PUNCHLINE COMING, LET'S HEAR IT.
AN INFORMANT OF MINE SAID THAT HE HEARD ONE OF THE ASSAILANTS CALL HAYES A "BONER."
AS IN "FLESH AND . . ." IT'S THE LATEST SLANG FOR SOMEONE THAT DOESN'T HAVE A SURROGATE.
NOW, I MAY BE NEW AT THIS, BUT NEWCOMB DOESN'T STRIKE ME AS THE KIND OF HANDS-ON DADDY THAT'D BE HIP TO ALL OF THE SCHOOLYARD PUT-DOWNS.

ARE WE ABOUT FINISHED HERE, DETECTIVE? MY CLIENT HAS HAD A TRYING DAY.

JUST ONE MORE QUESTION.

MR. NEWCOMB, COULD YOU EXPLAIN TO ME WHAT A "BONER" IS?

EXCUSE ME?

YOU HEARD ME. AND I DON'T MEAN THAT LITTLE *FISH RIB* YOU TICKLE YOUR WIFE WITH ON PAYDAY.

I DIDN'T THINK SO.

I'M CURIOUS... WHAT WAS YOUR *SON* DOING AT THE TIME OF TONIGHT'S MURDER?

DON'T ANSWER THAT, WYATT.

AS OF RIGHT NOW, THIS CONVERSATION IS *OVER*.

IN THAT CASE, YOUR CLIENT IS UNDER ARREST.

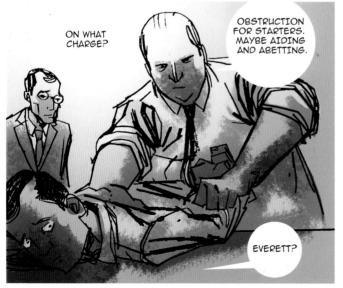

ON WHAT CHARGE?

OBSTRUCTION FOR STARTERS. MAYBE AIDING AND ABETTING.

EVERETT?

DON'T SAY ANYTHING, WYATT. I'LL HAVE YOU OUT BY MORNING.

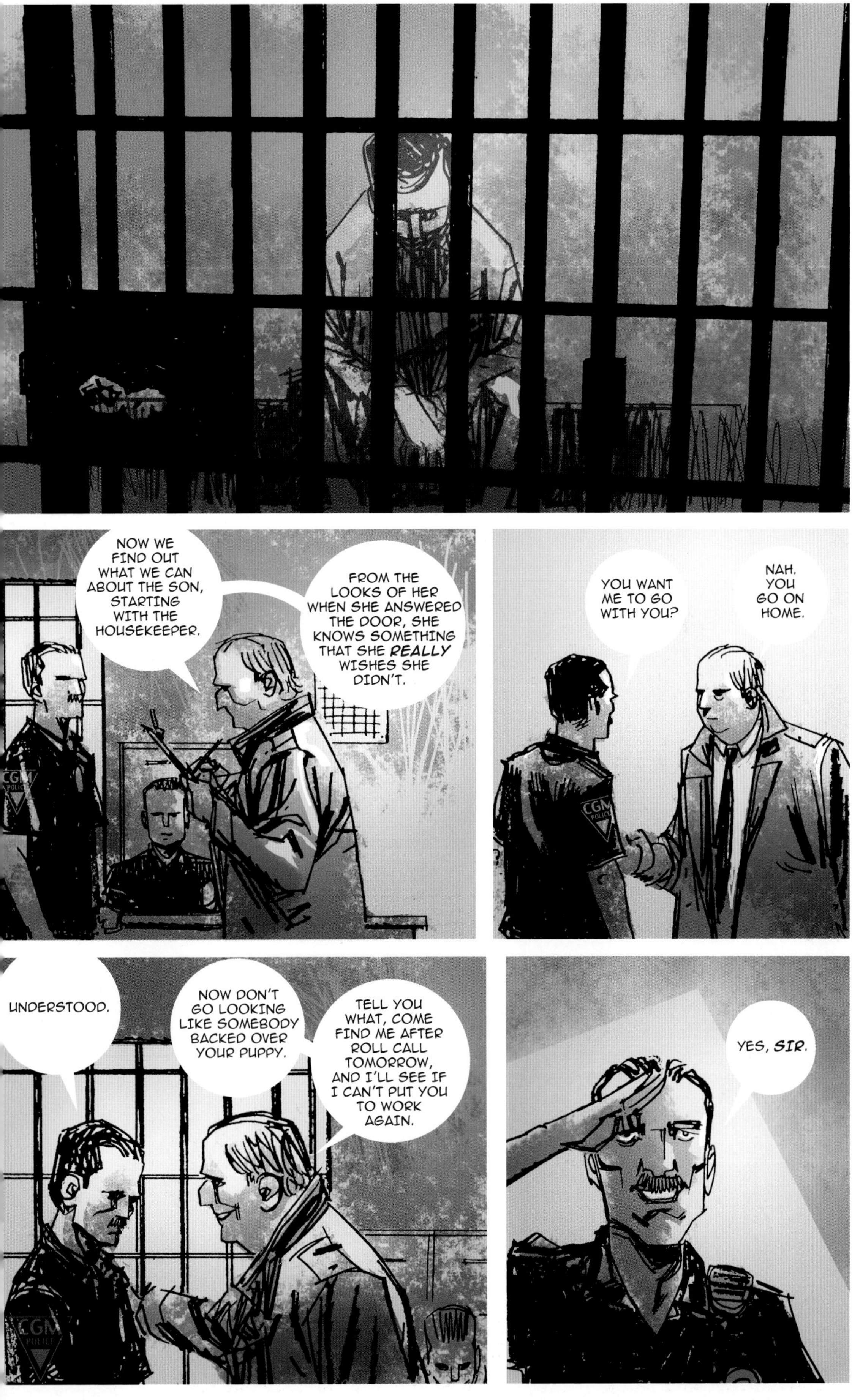
NOW WE FIND OUT WHAT WE CAN ABOUT THE SON, STARTING WITH THE HOUSEKEEPER.
FROM THE LOOKS OF HER WHEN SHE ANSWERED THE DOOR, SHE KNOWS SOMETHING THAT SHE REALLY WISHES SHE DIDN'T.
CGM POLICE
YOU WANT ME TO GO WITH YOU?
NAH. YOU GO ON HOME.
UNDERSTOOD.
NOW DON'T GO LOOKING LIKE SOMEBODY BACKED OVER YOUR PUPPY.
TELL YOU WHAT, COME FIND ME AFTER ROLL CALL TOMORROW, AND I'LL SEE IF I CAN'T PUT YOU TO WORK AGAIN.
YES, SIR.

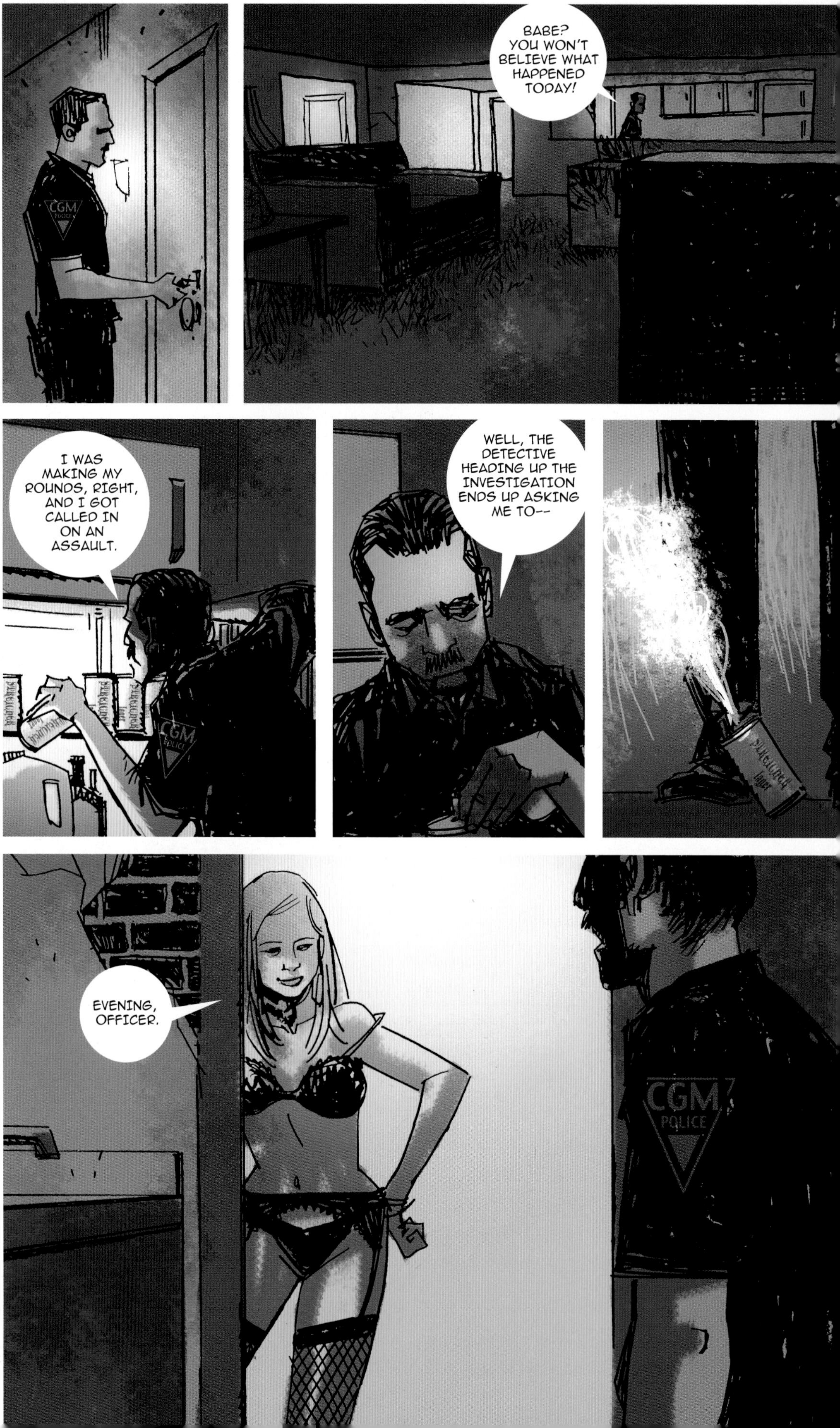
BABE? YOU WON'T BELIEVE WHAT HAPPENED TODAY!
I WAS MAKING MY ROUNDS, RIGHT, AND I GOT CALLED IN ON AN ASSAULT.
WELL, THE DETECTIVE HEADING UP THE INVESTIGATION ENDS UP ASKING ME TO--
EVENING, OFFICER.

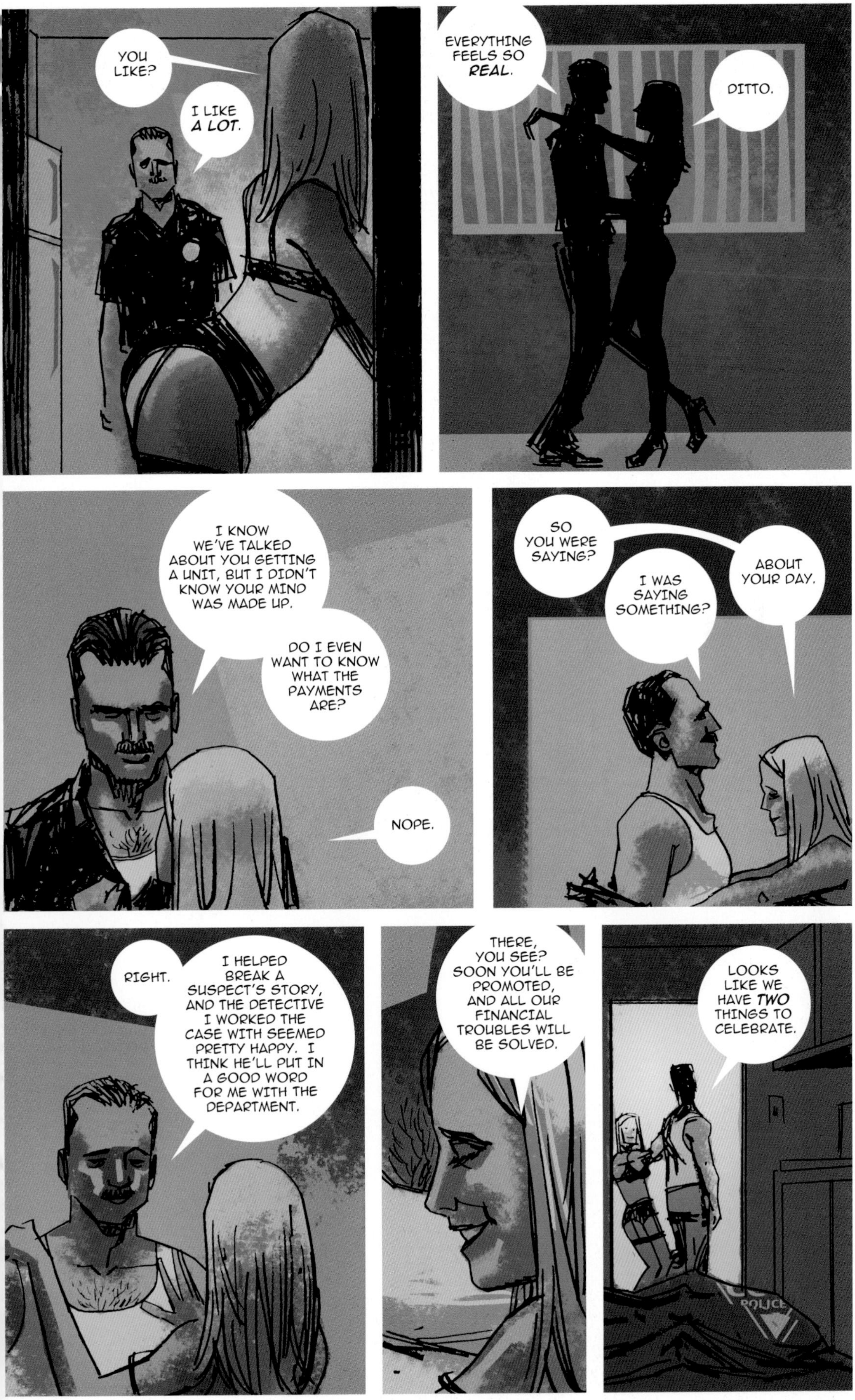
YOU LIKE?
I LIKE A LOT.
EVERYTHING FEELS SO REAL.
DITTO.
I KNOW WE'VE TALKED ABOUT YOU GETTING A UNIT, BUT I DIDN'T KNOW YOUR MIND WAS MADE UP.
DO I EVEN WANT TO KNOW WHAT THE PAYMENTS ARE?
NOPE.
SO YOU WERE SAYING?
I WAS SAYING SOMETHING?
ABOUT YOUR DAY.
RIGHT.
I HELPED BREAK A SUSPECT'S STORY, AND THE DETECTIVE I WORKED THE CASE WITH SEEMED PRETTY HAPPY. I THINK HE'LL PUT IN A GOOD WORD FOR ME WITH THE DEPARTMENT.
THERE, YOU SEE? SOON YOU'LL BE PROMOTED, AND ALL OUR FINANCIAL TROUBLES WILL BE SOLVED.
LOOKS LIKE WE HAVE TWO THINGS TO CELEBRATE.
POLICE

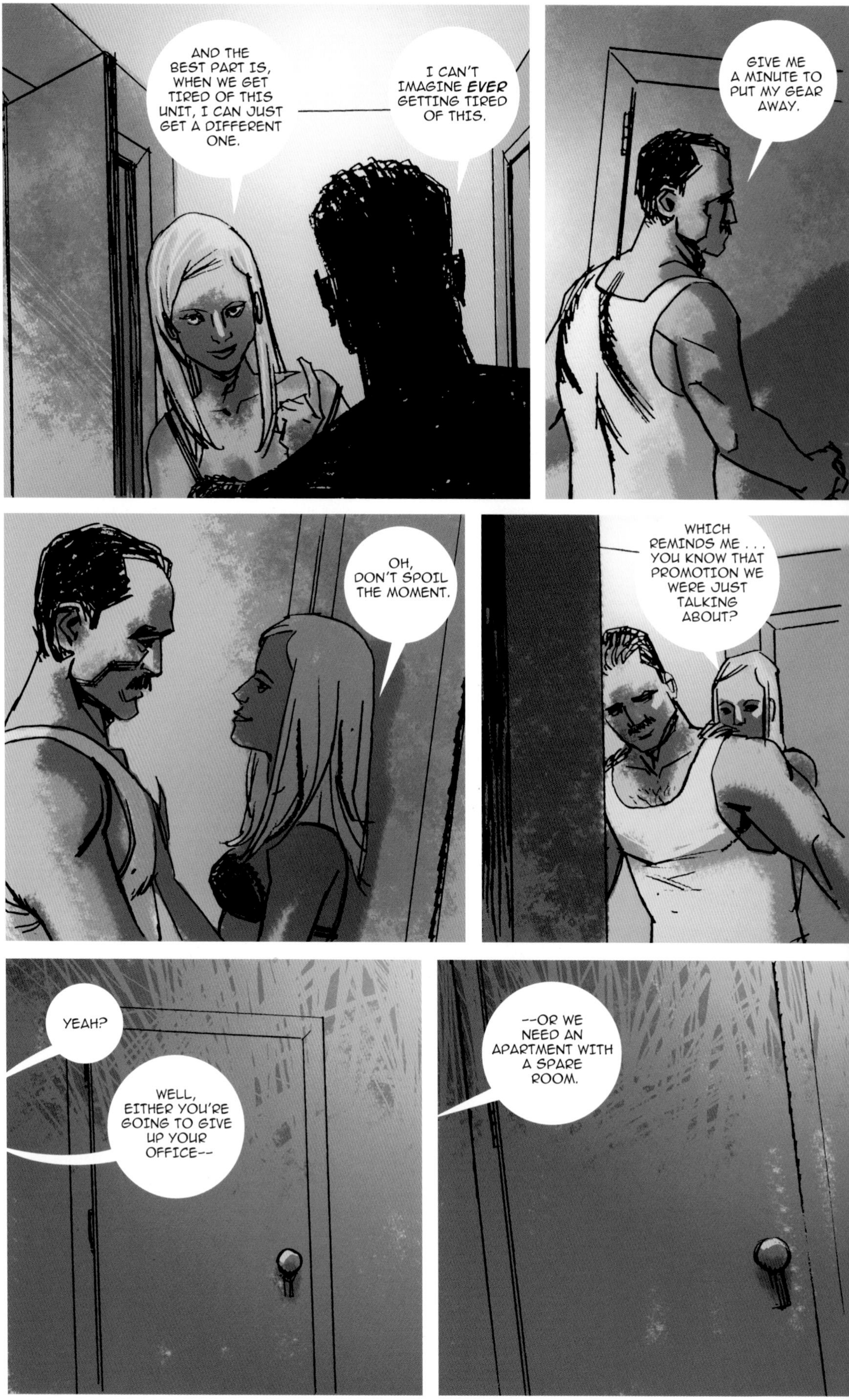
AND THE BEST PART IS, WHEN WE GET TIRED OF THIS UNIT, I CAN JUST GET A DIFFERENT ONE.
I CAN'T IMAGINE **EVER** GETTING TIRED OF THIS.
GIVE ME A MINUTE TO PUT MY GEAR AWAY.
OH, DON'T SPOIL THE MOMENT.
WHICH REMINDS ME . . . YOU KNOW THAT PROMOTION WE WERE JUST TALKING ABOUT?
YEAH?
WELL, EITHER YOU'RE GOING TO GIVE UP YOUR OFFICE--
--OR WE NEED AN APARTMENT WITH A SPARE ROOM.

Time for a reality check

—— OPINION

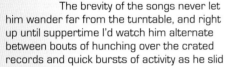

BY
MIKE
Daniels

I remember Sunday dinner at my grandparents' house: Ham in the oven, pie on the windowsill, and Grandpa in the living room with his phonograph. He owned an impressive collection of vintage 45s, painstakingly acquired during his youth and meticulously cared for so as to preserve the playability of the fragile wax disks. Danny & the Juniors (listen), Fats Domino (listen), and—of course—The King (listen).

The brevity of the songs never let him wander far from the turntable, and right up until suppertime I'd watch him alternate between bouts of hunching over the crated records and quick bursts of activity as he slid

At least, that's how I remember it today. At the time I was flabbergasted by the spectacle. Didn't he know about mp3s? He could fit a dozen songs easy on one CD (more, if we're talking about the quick hits from rock-'n'-roll's early days), push "play," and open up the rest of the afternoon to relaxation. Even better, he could transfer the entire collection to an iPod and leave the heavy crates at the curb for the trashman. Surely the upgrade would be worth the $1-per-song price tag, just on the grounds of convenience alone.

As was the case with just about everything back then, Grandpa already knew what I had yet to learn: *New* and *improved* may go well together on detergent boxes, but they seldom do in life. All of the convenience and neat-o capabilities of the digital music revolution carried another, hidden price tag—the loss of fidelity and pure, raw emotion that made those flawed 45s so crackling good.

Now the digital human revolution is upon us, and again we're faced with a choice between fidelity and flawlessness. The stakes are raised

ABOVE: Passersby admire a new window display at Virtual Self's showroom in the Fashion District.

the next selection from its original sleeve and set it beneath the arm. There was a soft crackle and hiss each time the needle found the groove, followed by music that sounded as though it had traveled across time for the sole purpose of reaching my ears.

to the nth degree, however, because in a world where technological substitutes allow us to remaster our selves, it won't be long until everyone plays the same. After all, following food and shelter, the third great human necessity is to be a "hottie." (Yes, I just dated myself with that word, but I've already used

MORE →

phonograph, so why not go whole hog.) We'll crate up all of our differences and imperfections and abandon them at the curb, and in the transfer we'll lose the qualities that, for better or for worse, make us who we are. No crackle. No hiss. Just the head-to-toe equivalent of vocal lilts and guitar twangs relegated to sterile, tinny precision.

To prevent myself from sounding like too much of a fuddy-duddy, I've got a promise for the twenty-something barista with acne scars at my local coffee shop, whose wrinkled clothes and too-long hair would never have passed muster in the diners of yore: You may get my order wrong three mornings out of five, but there'll be a little extra in your tip jar tomorrow, sport. Just for being you.

Quick bytes

DAILY DIGIT

– **17** The number of flash storms occurring in Fulton County this past May, according to a recent report released by the National Weather Service. The figure represents an increase of **6** from the same period last year, raising concerns that the damage caused by the storms will place excessive strain on county resources if the trend continues. May is traditionally the month that sees the highest level of flash storm activity.

TODAY IN HISTORY

– The first transcontinental telephone call connected New York and San Francisco on this day in **1914**. Though a more famous conversation between Alexander Graham Bell and Thomas Watson officially opened the line to commercial service on January 25, 1915, the true inaugural call was a trial conducted six months earlier by Theodore N. Vail, then president of the American Telephone & Telegraph Company (AT&T).

QUOTED

– "You can take the boy out of Georgia, but you can't take Georgia out of the boy," said Hollywood bad boy and Georgia native **Peyton Donovan** (search), on his recent purchase of a $6.2 million penthouse condo

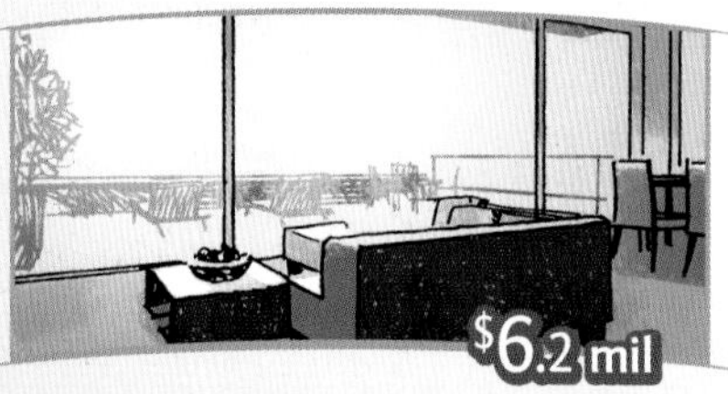
$6.2 mil

in downtown Central Georgia Metropolis. The actor spends the majority of his time in Los Angeles where he already owns a similarly spacious home, leading some critics to question the extravagance of the second residence.

Reality? Check.

—— OPPOSING VIEW

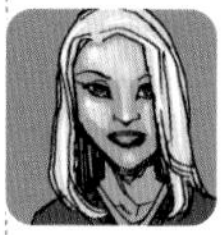

BY AMBER **Forbes**

Ever woken in the morning to cloudless skies, singing birds, and the overwhelming feeling that you're thrilled with the world exactly as it is?

Me neither.

"Older is better" is an absurd argument, that if followed to its logical conclusion would have patients undergoing root canal with nothing in the way of anesthesia save for scotch on the rocks. On second thought, better make that scotch neat; wouldn't want it tainted with any of that newfangled ice. It shouldn't surprise me that Mr. Daniels romanticizes the concept of old, though. We live in a world where men past the age of sixty are distinguished, and women past the age of sixty are divorced. I'd accuse him of being a hypocrite, if I didn't have it on good authority that he'd tapped out his editorial on the Southeast's only surviving functional typewriter. (How's *that* for throwback terminology?)

Okay, maybe that last one was a cheap shot, but the point is worth making. Decrying progress in the year 2039 seems to me a bit like lamenting your acrophobia (search) from the summit of Mount Everest—if the statement is true, then how the heck did you get all the way up there in the first place? Our society is comprised of every advance that has come before, from the discovery of fire to the invention of the combustion engine to the harnessing of solar power. Each of us is the beneficiary of myriad incremental changes that, when woven together, create the fabric of our daily lives, and you can't tug on a single thread without unraveling the whole. If not for the culture of one-click media distribution that began in earnest with mp3s, we can reason, we'd still be trudging down the driveway in slippers and robes every morning for the sake of door-to-door newspaper delivery.

The question I posed earlier is the only litmus test that's required here. If the day should ever arrive when the sun is shining, the birds are singing, and we're all satisfied with everything as it is, then our collective efforts to affect change—to weave more fabric—will stop. No one will have to tell us to stop, either. We'll inherently recognize that it's time to put down our shuttle and thread, and there will be nothing left to do except slip on the perfectly tailored garment and admire its fit. A pair of skinny jeans for the planet.

MORE →

And therein lies perhaps the simplest truth of all: It's not in our nature to settle for the status quo. We possess an intrinsic thirst for innovation that spurs mankind forward, pointing out the next hurdle even before our feet touch ground from clearing the previous one. It's the drive that led to the nonstick frying pan, the Martian landing, and, yes, even the personal surrogate. I suspect it's the same spirit that pushed Edison to invent Grandpa Daniels' beloved phonograph as well.

New *is* improved. And until such a time as our best minds devise the ability to create low-fat, calorically sensible meals that actually taste like food, you can find me combing the malls for a pair of jeans that won't make my butt look big.

Or maybe I'll buy a surrogate and wear whatever I want.

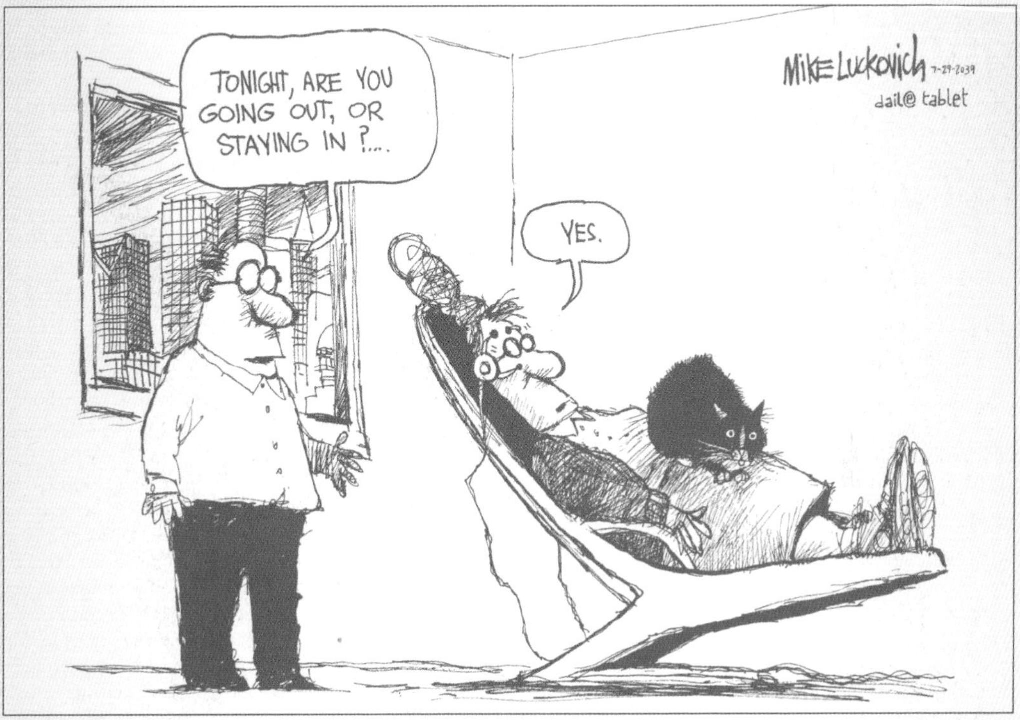
TONIGHT, ARE YOU GOING OUT, OR STAYING IN ?....
YES.
MIKE LUCKOVICH
dail@ tablet

Mass transit that actually gets it

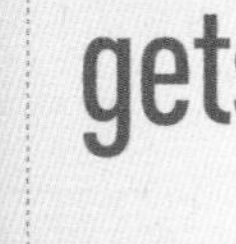

BY
LEE
Atterson
GUEST
COLUMNIST

Devising a means of reliable, commuter-friendly public transportation has proved to be America's great unsolvable riddle. With the nation's population moving from rural communities to urban centers in recent decades, countless initiatives have been launched in an effort to alleviate traffic congestion, improve air quality, and lessen the dependence on fossil fuels. Buses, trains, and carpools promised to move people in greater numbers and more efficiently, but commuters balked at the impact group travel would have on individual mobility. Vehicles powered by biodiesel, ethanol, and other alternative fuels were spawned by exorbitant gasoline prices, but the scattershot approach lacked the consistency needed to gain consensus among drivers who worried that an insufficient infrastructure would make refueling difficult. In every ensuing attempt, public acceptance remained similarly elusive.

With the new downtown skywalk system, civil engineering may at last trump public obstinacy. Skywalks reduce the number of cars on the road, the amount of CO_2 emissions produced by exhaust, and the barrels of oil consumed. At the same time they do not necessitate that individual mobility be sacrificed because skywalks, unlike buses or carpools, are always in motion, always available to meet the schedule of the commuter. While opponents are quick to point out that, for obvious reasons of safety, skywalks will never match the speed of automotive transportation, some of this is offset by the fact that they operate literally above the delays caused by peak travel hours, road repair, and traffic signals.

All of this is crucial because, as current behavioral studies suggest, the lesser the personal intrusion means the greater the chance of swaying opinion en masse. This is being borne out by the growing

MORE →

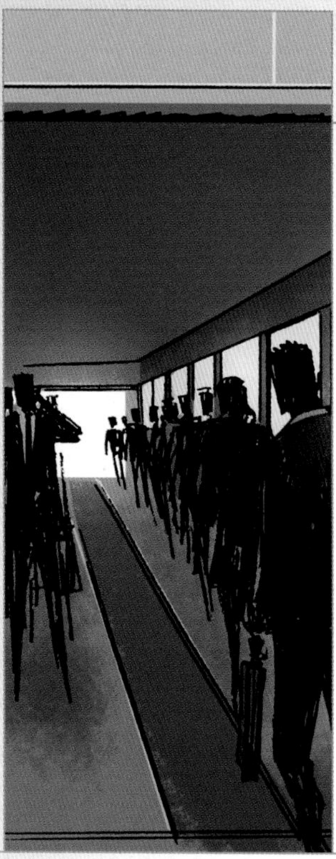

ABOVE: The skywalk above Marietta Street is one of the busiest in the metro area.

number of commuters taking to the skywalks here, as well as in other municipalities where similar initiatives have been implemented. Increased funding and an expansion of the skywalk system is sure to result, which in turn will attract additional commuters who find skywalks erected in their neighborhoods. One can envision our metropolitan areas being realigned by citizens who relocate to places where skywalks are prevalent, a shift that would effectively end the suburban mode of living that many recognize as already being in decline. Consumer automobiles could be rendered a secondary means of transportation, freeing up large amounts of disposable income to meet other needs. The impact on our cities would be profound.

→ **LEE ATTERSON** is author of the best-selling book *Sea Change: Behavioral Solutions to Modern Challenges.*

re:Action

READERS RESPOND TO THE JULY 22 EDITORIAL "Hiring Line"

(read)

I find the opposition of labor unions to surrogate-only hiring to be appalling. Removing the need for workman's comp insurance and other payroll costs from employers' balance sheets would lower the prices of goods for shoppers and make American products more competitive in the global marketplace. How many millions of jobs will have to move overseas before unions realize that they're a detriment to the cause of workers, not a benefit? In Asia, workers don't have unions. They have jobs.

— NORMAN WIZNIEWSKI,
Stone Mountain

Kudos to Mr. McGill and his union friends for standing up to the anti-worker establishment. Setting surrogate ownership as a condition of employment is no different than hiring someone because they are white or male. It discriminates against an entire segment of the population, and, worse, because many surrogate-only businesses fall under the category of blue-collar labor, it takes jobs away from the people who need a job most—those who don't have enough money to pay their rent, much less afford a surrogate. It's a new chapter in the same old story: The rich get richer, and the poor get poorer.

— TANDIE BONDERSON,
Jonesboro

Since when are business owners no longer allowed to determine their own hiring practices? Whether or not anyone thinks it's fair to replace workers with operators is irrelevant. In a free-market system, business decisions are either validated by profits or invalidated by bankruptcy. If consumers don't like the way a business is run, then they can take their patronage elsewhere. Once we start telling private businesses who they can and can't hire, then the concept of private business goes away.

— SHIRLEY RUVELLO,
Suwanee

I'm a licensed electrician with 25 years of experience in commercial installing. My whole life I worked for the same company, and I never had a single complaint about my work performance. Six months ago my boss told all of us he wanted us to start working through surrogates because it was cheaper to insure equipment than people. We were given 30 days to purchase a unit, otherwise we'd be out of a job. None of us were given raises to cover the additional expense, or to even help cover it. When the 30 days were up, me and five other longtime employees were let go and replaced with younger hires that already had their own surrogates. It doesn't seem fair that we should lose our jobs, or that buildings will have their wiring installed by the inexperienced crews that replaced us.

— CHARLES PEARSALL,
Vine City

What's your opinion?

The Dail-e Tablet welcomes readers to submit letters for publication. We reserve the right to truncate submissions to meet space requirements. Letters are accepted by email only. Please refrain from profanity, and include the title of the article you are responding to in the email's subject header. To submit a letter / click here

chapter
TWO

Spark

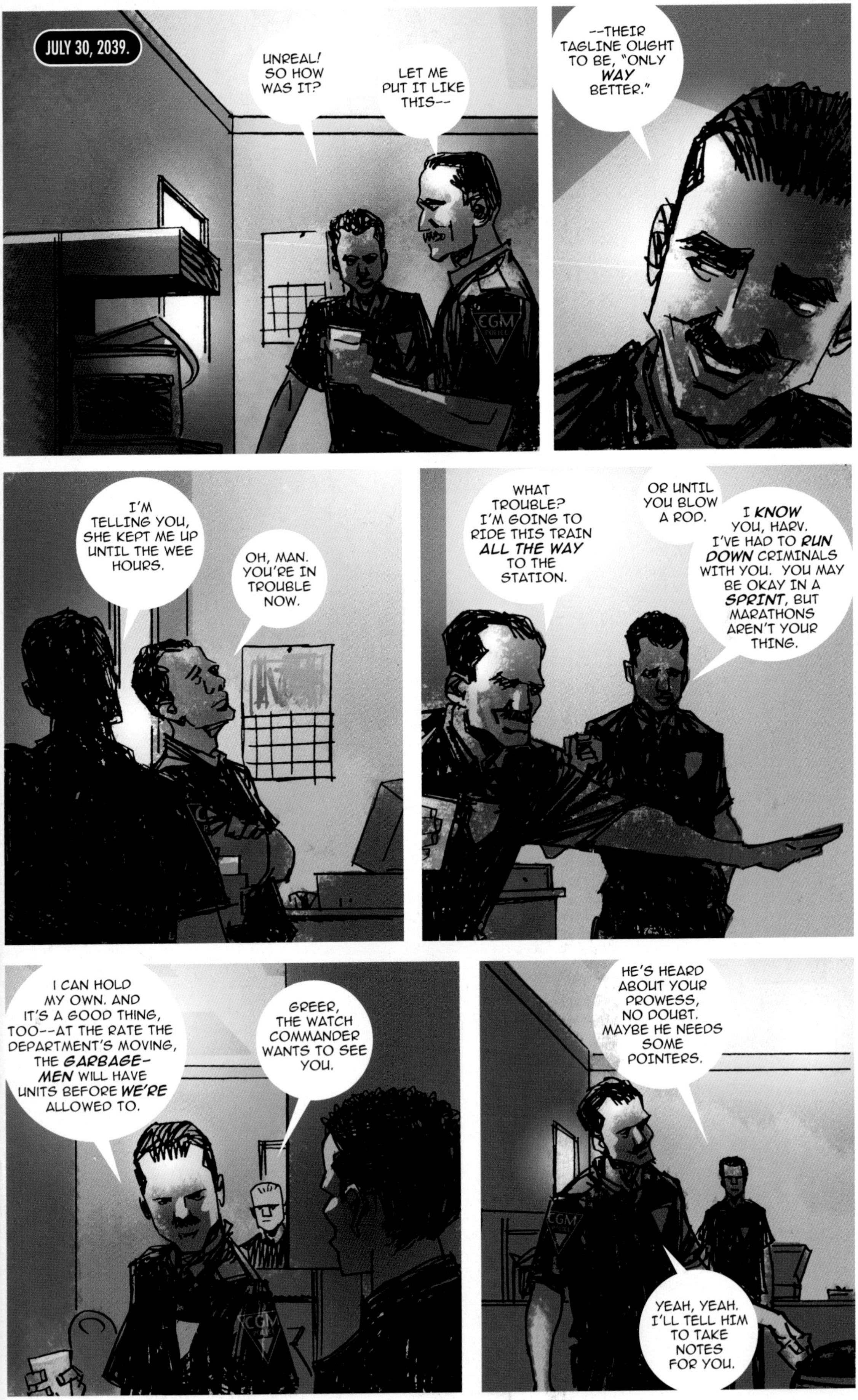
JULY 30, 2039.
UNREAL! SO HOW WAS IT?
LET ME PUT IT LIKE THIS--
--THEIR TAGLINE OUGHT TO BE, "ONLY WAY BETTER."
I'M TELLING YOU, SHE KEPT ME UP UNTIL THE WEE HOURS.
OH, MAN. YOU'RE IN TROUBLE NOW.
WHAT TROUBLE? I'M GOING TO RIDE THIS TRAIN ALL THE WAY TO THE STATION.
OR UNTIL YOU BLOW A ROD.
I KNOW YOU, HARV. I'VE HAD TO RUN DOWN CRIMINALS WITH YOU. YOU MAY BE OKAY IN A SPRINT, BUT MARATHONS AREN'T YOUR THING.
I CAN HOLD MY OWN. AND IT'S A GOOD THING, TOO--AT THE RATE THE DEPARTMENT'S MOVING, THE GARBAGE-MEN WILL HAVE UNITS BEFORE WE'RE ALLOWED TO.
GREER, THE WATCH COMMANDER WANTS TO SEE YOU.
HE'S HEARD ABOUT YOUR PROWESS, NO DOUBT. MAYBE HE NEEDS SOME POINTERS.
YEAH, YEAH. I'LL TELL HIM TO TAKE NOTES FOR YOU.

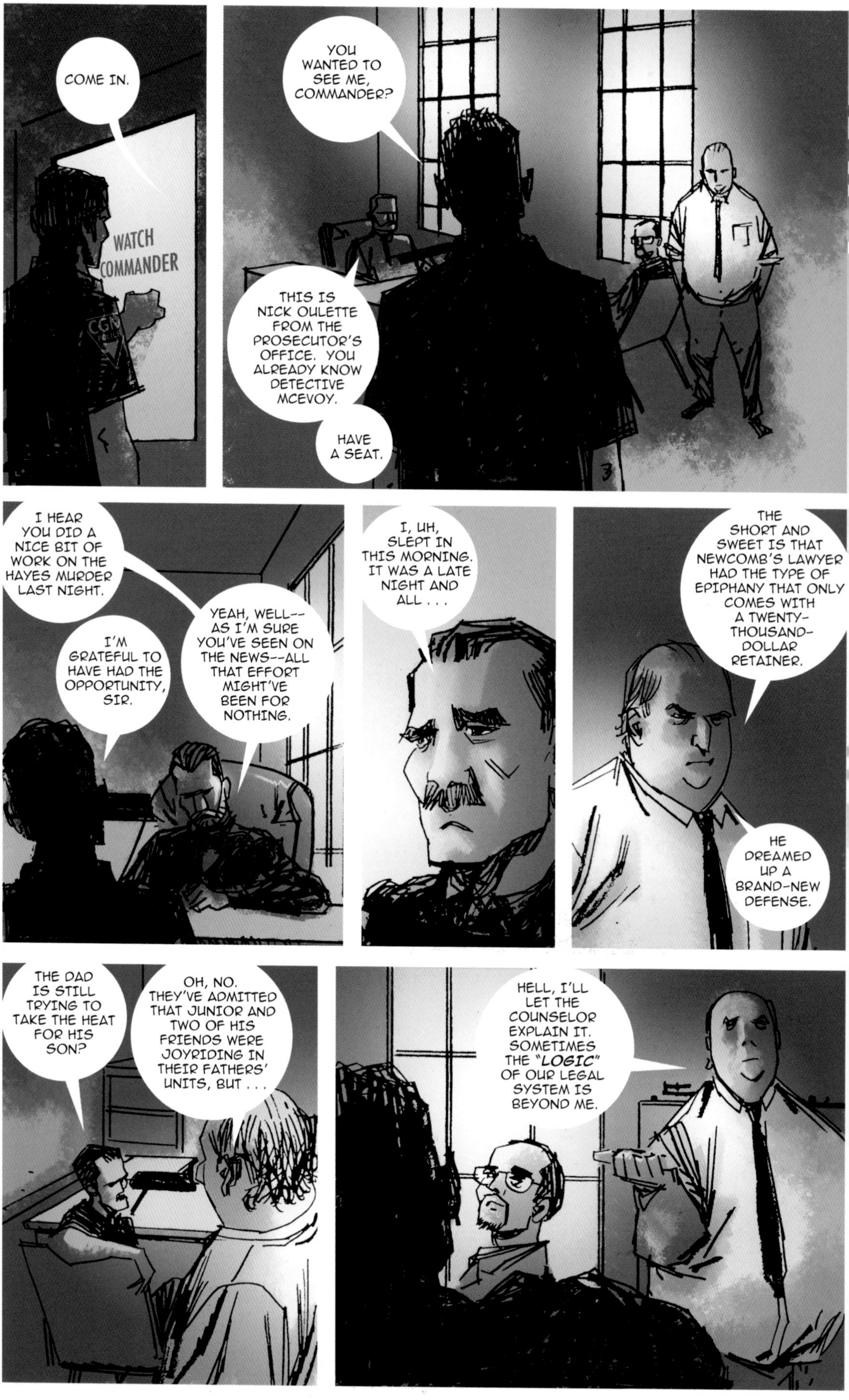
COME IN.
WATCH COMMANDER
YOU WANTED TO SEE ME, COMMANDER?
THIS IS NICK OULETTE FROM THE PROSECUTOR'S OFFICE. YOU ALREADY KNOW DETECTIVE MCEVOY.
HAVE A SEAT.
I HEAR YOU DID A NICE BIT OF WORK ON THE HAYES MURDER LAST NIGHT.
I'M GRATEFUL TO HAVE HAD THE OPPORTUNITY, SIR.
YEAH, WELL-- AS I'M SURE YOU'VE SEEN ON THE NEWS--ALL THAT EFFORT MIGHT'VE BEEN FOR NOTHING.
I, UH, SLEPT IN THIS MORNING. IT WAS A LATE NIGHT AND ALL . . .
THE SHORT AND SWEET IS THAT NEWCOMB'S LAWYER HAD THE TYPE OF EPIPHANY THAT ONLY COMES WITH A TWENTY-THOUSAND-DOLLAR RETAINER.
HE DREAMED UP A BRAND-NEW DEFENSE.
THE DAD IS STILL TRYING TO TAKE THE HEAT FOR HIS SON?
OH, NO. THEY'VE ADMITTED THAT JUNIOR AND TWO OF HIS FRIENDS WERE JOYRIDING IN THEIR FATHERS' UNITS, BUT . . .
HELL, I'LL LET THE COUNSELOR EXPLAIN IT. SOMETIMES THE "*LOGIC*" OF OUR LEGAL SYSTEM IS BEYOND ME.

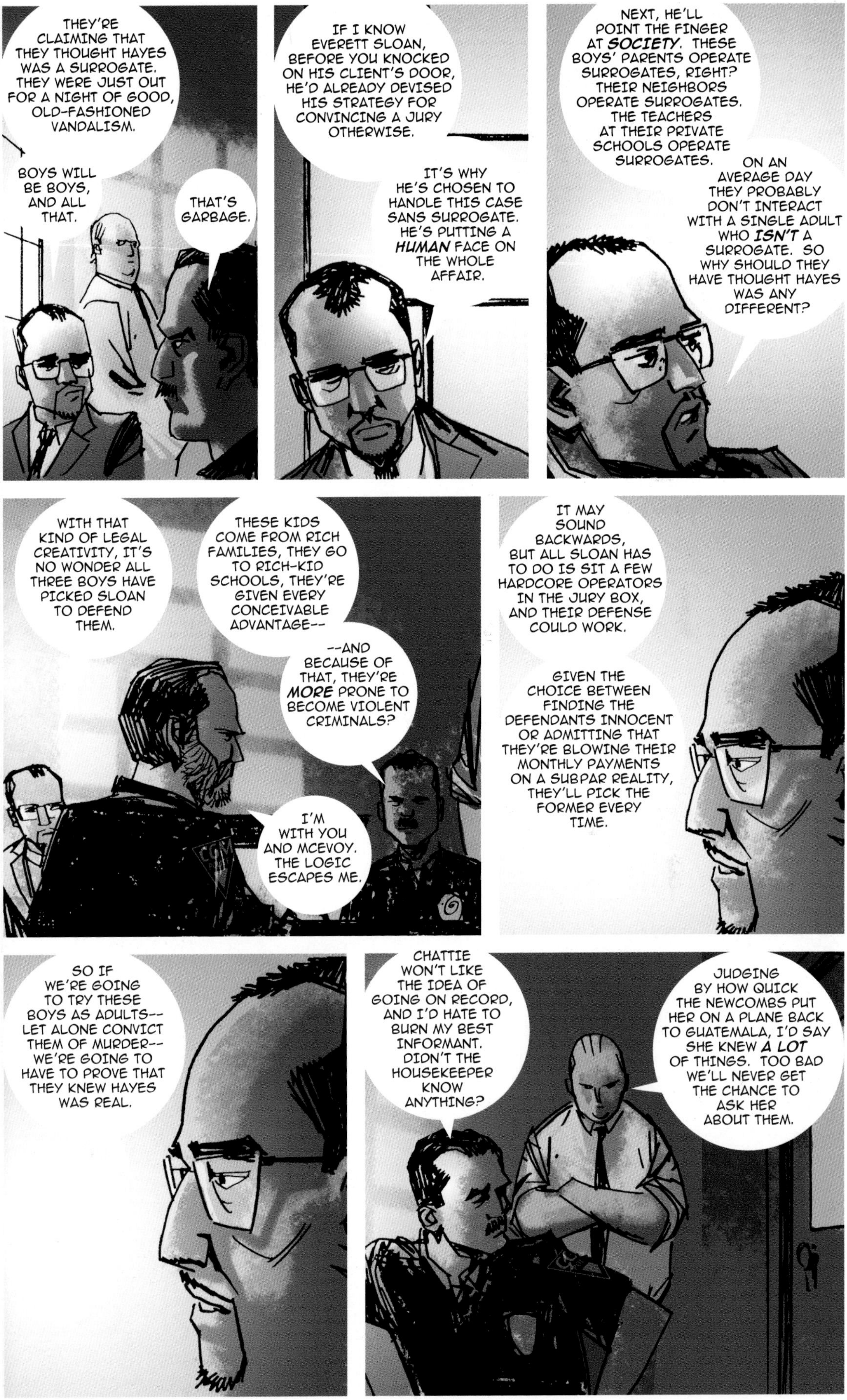
THEY'RE CLAIMING THAT THEY THOUGHT HAYES WAS A SURROGATE. THEY WERE JUST OUT FOR A NIGHT OF GOOD, OLD-FASHIONED VANDALISM.
BOYS WILL BE BOYS, AND ALL THAT.
THAT'S GARBAGE.
IF I KNOW EVERETT SLOAN, BEFORE YOU KNOCKED ON HIS CLIENT'S DOOR, HE'D ALREADY DEVISED HIS STRATEGY FOR CONVINCING A JURY OTHERWISE.
IT'S WHY HE'S CHOSEN TO HANDLE THIS CASE SANS SURROGATE. HE'S PUTTING A HUMAN FACE ON THE WHOLE AFFAIR.
NEXT, HE'LL POINT THE FINGER AT SOCIETY. THESE BOYS' PARENTS OPERATE SURROGATES, RIGHT? THEIR NEIGHBORS OPERATE SURROGATES. THE TEACHERS AT THEIR PRIVATE SCHOOLS OPERATE SURROGATES.
ON AN AVERAGE DAY THEY PROBABLY DON'T INTERACT WITH A SINGLE ADULT WHO ISN'T A SURROGATE. SO WHY SHOULD THEY HAVE THOUGHT HAYES WAS ANY DIFFERENT?
WITH THAT KIND OF LEGAL CREATIVITY, IT'S NO WONDER ALL THREE BOYS HAVE PICKED SLOAN TO DEFEND THEM.
THESE KIDS COME FROM RICH FAMILIES, THEY GO TO RICH-KID SCHOOLS, THEY'RE GIVEN EVERY CONCEIVABLE ADVANTAGE--
--AND BECAUSE OF THAT, THEY'RE MORE PRONE TO BECOME VIOLENT CRIMINALS?
I'M WITH YOU AND MCEVOY. THE LOGIC ESCAPES ME.
IT MAY SOUND BACKWARDS, BUT ALL SLOAN HAS TO DO IS SIT A FEW HARDCORE OPERATORS IN THE JURY BOX, AND THEIR DEFENSE COULD WORK.
GIVEN THE CHOICE BETWEEN FINDING THE DEFENDANTS INNOCENT OR ADMITTING THAT THEY'RE BLOWING THEIR MONTHLY PAYMENTS ON A SUBPAR REALITY, THEY'LL PICK THE FORMER EVERY TIME.
SO IF WE'RE GOING TO TRY THESE BOYS AS ADULTS-- LET ALONE CONVICT THEM OF MURDER-- WE'RE GOING TO HAVE TO PROVE THAT THEY KNEW HAYES WAS REAL.
CHATTIE WON'T LIKE THE IDEA OF GOING ON RECORD, AND I'D HATE TO BURN MY BEST INFORMANT. DIDN'T THE HOUSEKEEPER KNOW ANYTHING?
JUDGING BY HOW QUICK THE NEWCOMBS PUT HER ON A PLANE BACK TO GUATEMALA, I'D SAY SHE KNEW A LOT OF THINGS. TOO BAD WE'LL NEVER GET THE CHANCE TO ASK HER ABOUT THEM.

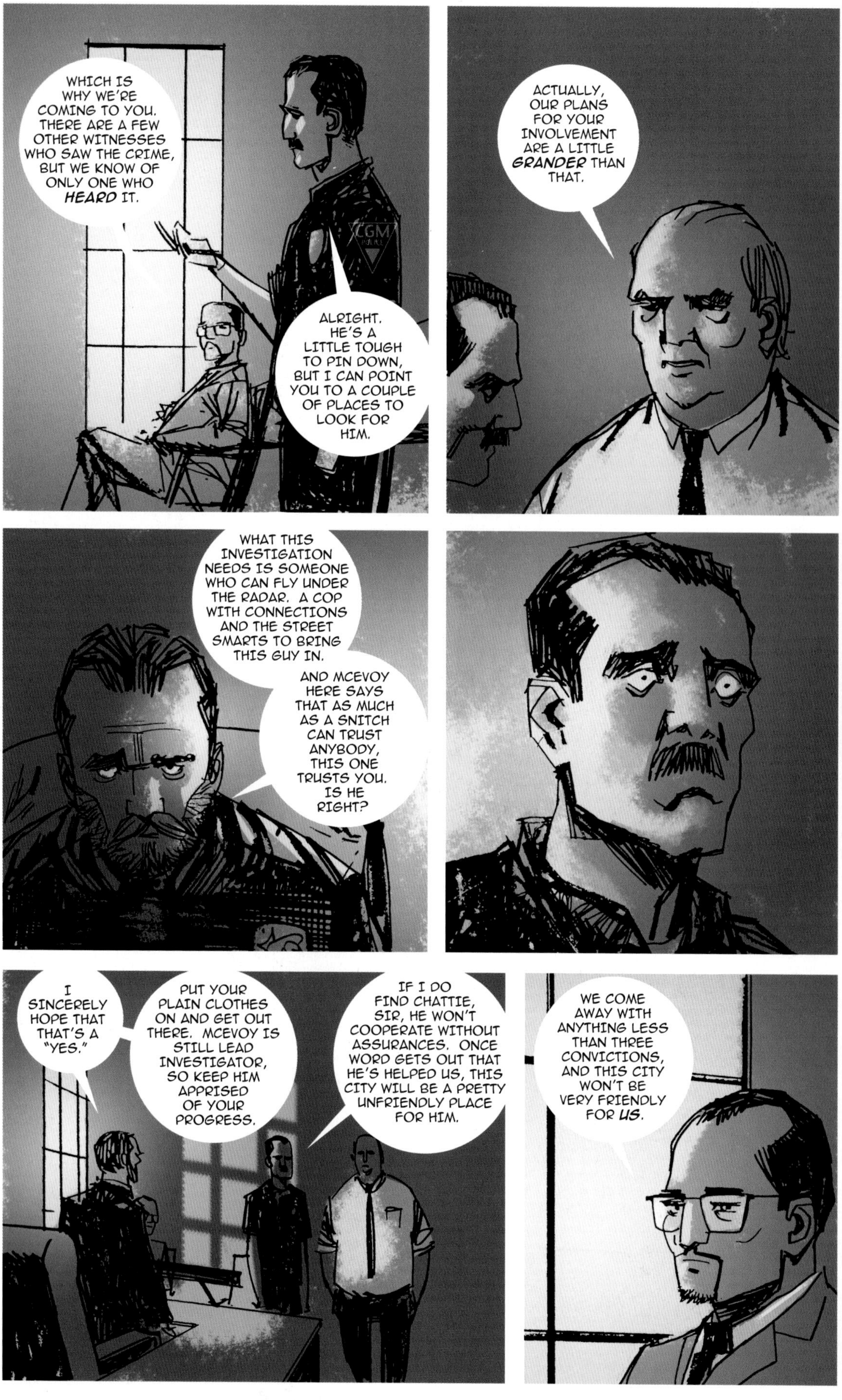

WHICH IS WHY WE'RE COMING TO YOU. THERE ARE A FEW OTHER WITNESSES WHO SAW THE CRIME, BUT WE KNOW OF ONLY ONE WHO *HEARD* IT.
ALRIGHT. HE'S A LITTLE TOUGH TO PIN DOWN, BUT I CAN POINT YOU TO A COUPLE OF PLACES TO LOOK FOR HIM.
ACTUALLY, OUR PLANS FOR YOUR INVOLVEMENT ARE A LITTLE *GRANDER* THAN THAT.
WHAT THIS INVESTIGATION NEEDS IS SOMEONE WHO CAN FLY UNDER THE RADAR. A COP WITH CONNECTIONS AND THE STREET SMARTS TO BRING THIS GUY IN.
AND MCEVOY HERE SAYS THAT AS MUCH AS A SNITCH CAN TRUST ANYBODY, THIS ONE TRUSTS YOU. IS HE RIGHT?
I SINCERELY HOPE THAT THAT'S A "YES."
PUT YOUR PLAIN CLOTHES ON AND GET OUT THERE. MCEVOY IS STILL LEAD INVESTIGATOR, SO KEEP HIM APPRISED OF YOUR PROGRESS.
IF I DO FIND CHATTIE, SIR, HE WON'T COOPERATE WITHOUT ASSURANCES. ONCE WORD GETS OUT THAT HE'S HELPED US, THIS CITY WILL BE A PRETTY UNFRIENDLY PLACE FOR HIM.
WE COME AWAY WITH ANYTHING LESS THAN THREE CONVICTIONS, AND THIS CITY WON'T BE VERY FRIENDLY FOR *US*.

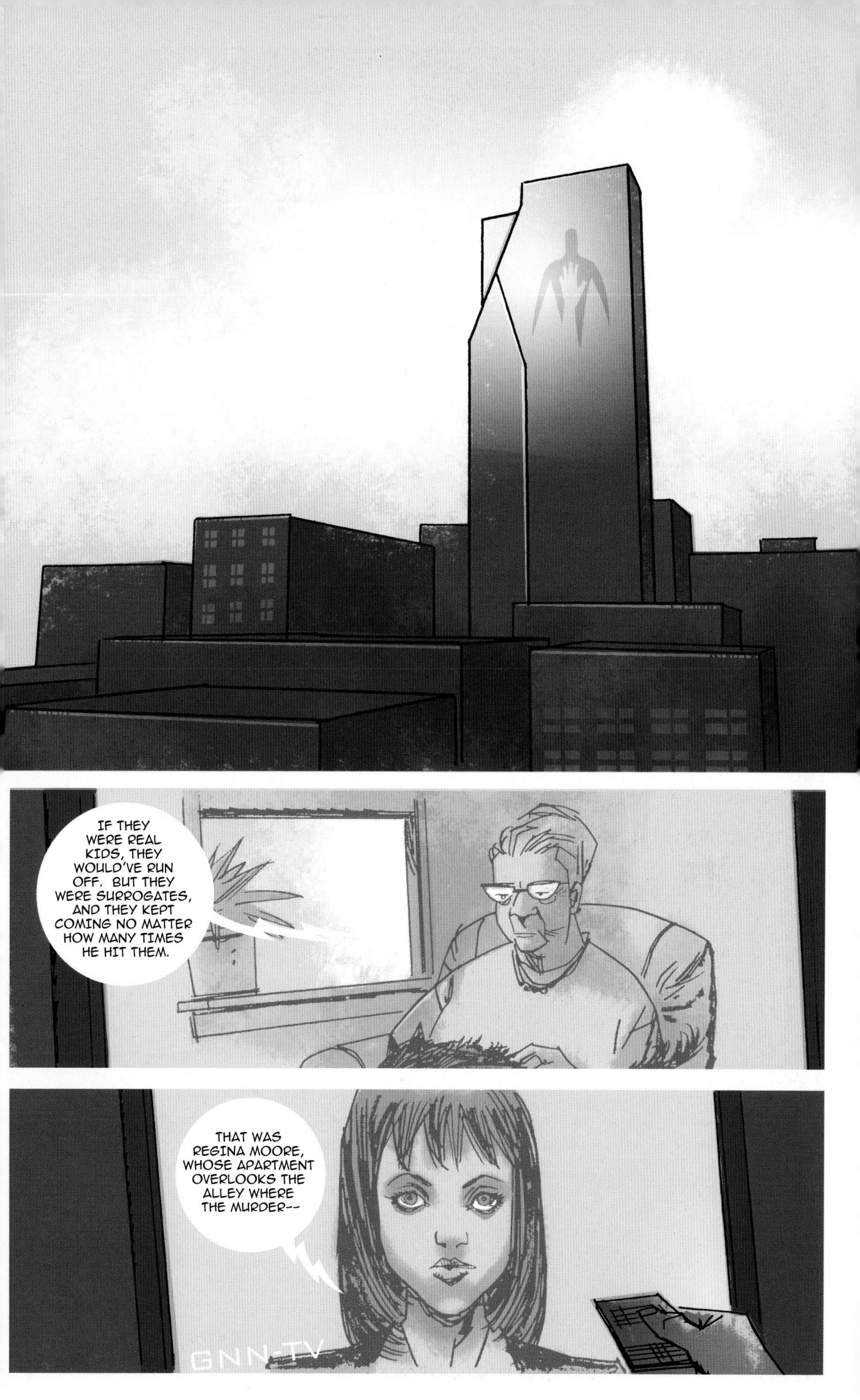
IF THEY WERE REAL KIDS, THEY WOULD'VE RUN OFF. BUT THEY WERE SURROGATES, AND THEY KEPT COMING NO MATTER HOW MANY TIMES HE HIT THEM.
THAT WAS REGINA MOORE, WHOSE APARTMENT OVERLOOKS THE ALLEY WHERE THE MURDER--
GNN-TV

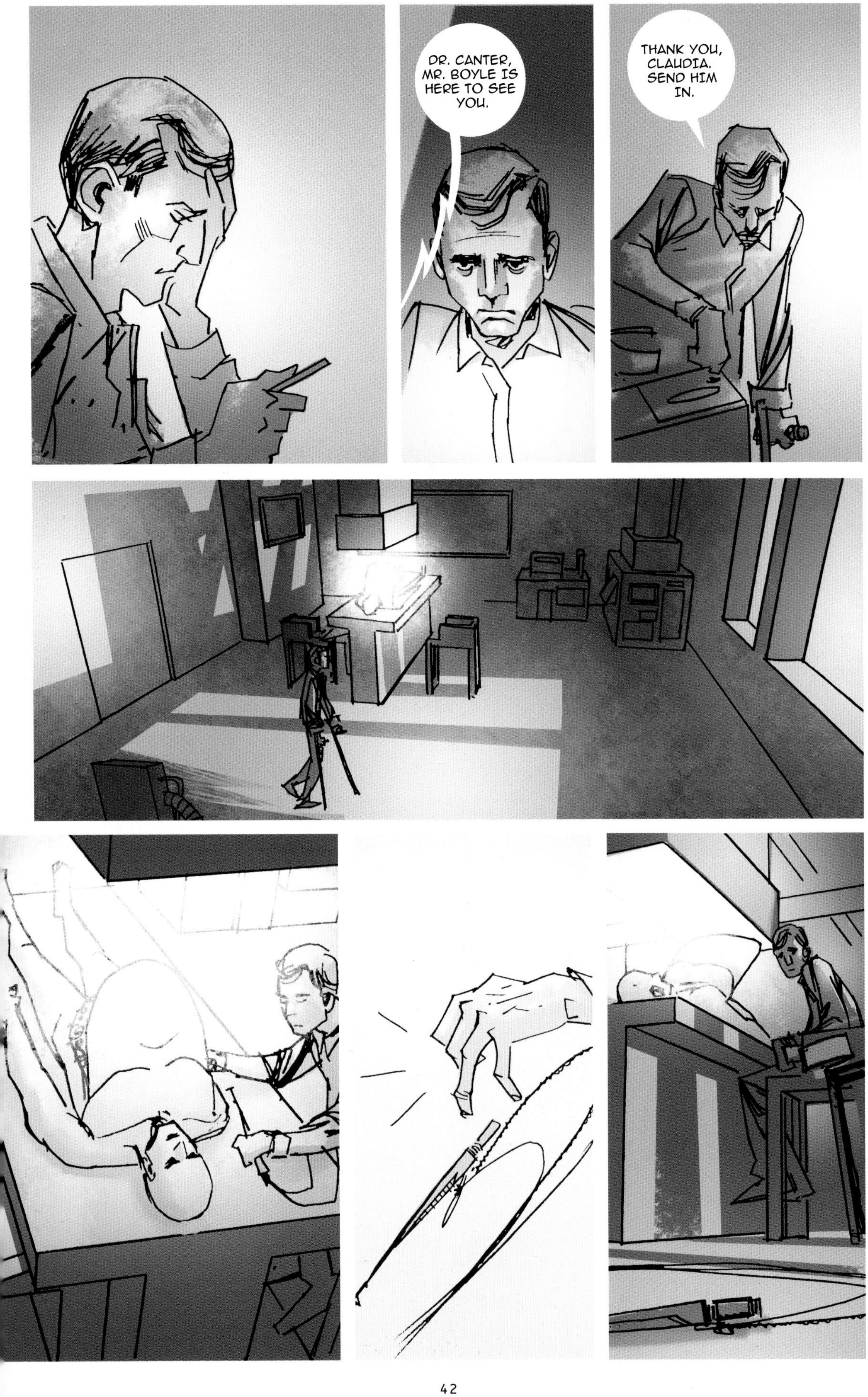
DR. CANTER, MR. BOYLE IS HERE TO SEE YOU.
THANK YOU, CLAUDIA. SEND HIM IN.

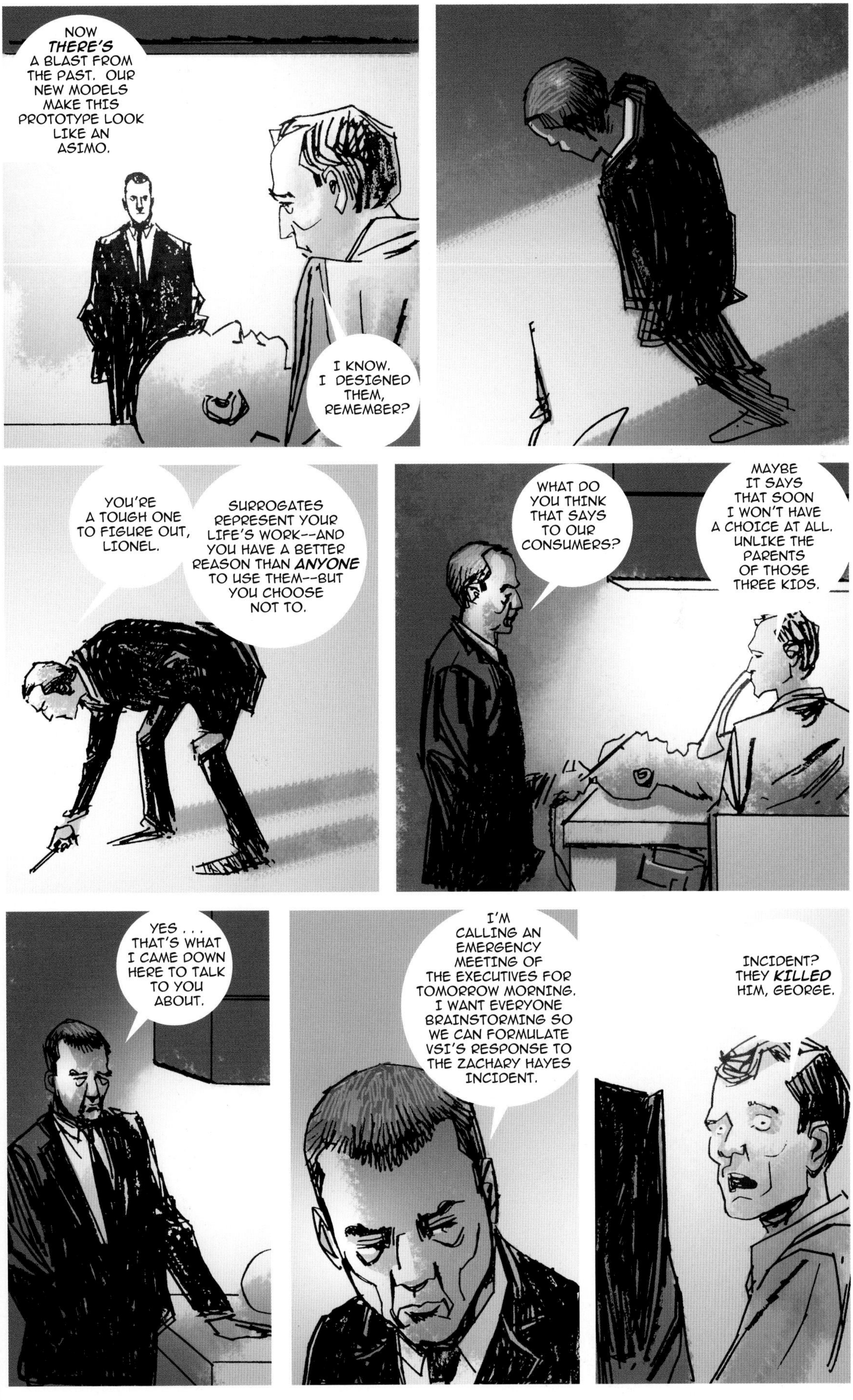
NOW THERE'S A BLAST FROM THE PAST. OUR NEW MODELS MAKE THIS PROTOTYPE LOOK LIKE AN ASIMO.
I KNOW. I DESIGNED THEM, REMEMBER?
YOU'RE A TOUGH ONE TO FIGURE OUT, LIONEL.
SURROGATES REPRESENT YOUR LIFE'S WORK--AND YOU HAVE A BETTER REASON THAN ANYONE TO USE THEM--BUT YOU CHOOSE NOT TO.
WHAT DO YOU THINK THAT SAYS TO OUR CONSUMERS?
MAYBE IT SAYS THAT SOON I WON'T HAVE A CHOICE AT ALL. UNLIKE THE PARENTS OF THOSE THREE KIDS.
YES . . . THAT'S WHAT I CAME DOWN HERE TO TALK TO YOU ABOUT.
I'M CALLING AN EMERGENCY MEETING OF THE EXECUTIVES FOR TOMORROW MORNING. I WANT EVERYONE BRAINSTORMING SO WE CAN FORMULATE VSI'S RESPONSE TO THE ZACHARY HAYES INCIDENT.
INCIDENT? THEY KILLED HIM, GEORGE.

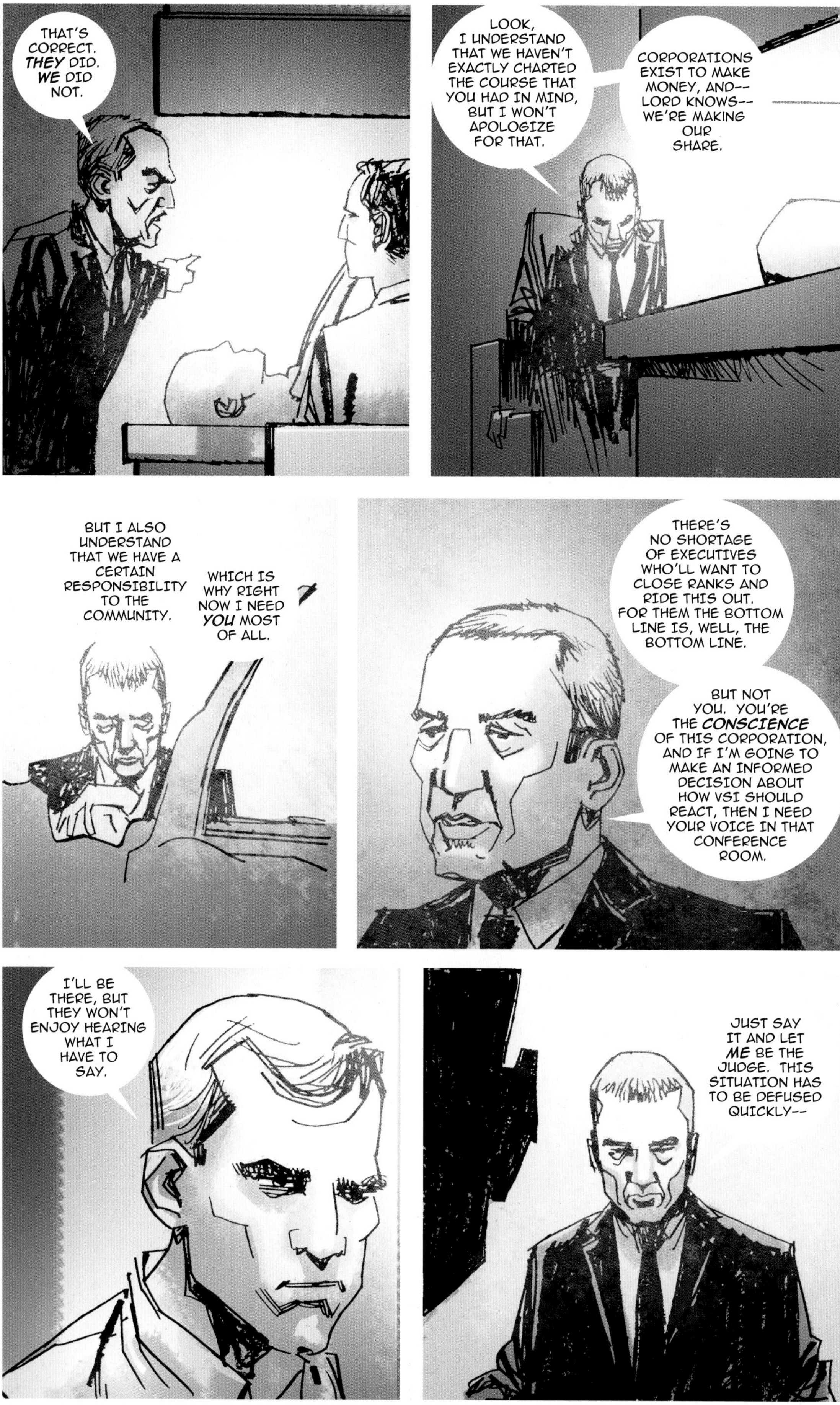
THAT'S CORRECT. THEY DID. WE DID NOT.
LOOK, I UNDERSTAND THAT WE HAVEN'T EXACTLY CHARTED THE COURSE THAT YOU HAD IN MIND, BUT I WON'T APOLOGIZE FOR THAT.
CORPORATIONS EXIST TO MAKE MONEY, AND-- LORD KNOWS-- WE'RE MAKING OUR SHARE.
BUT I ALSO UNDERSTAND THAT WE HAVE A CERTAIN RESPONSIBILITY TO THE COMMUNITY.
WHICH IS WHY RIGHT NOW I NEED YOU MOST OF ALL.
THERE'S NO SHORTAGE OF EXECUTIVES WHO'LL WANT TO CLOSE RANKS AND RIDE THIS OUT. FOR THEM THE BOTTOM LINE IS, WELL, THE BOTTOM LINE.
BUT NOT YOU. YOU'RE THE CONSCIENCE OF THIS CORPORATION, AND IF I'M GOING TO MAKE AN INFORMED DECISION ABOUT HOW VSI SHOULD REACT, THEN I NEED YOUR VOICE IN THAT CONFERENCE ROOM.
I'LL BE THERE, BUT THEY WON'T ENJOY HEARING WHAT I HAVE TO SAY.
JUST SAY IT AND LET ME BE THE JUDGE. THIS SITUATION HAS TO BE DEFUSED QUICKLY--

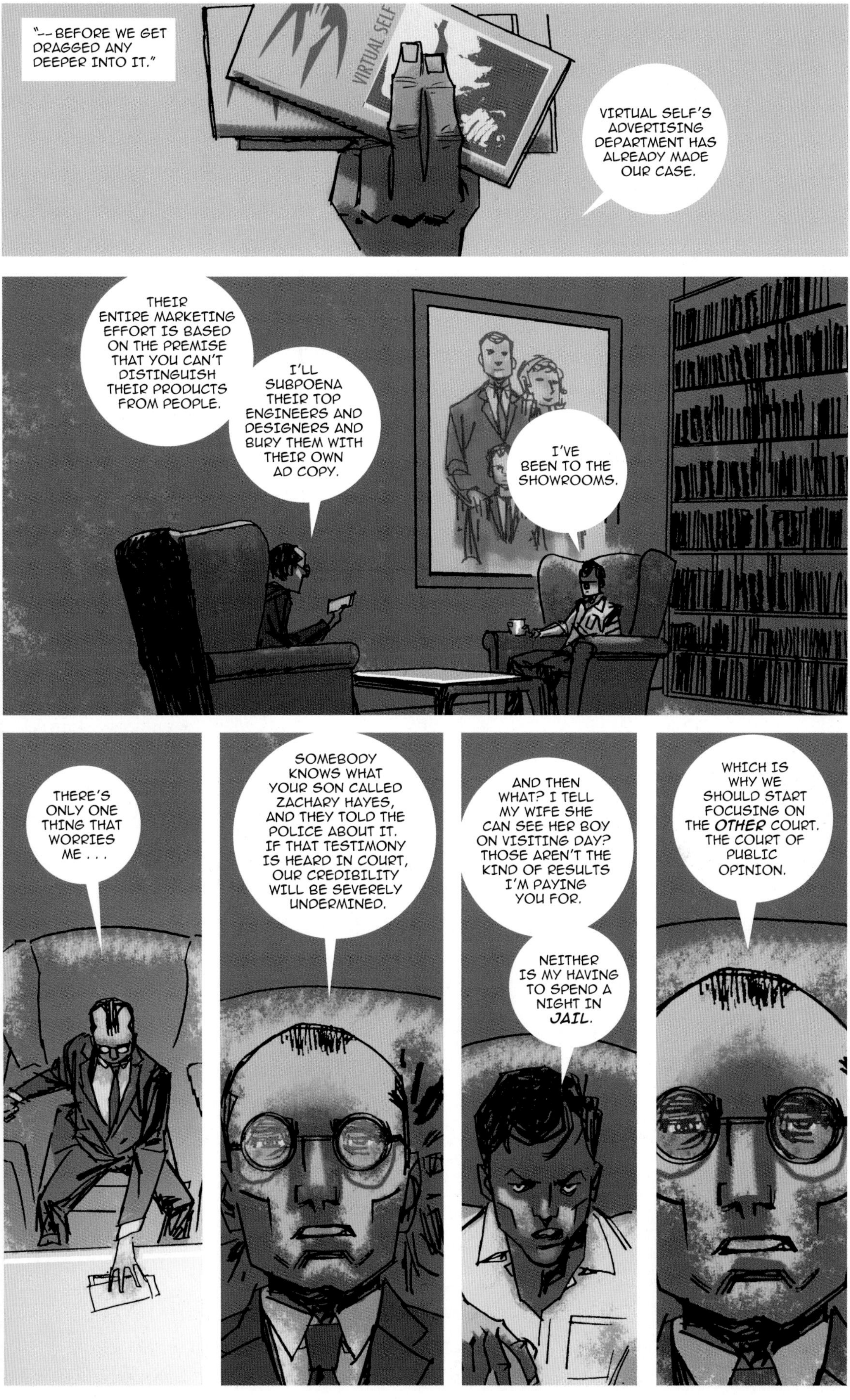
"--BEFORE WE GET DRAGGED ANY DEEPER INTO IT."
VIRTUAL SELF'S ADVERTISING DEPARTMENT HAS ALREADY MADE OUR CASE.
THEIR ENTIRE MARKETING EFFORT IS BASED ON THE PREMISE THAT YOU CAN'T DISTINGUISH THEIR PRODUCTS FROM PEOPLE.
I'LL SUBPOENA THEIR TOP ENGINEERS AND DESIGNERS AND BURY THEM WITH THEIR OWN AD COPY.
I'VE BEEN TO THE SHOWROOMS.
THERE'S ONLY ONE THING THAT WORRIES ME . . .
SOMEBODY KNOWS WHAT YOUR SON CALLED ZACHARY HAYES, AND THEY TOLD THE POLICE ABOUT IT. IF THAT TESTIMONY IS HEARD IN COURT, OUR CREDIBILITY WILL BE SEVERELY UNDERMINED.
AND THEN WHAT? I TELL MY WIFE SHE CAN SEE HER BOY ON VISITING DAY? THOSE AREN'T THE KIND OF RESULTS I'M PAYING YOU FOR.
NEITHER IS MY HAVING TO SPEND A NIGHT IN JAIL.
WHICH IS WHY WE SHOULD START FOCUSING ON THE OTHER COURT. THE COURT OF PUBLIC OPINION.

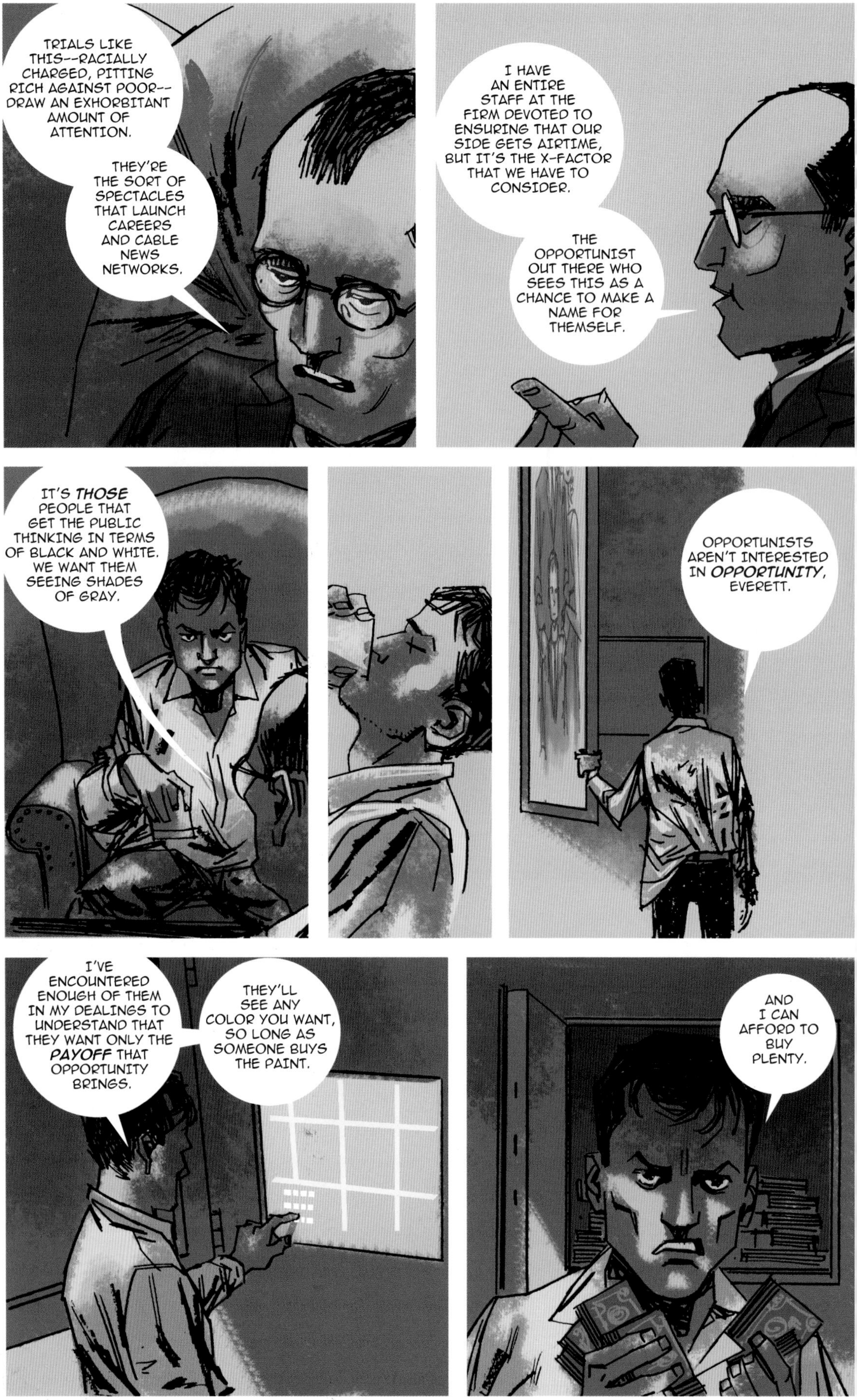
TRIALS LIKE THIS--RACIALLY CHARGED, PITTING RICH AGAINST POOR--DRAW AN EXHORBITANT AMOUNT OF ATTENTION.
THEY'RE THE SORT OF SPECTACLES THAT LAUNCH CAREERS AND CABLE NEWS NETWORKS.
I HAVE AN ENTIRE STAFF AT THE FIRM DEVOTED TO ENSURING THAT OUR SIDE GETS AIRTIME, BUT IT'S THE X-FACTOR THAT WE HAVE TO CONSIDER.
THE OPPORTUNIST OUT THERE WHO SEES THIS AS A CHANCE TO MAKE A NAME FOR THEMSELF.
IT'S *THOSE* PEOPLE THAT GET THE PUBLIC THINKING IN TERMS OF BLACK AND WHITE. WE WANT THEM SEEING SHADES OF GRAY.
OPPORTUNISTS AREN'T INTERESTED IN *OPPORTUNITY*, EVERETT.
I'VE ENCOUNTERED ENOUGH OF THEM IN MY DEALINGS TO UNDERSTAND THAT THEY WANT ONLY THE *PAYOFF* THAT OPPORTUNITY BRINGS.
THEY'LL SEE ANY COLOR YOU WANT, SO LONG AS SOMEONE BUYS THE PAINT.
AND I CAN AFFORD TO BUY PLENTY.

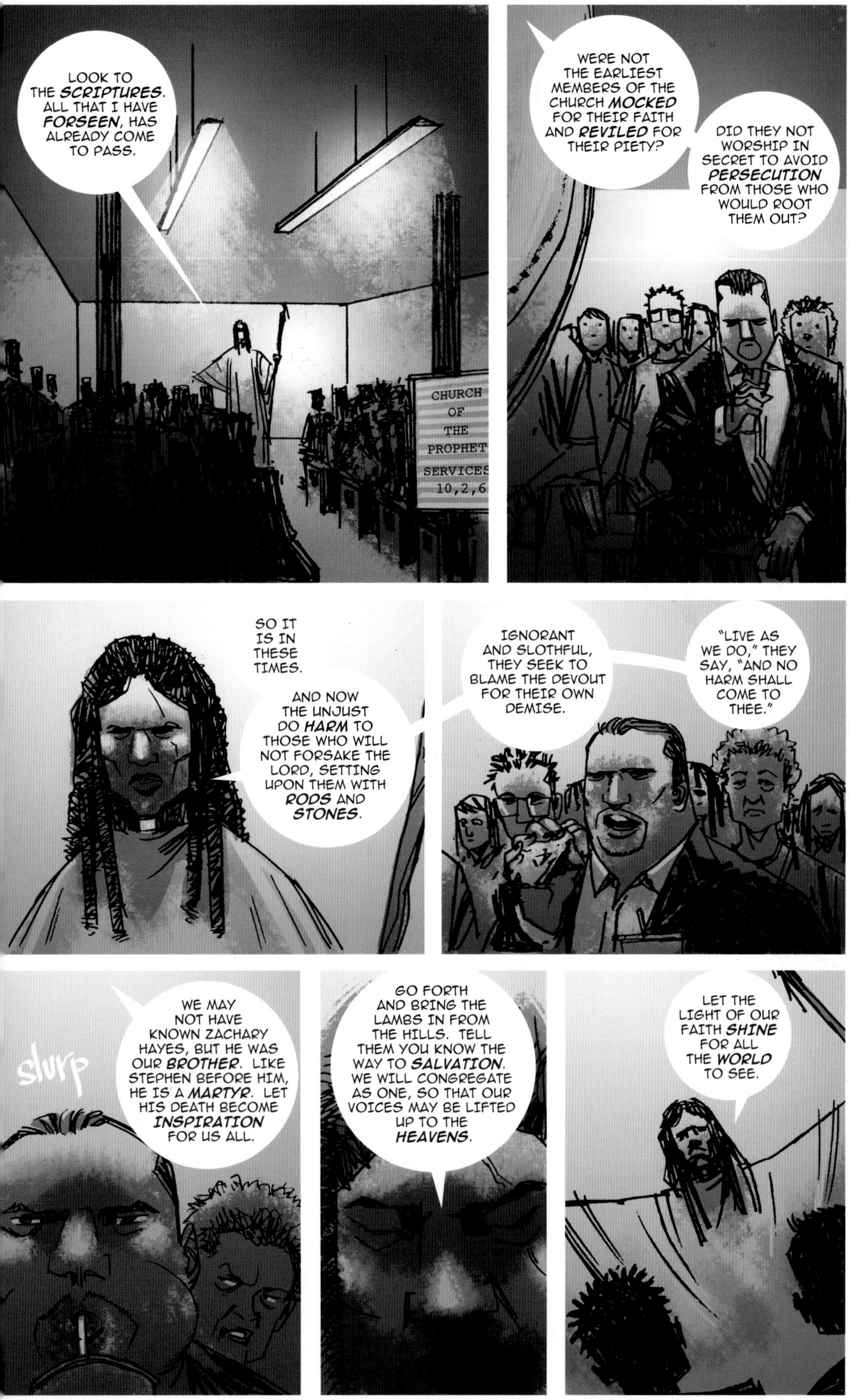
LOOK TO THE SCRIPTURES. ALL THAT I HAVE FORSEEN, HAS ALREADY COME TO PASS.
CHURCH OF THE PROPHET SERVICES 10,2,6
WERE NOT THE EARLIEST MEMBERS OF THE CHURCH MOCKED FOR THEIR FAITH AND REVILED FOR THEIR PIETY?
DID THEY NOT WORSHIP IN SECRET TO AVOID PERSECUTION FROM THOSE WHO WOULD ROOT THEM OUT?
SO IT IS IN THESE TIMES.
AND NOW THE UNJUST DO HARM TO THOSE WHO WILL NOT FORSAKE THE LORD, SETTING UPON THEM WITH RODS AND STONES.
IGNORANT AND SLOTHFUL, THEY SEEK TO BLAME THE DEVOUT FOR THEIR OWN DEMISE.
"LIVE AS WE DO," THEY SAY, "AND NO HARM SHALL COME TO THEE."
slurp
WE MAY NOT HAVE KNOWN ZACHARY HAYES, BUT HE WAS OUR BROTHER. LIKE STEPHEN BEFORE HIM, HE IS A MARTYR. LET HIS DEATH BECOME INSPIRATION FOR US ALL.
GO FORTH AND BRING THE LAMBS IN FROM THE HILLS. TELL THEM YOU KNOW THE WAY TO SALVATION. WE WILL CONGREGATE AS ONE, SO THAT OUR VOICES MAY BE LIFTED UP TO THE HEAVENS.
LET THE LIGHT OF OUR FAITH SHINE FOR ALL THE WORLD TO SEE.

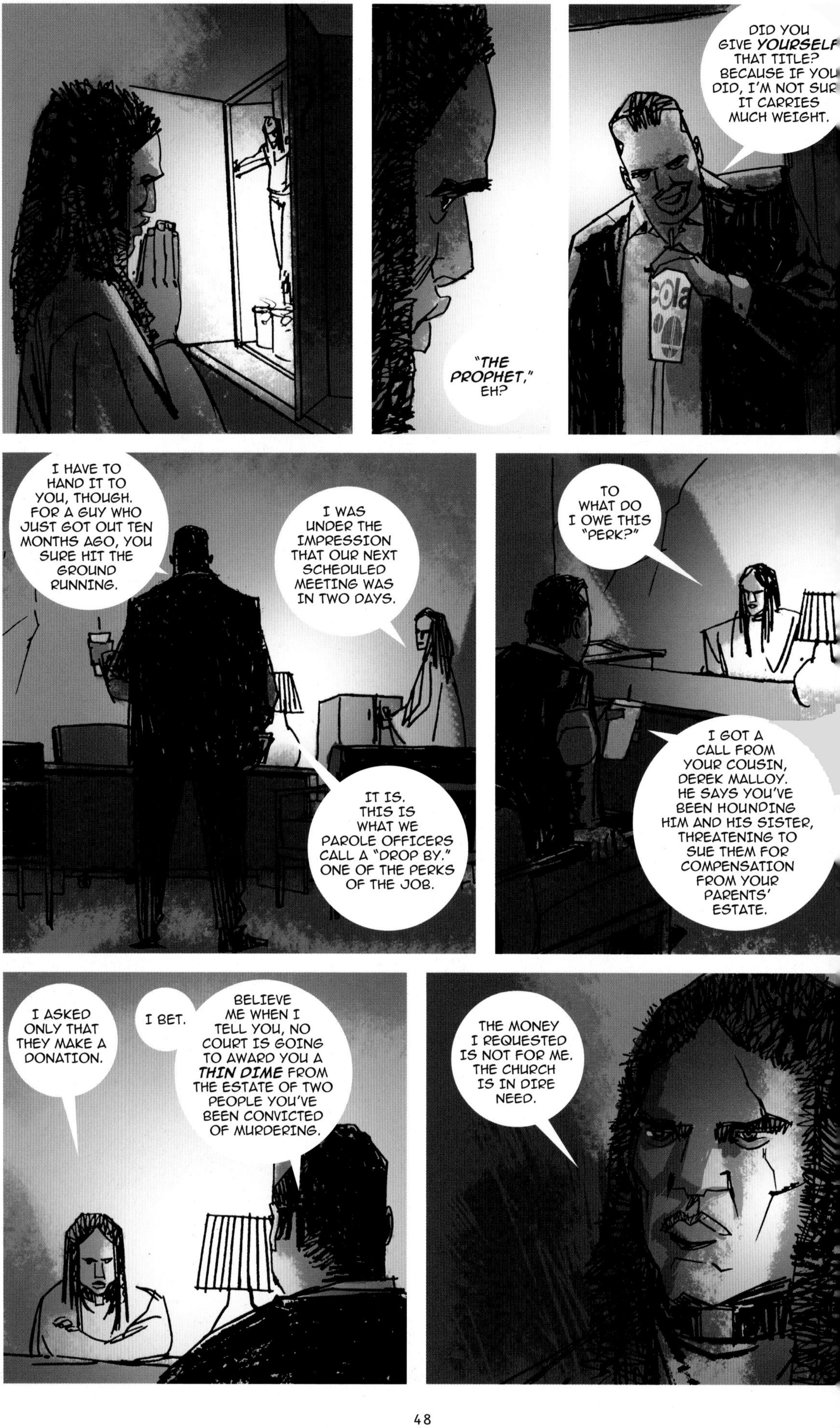
"THE PROPHET," EH?
DID YOU GIVE YOURSELF THAT TITLE? BECAUSE IF YOU DID, I'M NOT SUR IT CARRIES MUCH WEIGHT.
I HAVE TO HAND IT TO YOU, THOUGH. FOR A GUY WHO JUST GOT OUT TEN MONTHS AGO, YOU SURE HIT THE GROUND RUNNING.
I WAS UNDER THE IMPRESSION THAT OUR NEXT SCHEDULED MEETING WAS IN TWO DAYS.
IT IS. THIS IS WHAT WE PAROLE OFFICERS CALL A "DROP BY." ONE OF THE PERKS OF THE JOB.
TO WHAT DO I OWE THIS "PERK?"
I GOT A CALL FROM YOUR COUSIN, DEREK MALLOY. HE SAYS YOU'VE BEEN HOUNDING HIM AND HIS SISTER, THREATENING TO SUE THEM FOR COMPENSATION FROM YOUR PARENTS' ESTATE.
I ASKED ONLY THAT THEY MAKE A DONATION.
I BET.
BELIEVE ME WHEN I TELL YOU, NO COURT IS GOING TO AWARD YOU A THIN DIME FROM THE ESTATE OF TWO PEOPLE YOU'VE BEEN CONVICTED OF MURDERING.
THE MONEY I REQUESTED IS NOT FOR ME. THE CHURCH IS IN DIRE NEED.

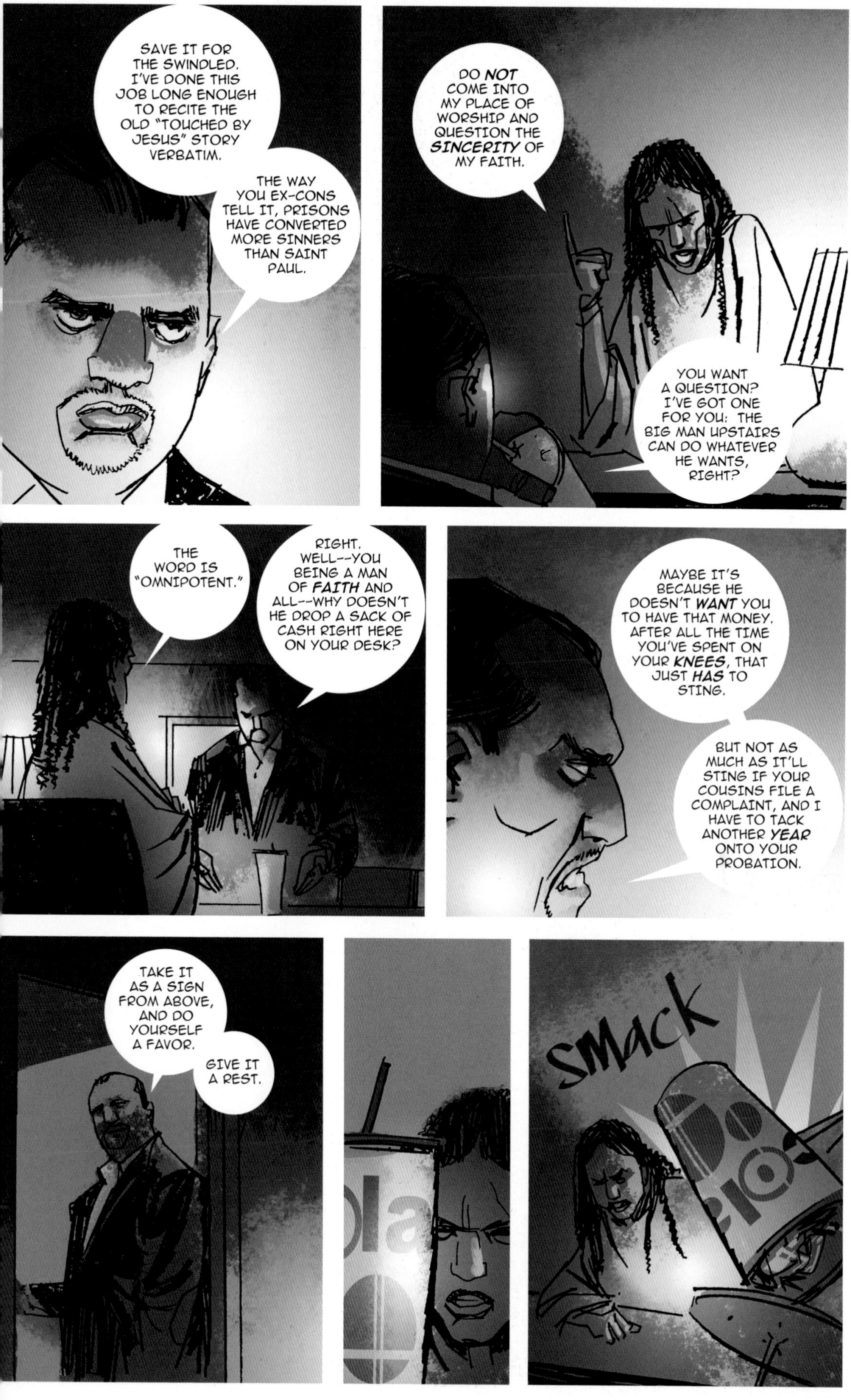
SAVE IT FOR THE SWINDLED. I'VE DONE THIS JOB LONG ENOUGH TO RECITE THE OLD "TOUCHED BY JESUS" STORY VERBATIM.
THE WAY YOU EX-CONS TELL IT, PRISONS HAVE CONVERTED MORE SINNERS THAN SAINT PAUL.
DO **NOT** COME INTO MY PLACE OF WORSHIP AND QUESTION THE **SINCERITY** OF MY FAITH.
YOU WANT A QUESTION? I'VE GOT ONE FOR YOU: THE BIG MAN UPSTAIRS CAN DO WHATEVER HE WANTS, RIGHT?
THE WORD IS "OMNIPOTENT."
RIGHT. WELL--YOU BEING A MAN OF **FAITH** AND ALL--WHY DOESN'T HE DROP A SACK OF CASH RIGHT HERE ON YOUR DESK?
MAYBE IT'S BECAUSE HE DOESN'T **WANT** YOU TO HAVE THAT MONEY. AFTER ALL THE TIME YOU'VE SPENT ON YOUR **KNEES**, THAT JUST **HAS** TO STING.
BUT NOT AS MUCH AS IT'LL STING IF YOUR COUSINS FILE A COMPLAINT, AND I HAVE TO TACK ANOTHER **YEAR** ONTO YOUR PROBATION.
TAKE IT AS A SIGN FROM ABOVE, AND DO YOURSELF A FAVOR.
GIVE IT A REST.
SMACK

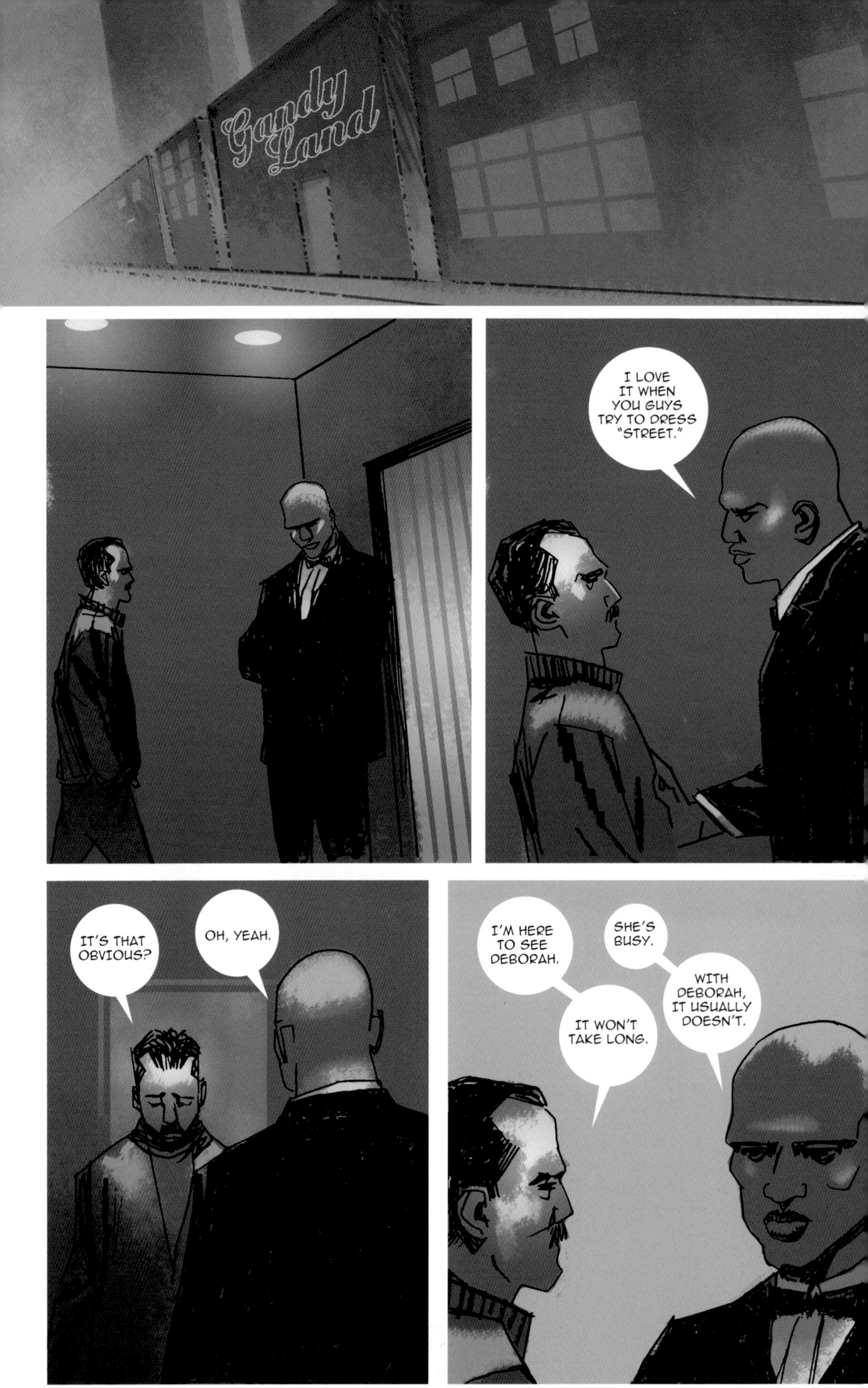
Candy Land
I LOVE IT WHEN YOU GUYS TRY TO DRESS "STREET."
IT'S THAT OBVIOUS?
OH, YEAH.
I'M HERE TO SEE DEBORAH.
SHE'S BUSY.
IT WON'T TAKE LONG.
WITH DEBORAH, IT USUALLY DOESN'T.

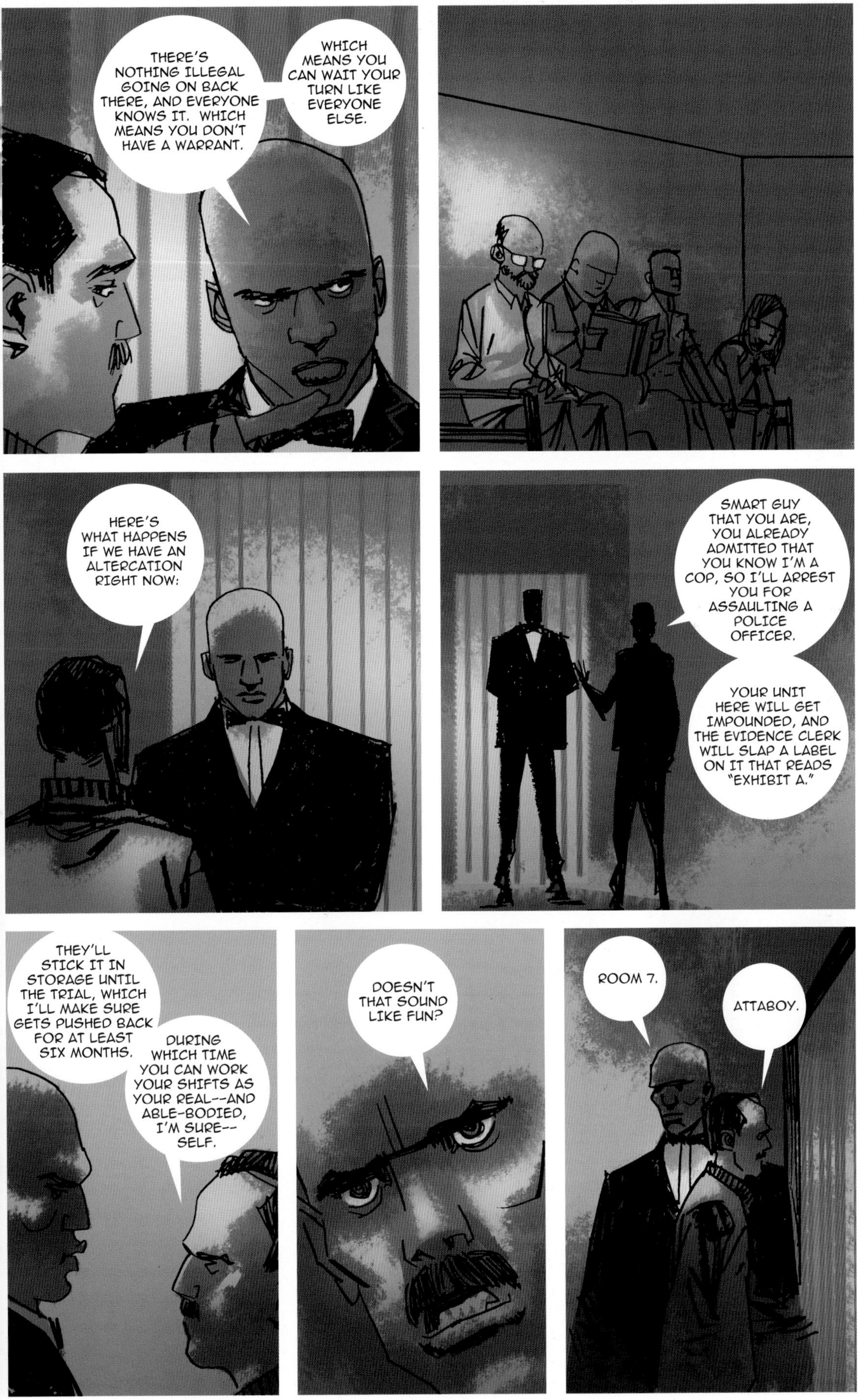
THERE'S NOTHING ILLEGAL GOING ON BACK THERE, AND EVERYONE KNOWS IT. WHICH MEANS YOU DON'T HAVE A WARRANT.
WHICH MEANS YOU CAN WAIT YOUR TURN LIKE EVERYONE ELSE.
HERE'S WHAT HAPPENS IF WE HAVE AN ALTERCATION RIGHT NOW:
SMART GUY THAT YOU ARE, YOU ALREADY ADMITTED THAT YOU KNOW I'M A COP, SO I'LL ARREST YOU FOR ASSAULTING A POLICE OFFICER.
YOUR UNIT HERE WILL GET IMPOUNDED, AND THE EVIDENCE CLERK WILL SLAP A LABEL ON IT THAT READS "EXHIBIT A."
THEY'LL STICK IT IN STORAGE UNTIL THE TRIAL, WHICH I'LL MAKE SURE GETS PUSHED BACK FOR AT LEAST SIX MONTHS.
DURING WHICH TIME YOU CAN WORK YOUR SHIFTS AS YOUR REAL--AND ABLE-BODIED, I'M SURE--SELF.
DOESN'T THAT SOUND LIKE FUN?
ROOM 7.
ATTABOY.

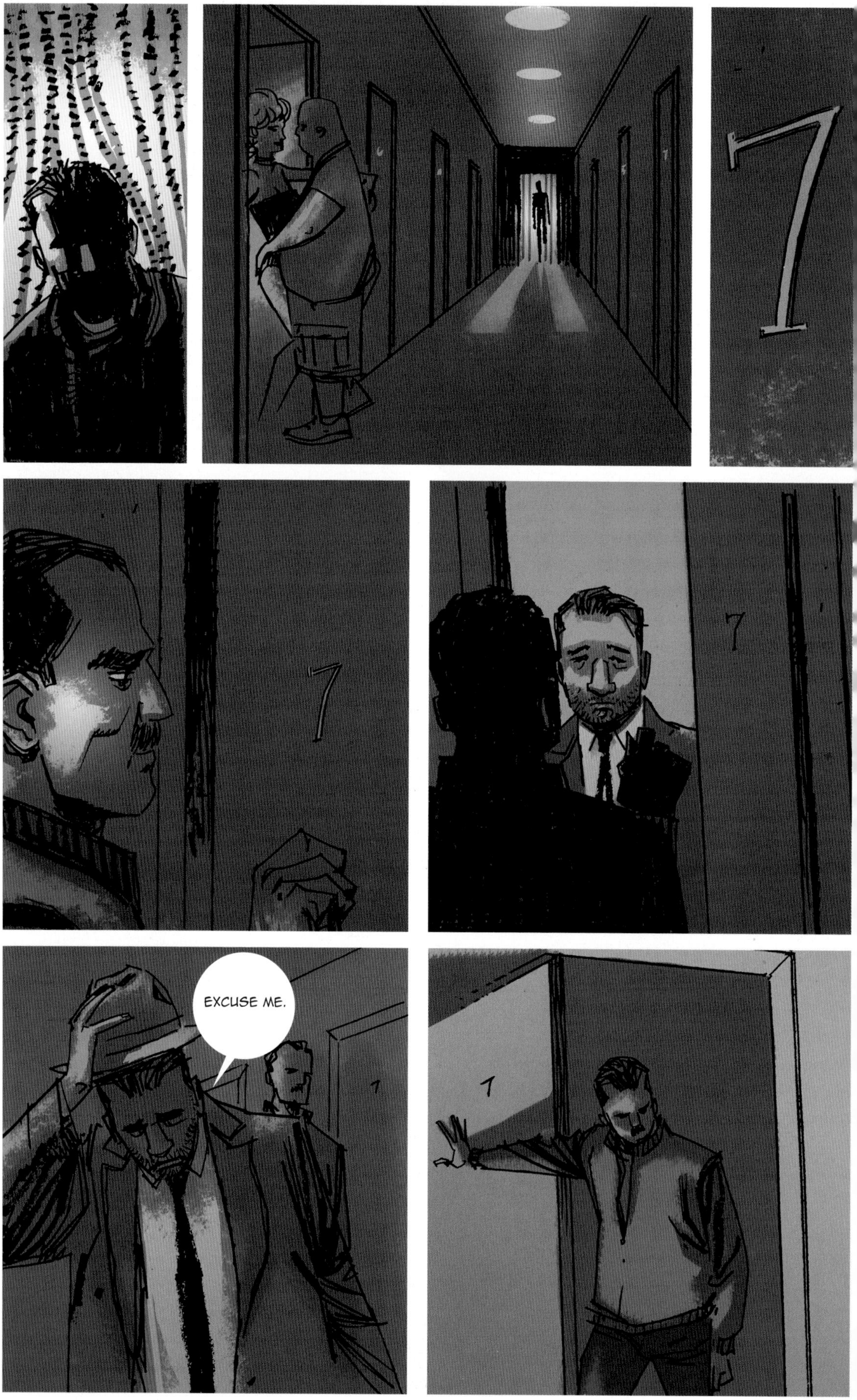
7
7
7
EXCUSE ME.
7
7

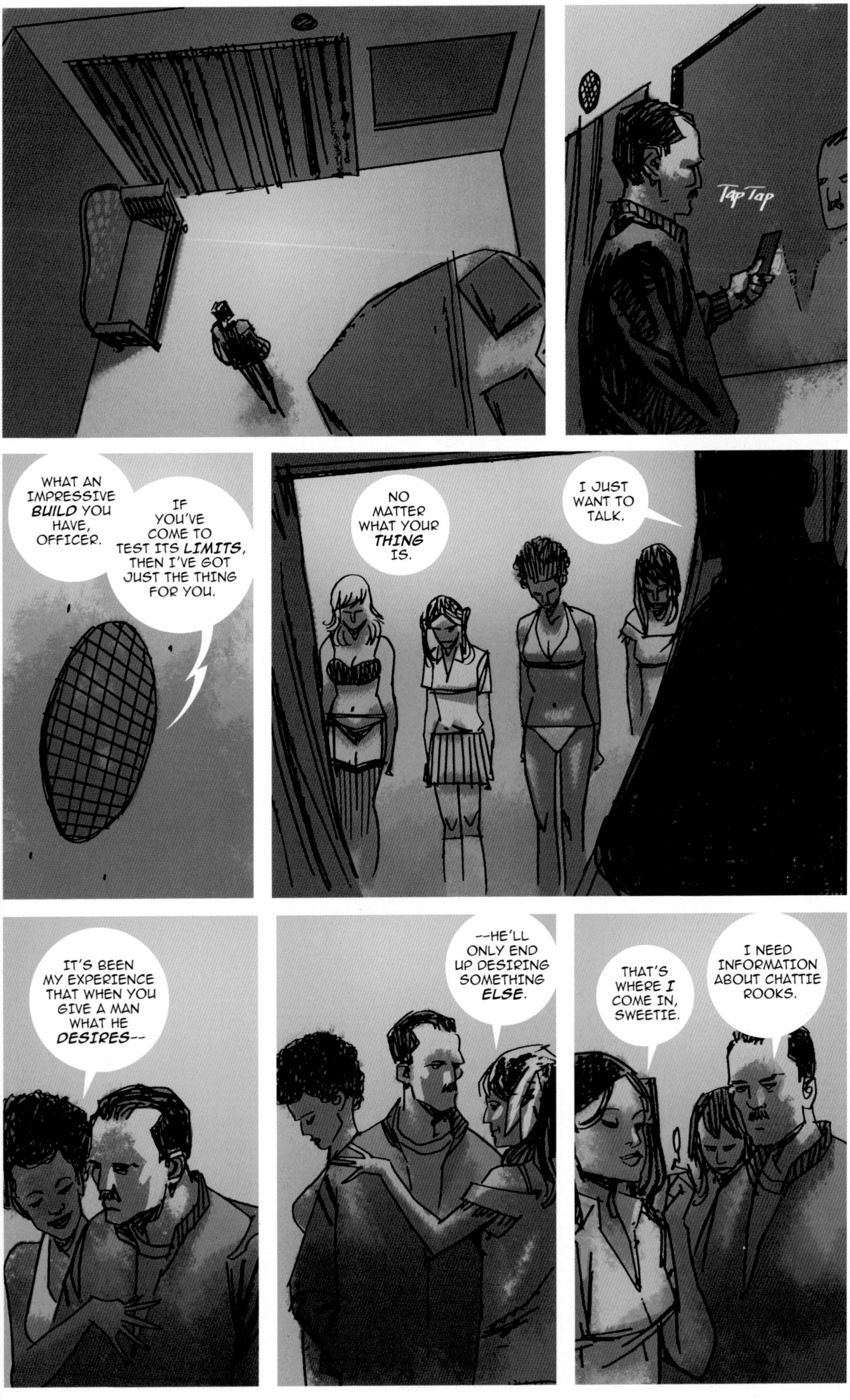
TAP TAP
WHAT AN IMPRESSIVE BUILD YOU HAVE, OFFICER.
IF YOU'VE COME TO TEST ITS LIMITS, THEN I'VE GOT JUST THE THING FOR YOU.
NO MATTER WHAT YOUR THING IS.
I JUST WANT TO TALK.
IT'S BEEN MY EXPERIENCE THAT WHEN YOU GIVE A MAN WHAT HE DESIRES--
--HE'LL ONLY END UP DESIRING SOMETHING ELSE.
THAT'S WHERE I COME IN, SWEETIE.
I NEED INFORMATION ABOUT CHATTIE ROOKS.

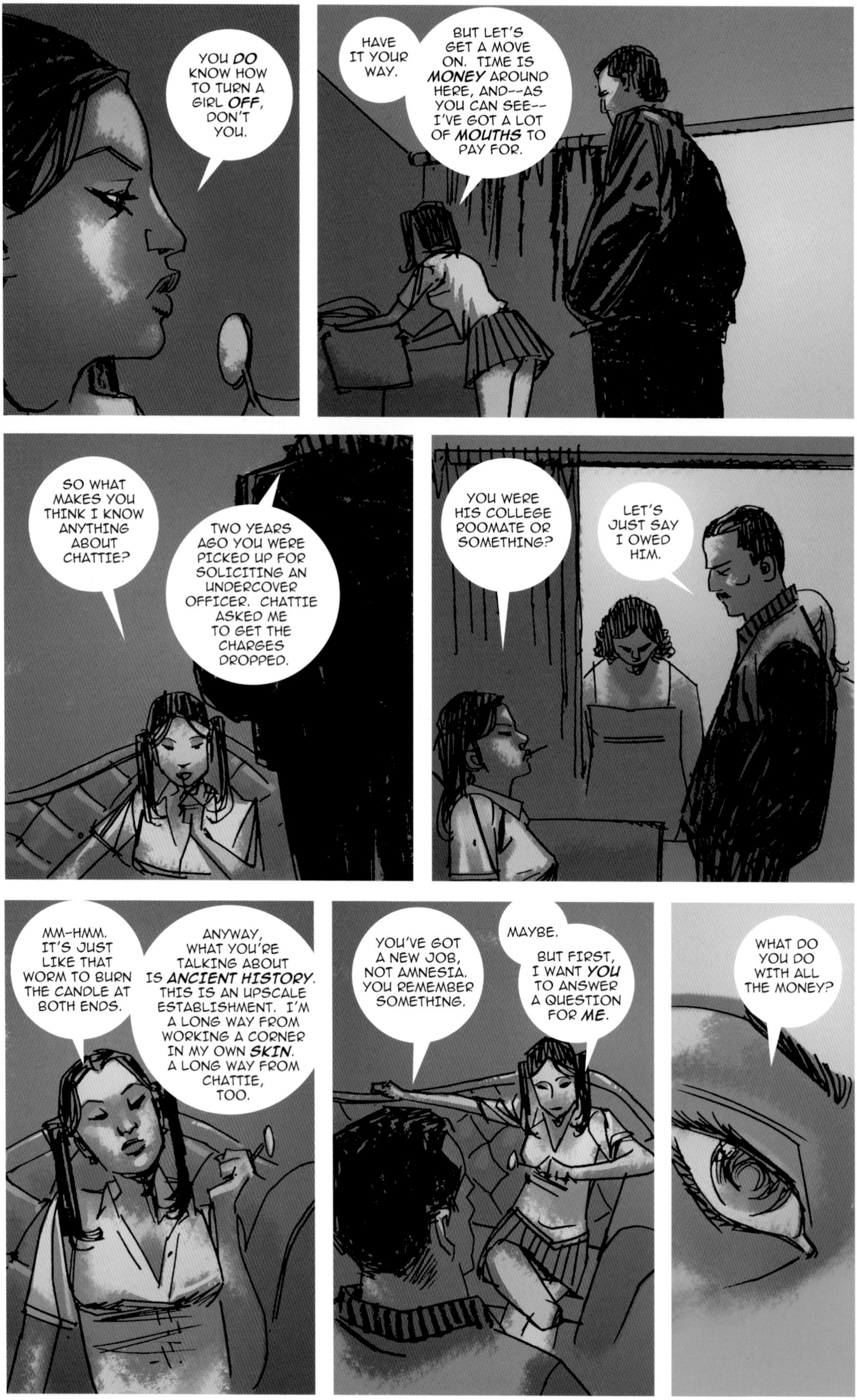

YOU DO KNOW HOW TO TURN A GIRL OFF, DON'T YOU.
HAVE IT YOUR WAY.
BUT LET'S GET A MOVE ON. TIME IS MONEY AROUND HERE, AND--AS YOU CAN SEE--I'VE GOT A LOT OF MOUTHS TO PAY FOR.
SO WHAT MAKES YOU THINK I KNOW ANYTHING ABOUT CHATTIE?
TWO YEARS AGO YOU WERE PICKED UP FOR SOLICITING AN UNDERCOVER OFFICER. CHATTIE ASKED ME TO GET THE CHARGES DROPPED.
YOU WERE HIS COLLEGE ROOMATE OR SOMETHING?
LET'S JUST SAY I OWED HIM.
MM-HMM. IT'S JUST LIKE THAT WORM TO BURN THE CANDLE AT BOTH ENDS.
ANYWAY, WHAT YOU'RE TALKING ABOUT IS ANCIENT HISTORY. THIS IS AN UPSCALE ESTABLISHMENT. I'M A LONG WAY FROM WORKING A CORNER IN MY OWN SKIN. A LONG WAY FROM CHATTIE, TOO.
YOU'VE GOT A NEW JOB, NOT AMNESIA. YOU REMEMBER SOMETHING.
MAYBE.
BUT FIRST, I WANT YOU TO ANSWER A QUESTION FOR ME.
WHAT DO YOU DO WITH ALL THE MONEY?

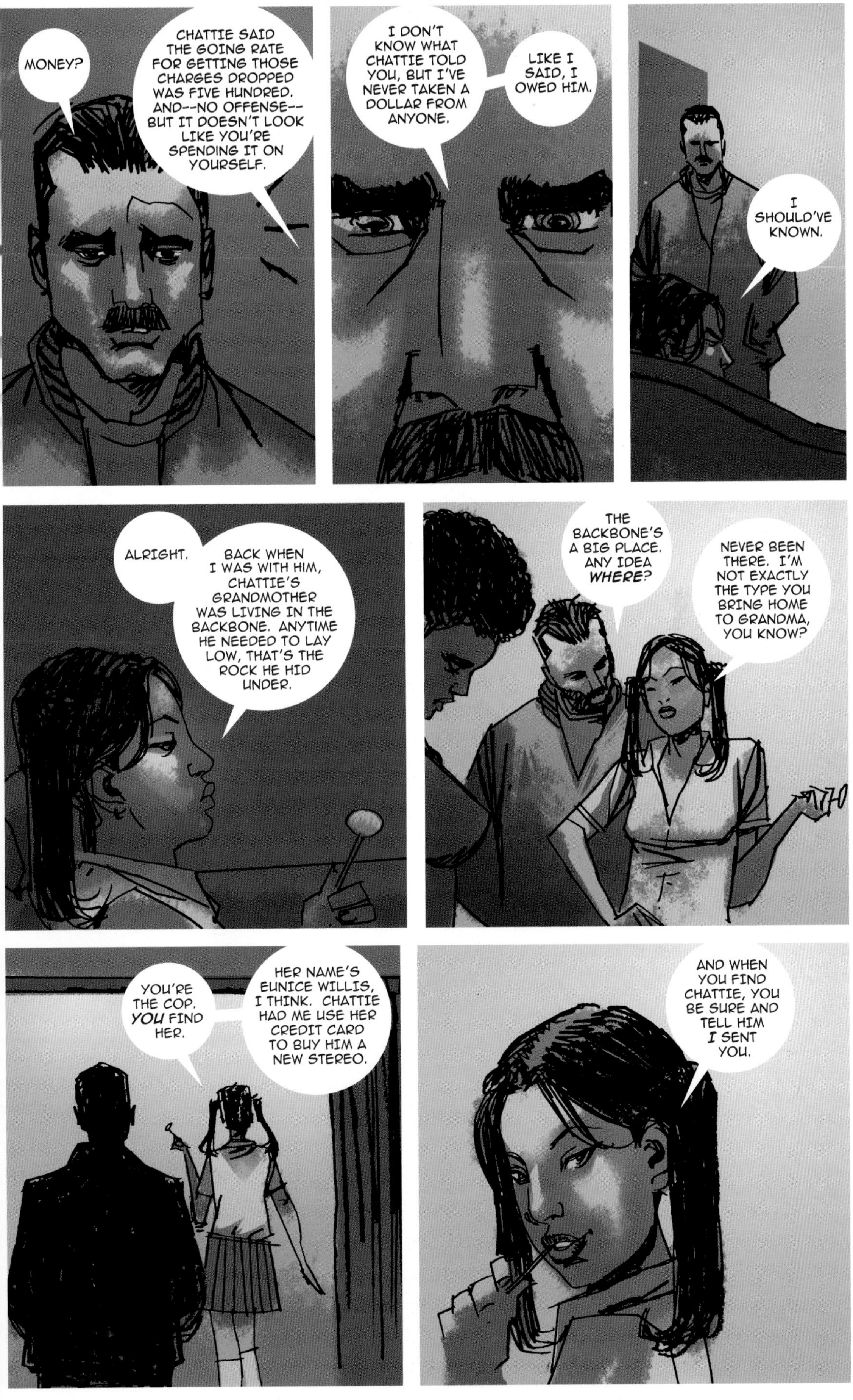

MONEY?
CHATTIE SAID THE GOING RATE FOR GETTING THOSE CHARGES DROPPED WAS FIVE HUNDRED. AND--NO OFFENSE--BUT IT DOESN'T LOOK LIKE YOU'RE SPENDING IT ON YOURSELF.
I DON'T KNOW WHAT CHATTIE TOLD YOU, BUT I'VE NEVER TAKEN A DOLLAR FROM ANYONE.
LIKE I SAID, I OWED HIM.
I SHOULD'VE KNOWN.
ALRIGHT.
BACK WHEN I WAS WITH HIM, CHATTIE'S GRANDMOTHER WAS LIVING IN THE BACKBONE. ANYTIME HE NEEDED TO LAY LOW, THAT'S THE ROCK HE HID UNDER.
THE BACKBONE'S A BIG PLACE. ANY IDEA WHERE?
NEVER BEEN THERE. I'M NOT EXACTLY THE TYPE YOU BRING HOME TO GRANDMA, YOU KNOW?
YOU'RE THE COP. YOU FIND HER.
HER NAME'S EUNICE WILLIS, I THINK. CHATTIE HAD ME USE HER CREDIT CARD TO BUY HIM A NEW STEREO.
AND WHEN YOU FIND CHATTIE, YOU BE SURE AND TELL HIM I SENT YOU.

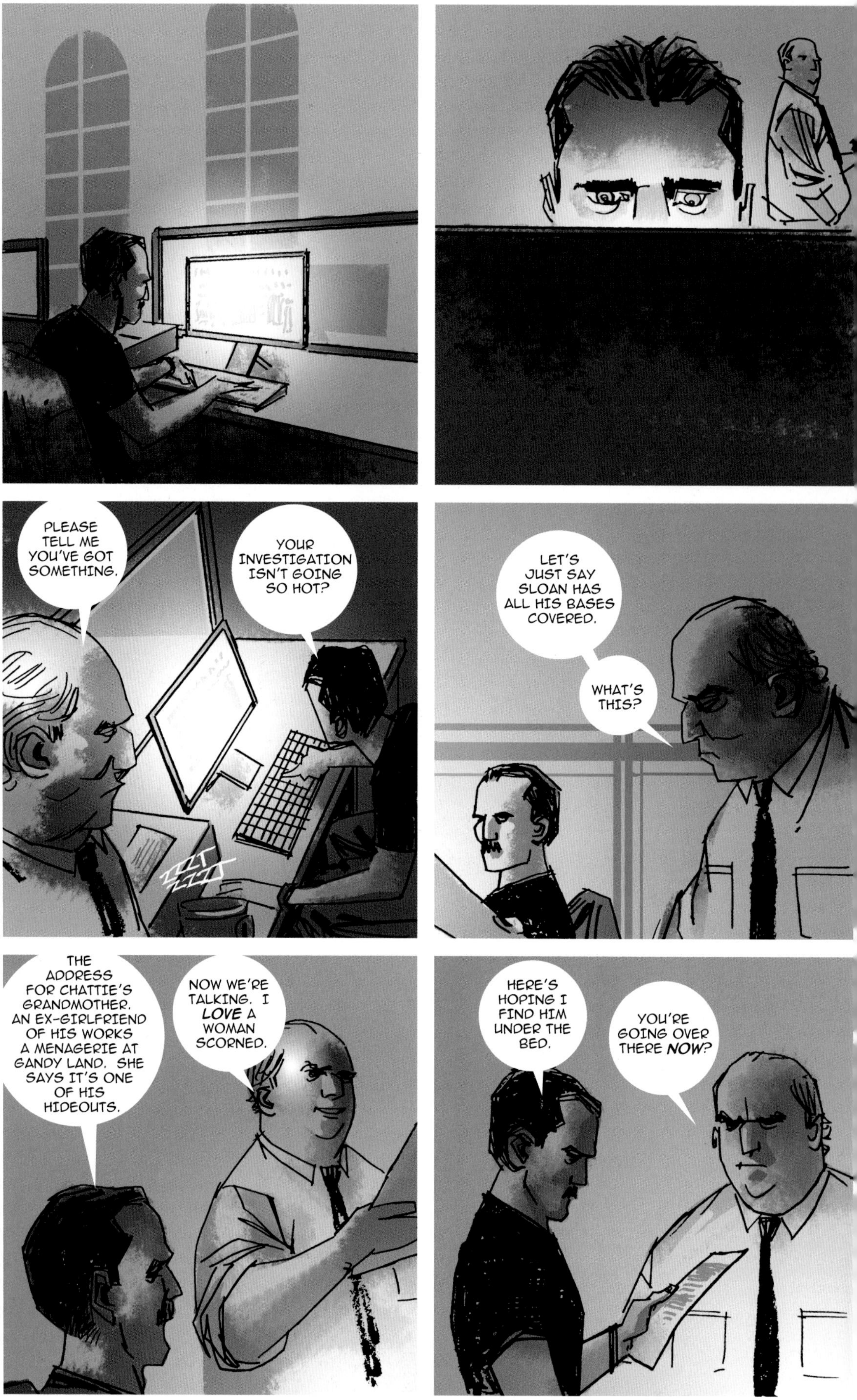

PLEASE TELL ME YOU'VE GOT SOMETHING.
YOUR INVESTIGATION ISN'T GOING SO HOT?
LET'S JUST SAY SLOAN HAS ALL HIS BASES COVERED.
WHAT'S THIS?
THE ADDRESS FOR CHATTIE'S GRANDMOTHER. AN EX-GIRLFRIEND OF HIS WORKS A MENAGERIE AT GANDY LAND. SHE SAYS IT'S ONE OF HIS HIDEOUTS.
NOW WE'RE TALKING. I *LOVE* A WOMAN SCORNED.
HERE'S HOPING I FIND HIM UNDER THE BED.
YOU'RE GOING OVER THERE *NOW*?

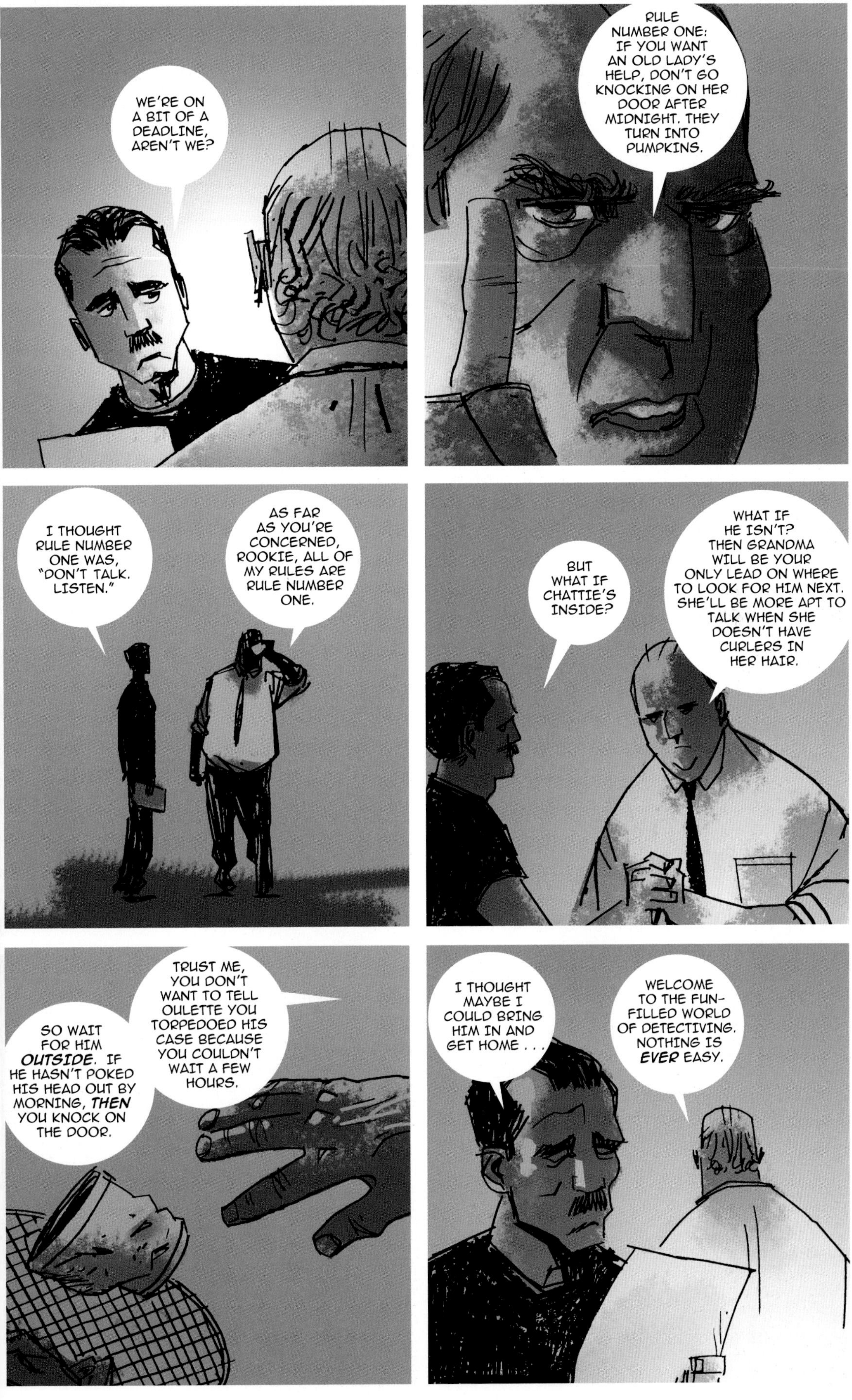
WE'RE ON A BIT OF A DEADLINE, AREN'T WE?
RULE NUMBER ONE: IF YOU WANT AN OLD LADY'S HELP, DON'T GO KNOCKING ON HER DOOR AFTER MIDNIGHT. THEY TURN INTO PUMPKINS.
I THOUGHT RULE NUMBER ONE WAS, "DON'T TALK. LISTEN."
AS FAR AS YOU'RE CONCERNED, ROOKIE, ALL OF MY RULES ARE RULE NUMBER ONE.
BUT WHAT IF CHATTIE'S INSIDE?
WHAT IF HE ISN'T? THEN GRANDMA WILL BE YOUR ONLY LEAD ON WHERE TO LOOK FOR HIM NEXT. SHE'LL BE MORE APT TO TALK WHEN SHE DOESN'T HAVE CURLERS IN HER HAIR.
SO WAIT FOR HIM **OUTSIDE**. IF HE HASN'T POKED HIS HEAD OUT BY MORNING, **THEN** YOU KNOCK ON THE DOOR.
TRUST ME, YOU DON'T WANT TO TELL OULETTE YOU TORPEDOED HIS CASE BECAUSE YOU COULDN'T WAIT A FEW HOURS.
I THOUGHT MAYBE I COULD BRING HIM IN AND GET HOME . . .
WELCOME TO THE FUN-FILLED WORLD OF DETECTIVING. NOTHING IS **EVER** EASY.

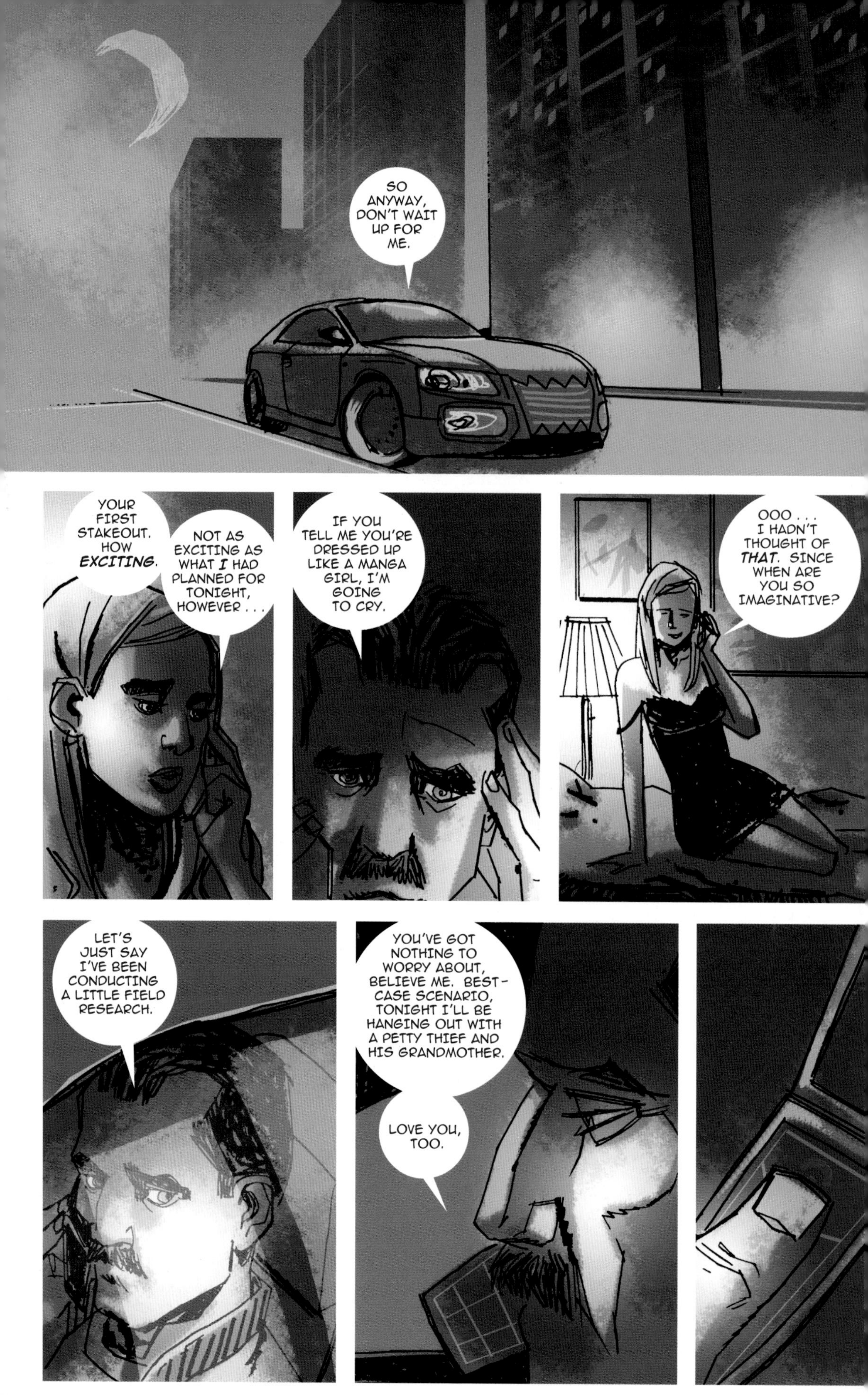
SO ANYWAY, DON'T WAIT UP FOR ME.
YOUR FIRST STAKEOUT. HOW **EXCITING**.
NOT AS EXCITING AS WHAT ***I*** HAD PLANNED FOR TONIGHT, HOWEVER . . .
IF YOU TELL ME YOU'RE DRESSED UP LIKE A MANGA GIRL, I'M GOING TO CRY.
OOO . . . I HADN'T THOUGHT OF ***THAT***. SINCE WHEN ARE YOU SO IMAGINATIVE?
LET'S JUST SAY I'VE BEEN CONDUCTING A LITTLE FIELD RESEARCH.
YOU'VE GOT NOTHING TO WORRY ABOUT, BELIEVE ME. BEST-CASE SCENARIO, TONIGHT I'LL BE HANGING OUT WITH A PETTY THIEF AND HIS GRANDMOTHER.
LOVE YOU, TOO.

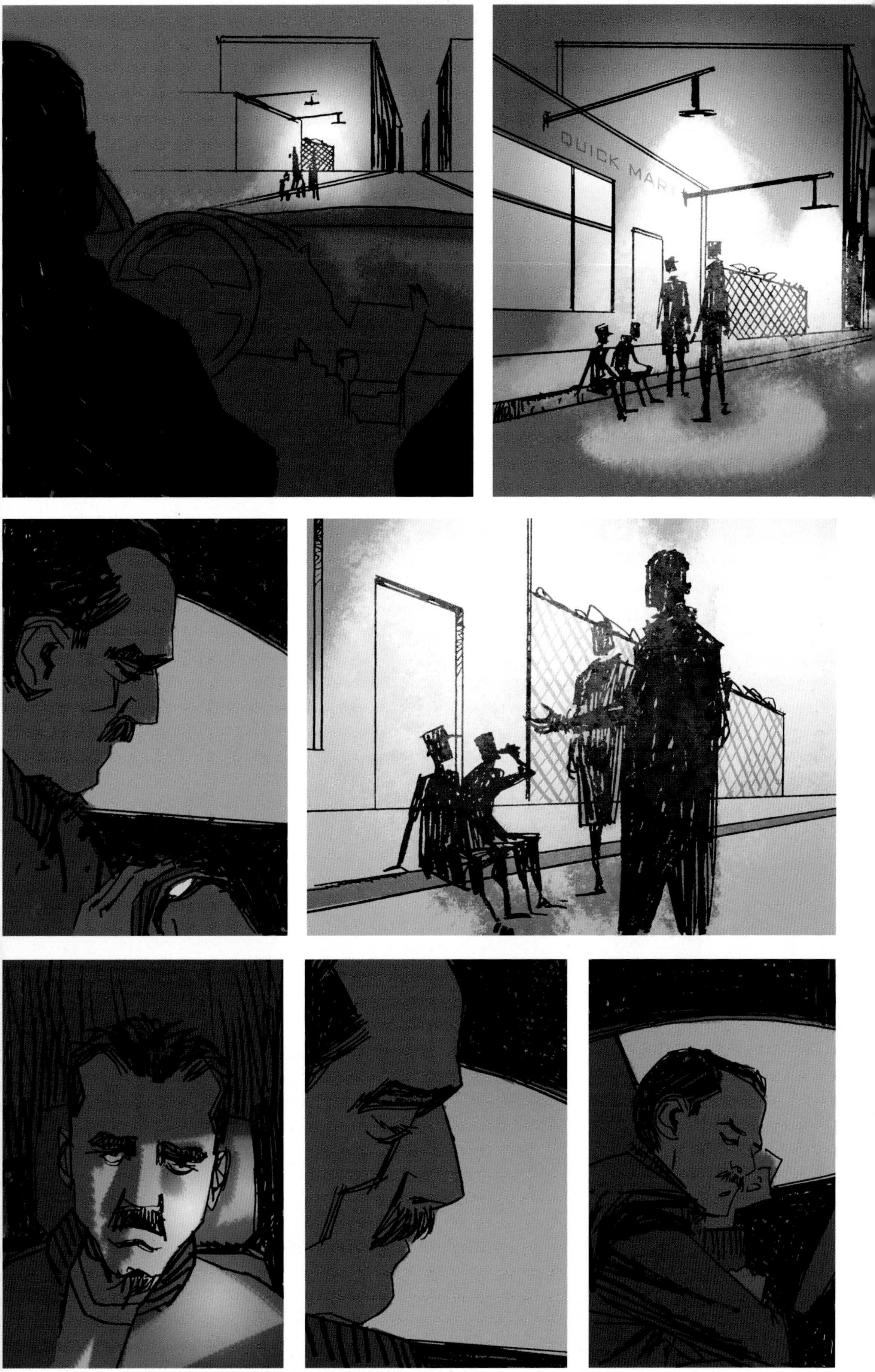
QUICK MAR

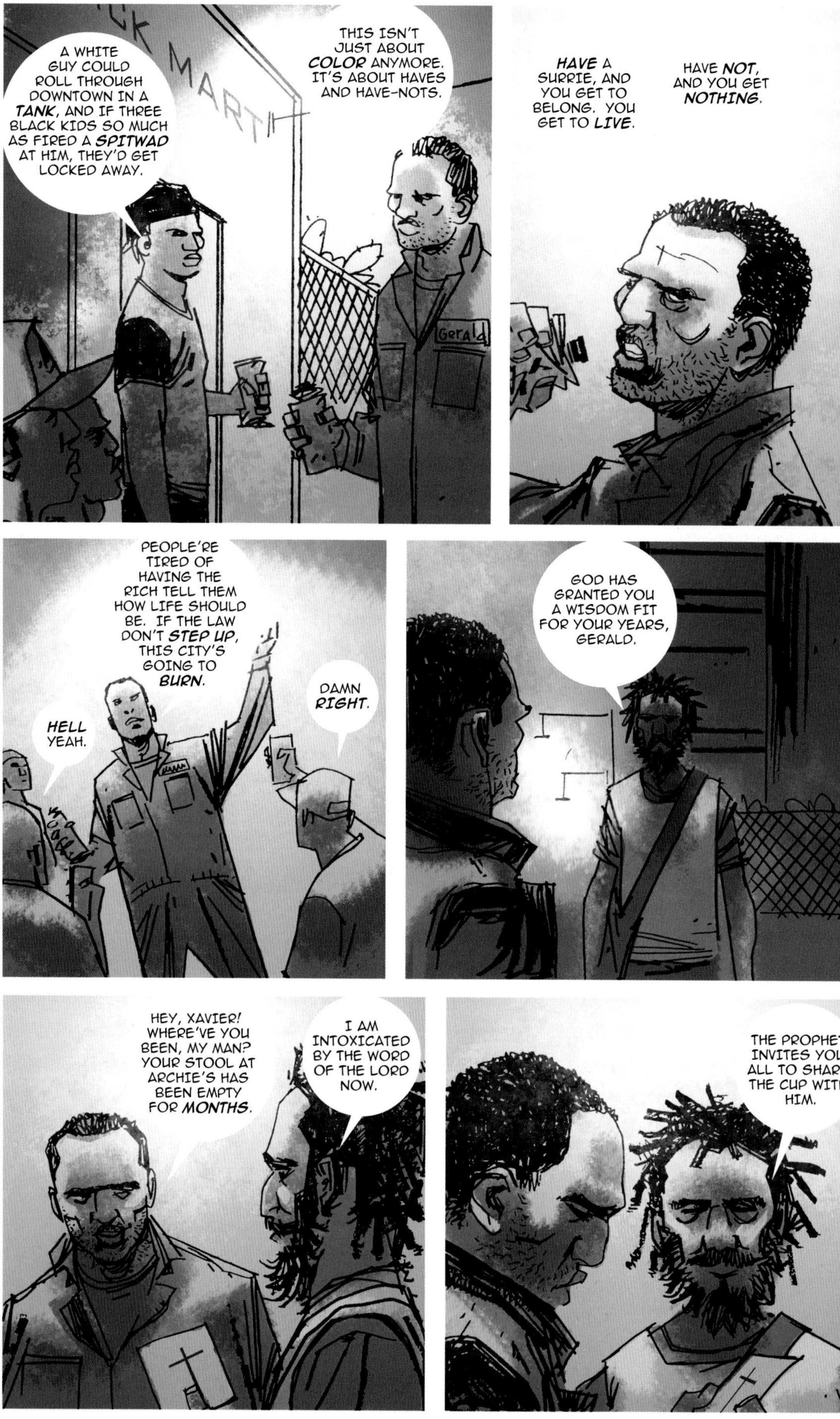

A WHITE GUY COULD ROLL THROUGH DOWNTOWN IN A TANK, AND IF THREE BLACK KIDS SO MUCH AS FIRED A SPITWAD AT HIM, THEY'D GET LOCKED AWAY.
THIS ISN'T JUST ABOUT COLOR ANYMORE. IT'S ABOUT HAVES AND HAVE-NOTS.
MART
Gerald
HAVE A SURRIE, AND YOU GET TO BELONG. YOU GET TO LIVE.
HAVE NOT, AND YOU GET NOTHING.
PEOPLE'RE TIRED OF HAVING THE RICH TELL THEM HOW LIFE SHOULD BE. IF THE LAW DON'T STEP UP, THIS CITY'S GOING TO BURN.
HELL YEAH.
DAMN RIGHT.
GOD HAS GRANTED YOU A WISDOM FIT FOR YOUR YEARS, GERALD.
HEY, XAVIER! WHERE'VE YOU BEEN, MY MAN? YOUR STOOL AT ARCHIE'S HAS BEEN EMPTY FOR MONTHS.
I AM INTOXICATED BY THE WORD OF THE LORD NOW.
THE PROPHET INVITES YOU ALL TO SHARE THE CUP WITH HIM.

THERE IS AFTER ALL REWARD
FOR THE RIGHTEOUS;

THERE IS AFTER ALL A GOD
WHO DISPENSES JUSTICE ON EARTH.

-- PSALM 58:11

EARTHLY POSSESSIONS BRING SUFFERING, NOT JOY.

Much emphasis is placed on the things we acquire. Advertisements, popular music, television shows . . . we are constantly assaulted with people telling us that what we own decides if we are worthy. There were no ads or TVs in Jesus' day, but there was this same obsession with material goods. In Mark 10:25, Jesus tells his disciples that *It is easier for a camel to pass through the eye of a needle than for a rich man to enter the kingdom of God.* What did he mean by this? He meant that salvation cannot be gained through trinkets and possessions. Quite the opposite, the more we surround ourselves with objects, the farther we getfrom true riches. Ask yourself: Has there ever been a time in history when people were more defined by what they own -- or do not own? In Luke 6:24-25, Jesus gives a dire warning to all who fall into such traps:

JUDAS WENT TO GREAT LENGTHS
TO GET HIS POUCHFUL OF SILVER.
DID IT BRING HIM JOY?

*But alas for you who are rich;
you have had your time of happiness.*

*Alas for you who are well fed now;
you will go hungry.*

*Alas for you who laugh now;
you will mourn and weep.*

Christ, too, was an outcast.

The righteous road is often a lonely one. No one experienced this more than Jesus himself. Branded a renegade by the leaders of his day, Jesus' followers were those whom society had rejected. The disciple Matthew was reviled for being a tax collector. Mary Magdalene was a former prostitute. Others were fishermen, shepherds, sickly or infirm. Commoners at best, they were hardly members of the elite. And as though their troubles were not already many, taking up the cross of Christ only worsened their status as pariahs. Jesus welcomes his converts in Matthew 5:11-12, and lets them know that their predicaments do not go unnoticed:

Blessed are you, when you suffer insults and persecution and calumnies of every kind for my sake. Exult and be glad, for you have a rich reward in heaven.

While the forces of society swept the masses in one direction, Jesus and his followers forged a different path. To be outnumbered is the definition of being a minority. But great deeds have been done by those who -- though they may be just -- were in the minority. Great deeds await you as well. Will you answer God's call?

<u>God</u> has <u>**not**</u> <u>forgotten</u> <u>you</u>.

As the unfaithful around us are seemingly rewarded for their sins, its easy to question God's presence in our lives. However, one need look no farther than the Bible to find proof that He stands beside us even in our darkest hour. The prophet Daniel was cast among the lions in the pit, only to be taken out unscathed. When Shadrach, Meshach, and Abednego emerged from the blazing fire of Nebuchadnezzar's furnace, *The hair of their heads had not been singed, their trousers were untouched, and no smell of fire lingered about them* (Daniel 3:27). This is in fulfillment of God's promise in Isaiah 49:15-16:

I shall never forget you.
I have inscribed you on the palms of my hands.

But such divine protection carries the price of our obedience. Even Jesus himself, God's only son, suffered torments unimaginable in service of the Father's will. If we make our lives examples of faith, then Isaiah 49:26 says that God will do more than simply remember us:

I shall make your oppressors eat their own flesh,
and they will be drunk with their own blood as if with wine,
and all mankind will know that I the Lord am your Deliverer.

How will you show God your obedience?

THE CHURCH OF THE PROPHET INVITES ALL WHO WISH TO KNOW MORE ABOUT GOD'S PLAN TO JOIN OUR CONGREGATION.

Services held daily at
10 a.m., 2 p.m. and 6 p.m.

For our address and directions,
visit our website:

www.churchoftheprophet.com

Our Parish Prayer

*Heavenly Father, Giver of life
and Creator of all things:*

*Bestow upon us the wisdom
to recognize your will and
reject those who act against it;*

*Grant us fortitude,
so that we may live righteously,
even when doing so
requires sacrifice;*

*Inspire in us the faith
to accept your plan,
though its entirety may not
be revealed;*

*Strengthen our resolve,
and we will do what is necessary
to restore your glory on Earth.*

*We ask this in the name
of your beloved son,
Jesus Christ our Lord.
Amen.*

chapter
THREE

Flame

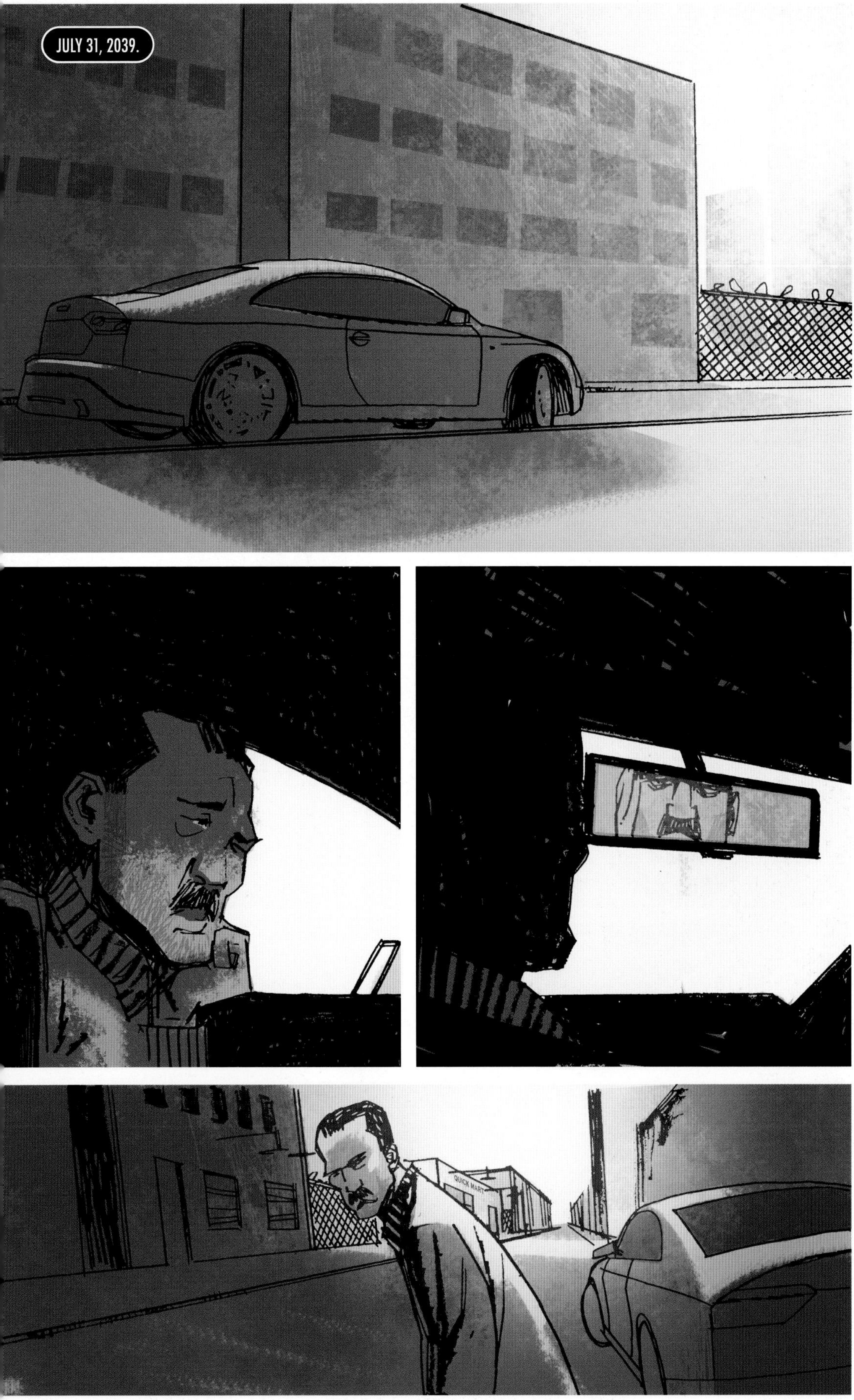
JULY 31, 2039.
QUICK MART

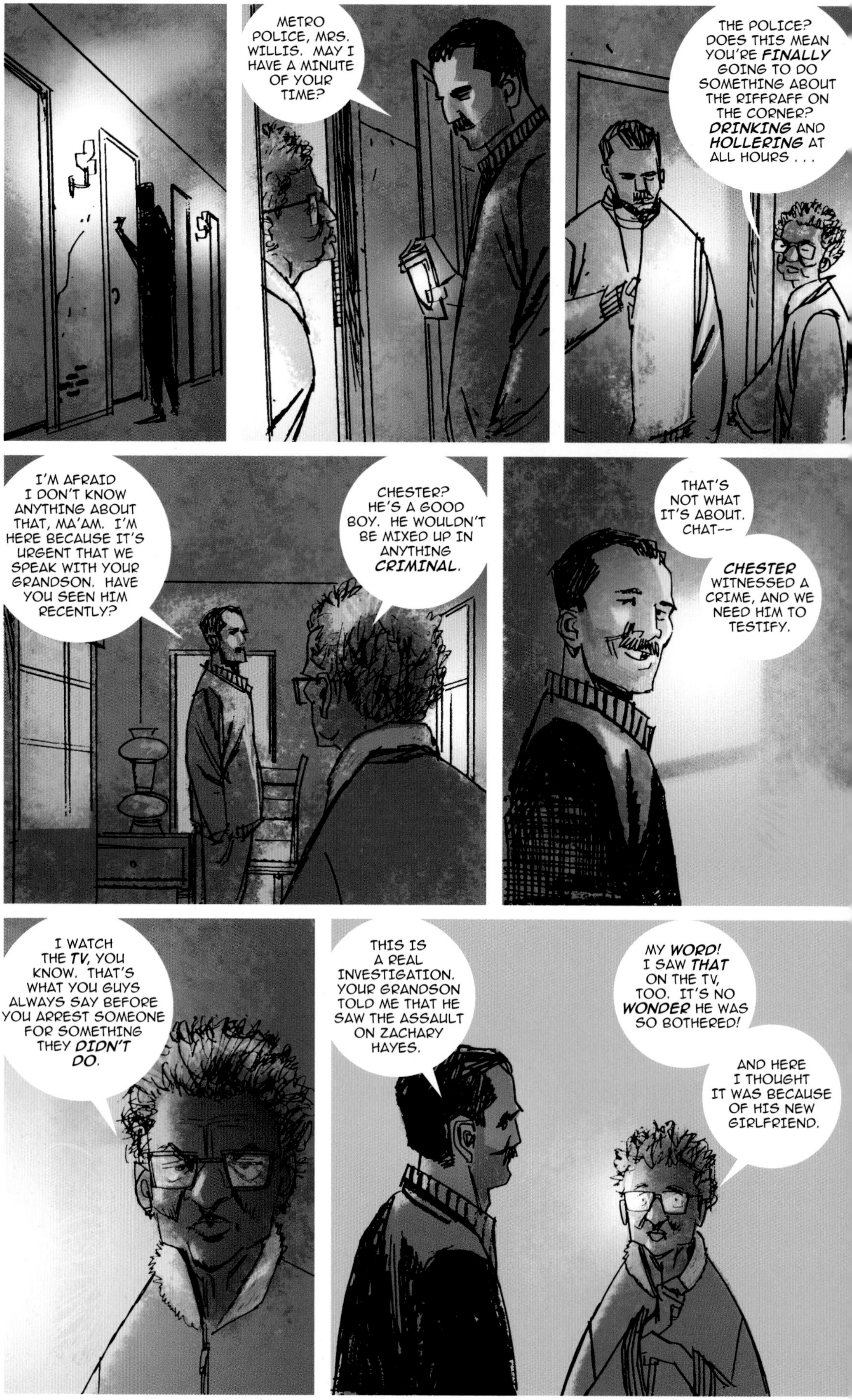
METRO POLICE, MRS. WILLIS. MAY I HAVE A MINUTE OF YOUR TIME?
THE POLICE? DOES THIS MEAN YOU'RE FINALLY GOING TO DO SOMETHING ABOUT THE RIFFRAFF ON THE CORNER? DRINKING AND HOLLERING AT ALL HOURS . . .
I'M AFRAID I DON'T KNOW ANYTHING ABOUT THAT, MA'AM. I'M HERE BECAUSE IT'S URGENT THAT WE SPEAK WITH YOUR GRANDSON. HAVE YOU SEEN HIM RECENTLY?
CHESTER? HE'S A GOOD BOY. HE WOULDN'T BE MIXED UP IN ANYTHING CRIMINAL.
THAT'S NOT WHAT IT'S ABOUT. CHAT--
CHESTER WITNESSED A CRIME, AND WE NEED HIM TO TESTIFY.
I WATCH THE TV, YOU KNOW. THAT'S WHAT YOU GUYS ALWAYS SAY BEFORE YOU ARREST SOMEONE FOR SOMETHING THEY DIDN'T DO.
THIS IS A REAL INVESTIGATION. YOUR GRANDSON TOLD ME THAT HE SAW THE ASSAULT ON ZACHARY HAYES.
MY WORD! I SAW THAT ON THE TV, TOO. IT'S NO WONDER HE WAS SO BOTHERED!
AND HERE I THOUGHT IT WAS BECAUSE OF HIS NEW GIRLFRIEND.

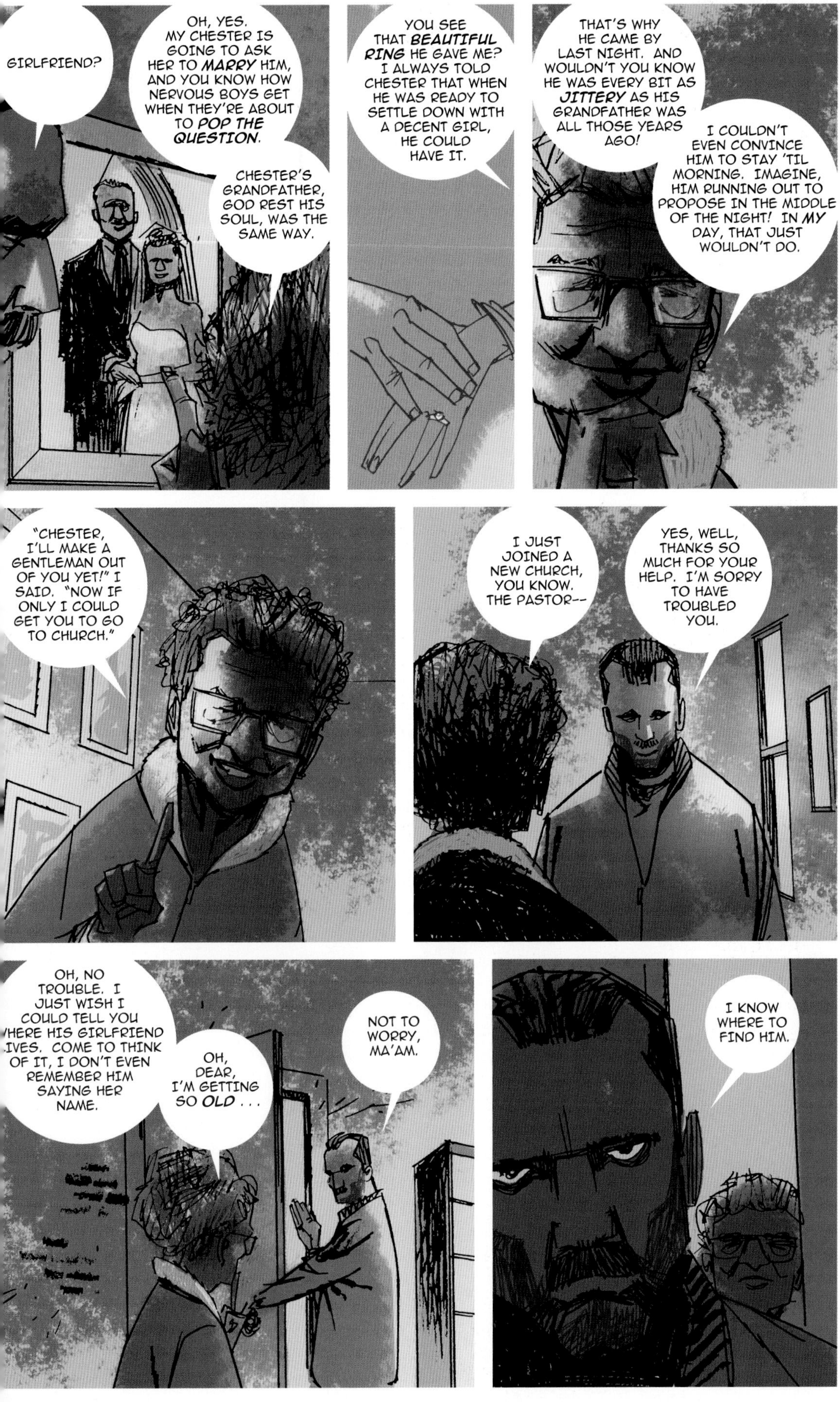
GIRLFRIEND?
OH, YES. MY CHESTER IS GOING TO ASK HER TO *MARRY* HIM, AND YOU KNOW HOW NERVOUS BOYS GET WHEN THEY'RE ABOUT TO *POP THE QUESTION*.
CHESTER'S GRANDFATHER, GOD REST HIS SOUL, WAS THE SAME WAY.
YOU SEE THAT *BEAUTIFUL RING* HE GAVE ME? I ALWAYS TOLD CHESTER THAT WHEN HE WAS READY TO SETTLE DOWN WITH A DECENT GIRL, HE COULD HAVE IT.
THAT'S WHY HE CAME BY LAST NIGHT. AND WOULDN'T YOU KNOW HE WAS EVERY BIT AS *JITTERY* AS HIS GRANDFATHER WAS ALL THOSE YEARS AGO!
I COULDN'T EVEN CONVINCE HIM TO STAY 'TIL MORNING. IMAGINE, HIM RUNNING OUT TO PROPOSE IN THE MIDDLE OF THE NIGHT! IN *MY* DAY, THAT JUST WOULDN'T DO.
"CHESTER, I'LL MAKE A GENTLEMAN OUT OF YOU YET!" I SAID. "NOW IF ONLY I COULD GET YOU TO GO TO CHURCH."
I JUST JOINED A NEW CHURCH, YOU KNOW. THE PASTOR--
YES, WELL, THANKS SO MUCH FOR YOUR HELP. I'M SORRY TO HAVE TROUBLED YOU.
OH, NO TROUBLE. I JUST WISH I COULD TELL YOU HERE HIS GIRLFRIEND IVES. COME TO THINK OF IT, I DON'T EVEN REMEMBER HIM SAYING HER NAME.
OH, DEAR, I'M GETTING SO *OLD* . . .
NOT TO WORRY, MA'AM.
I KNOW WHERE TO FIND HIM.

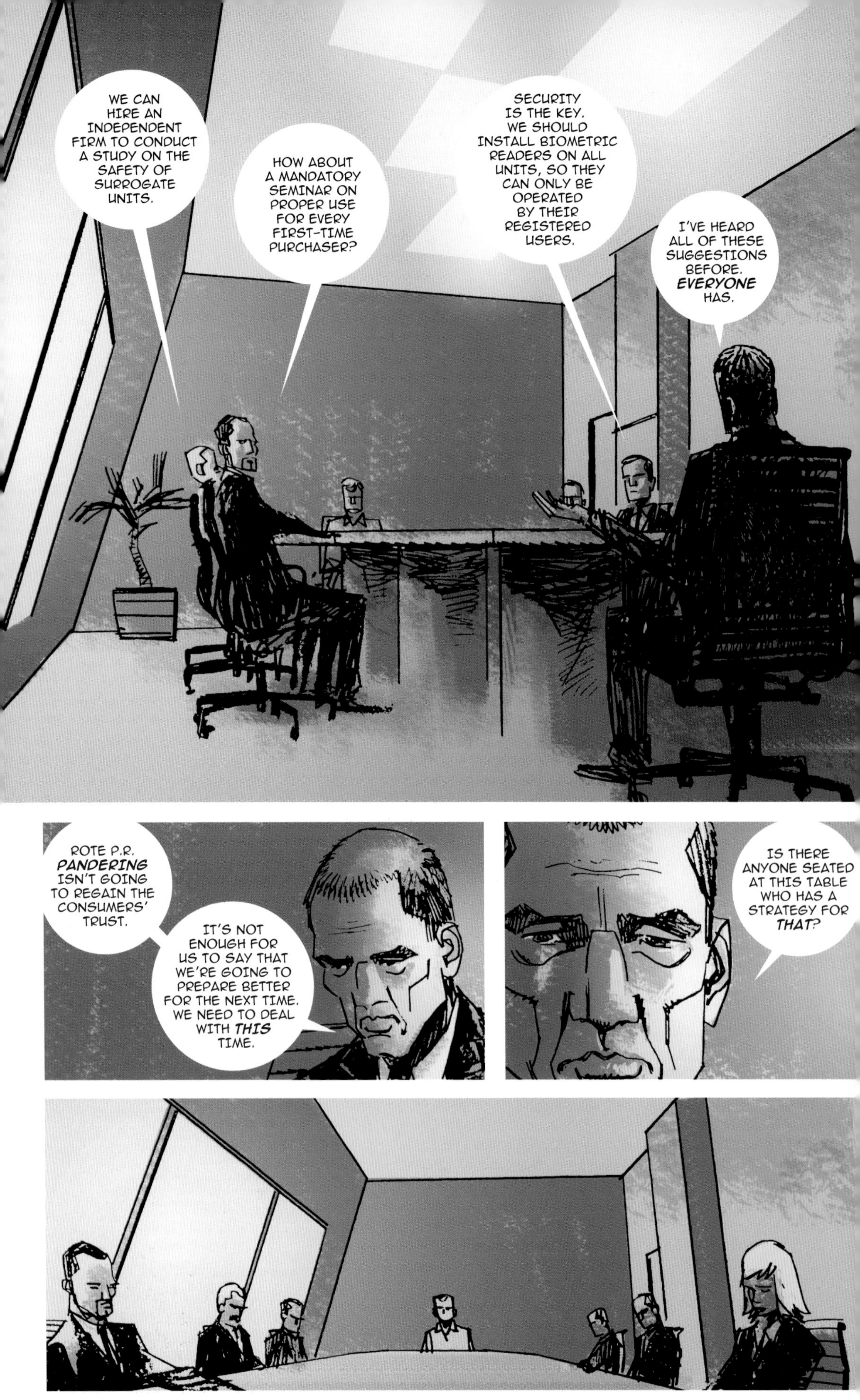

WE CAN HIRE AN INDEPENDENT FIRM TO CONDUCT A STUDY ON THE SAFETY OF SURROGATE UNITS.
HOW ABOUT A MANDATORY SEMINAR ON PROPER USE FOR EVERY FIRST-TIME PURCHASER?
SECURITY IS THE KEY. WE SHOULD INSTALL BIOMETRIC READERS ON ALL UNITS, SO THEY CAN ONLY BE OPERATED BY THEIR REGISTERED USERS.
I'VE HEARD ALL OF THESE SUGGESTIONS BEFORE. ***EVERYONE*** HAS.
ROTE P.R. ***PANDERING*** ISN'T GOING TO REGAIN THE CONSUMERS' TRUST.
IT'S NOT ENOUGH FOR US TO SAY THAT WE'RE GOING TO PREPARE BETTER FOR THE NEXT TIME. WE NEED TO DEAL WITH ***THIS*** TIME.
IS THERE ANYONE SEATED AT THIS TABLE WHO HAS A STRATEGY FOR ***THAT***?

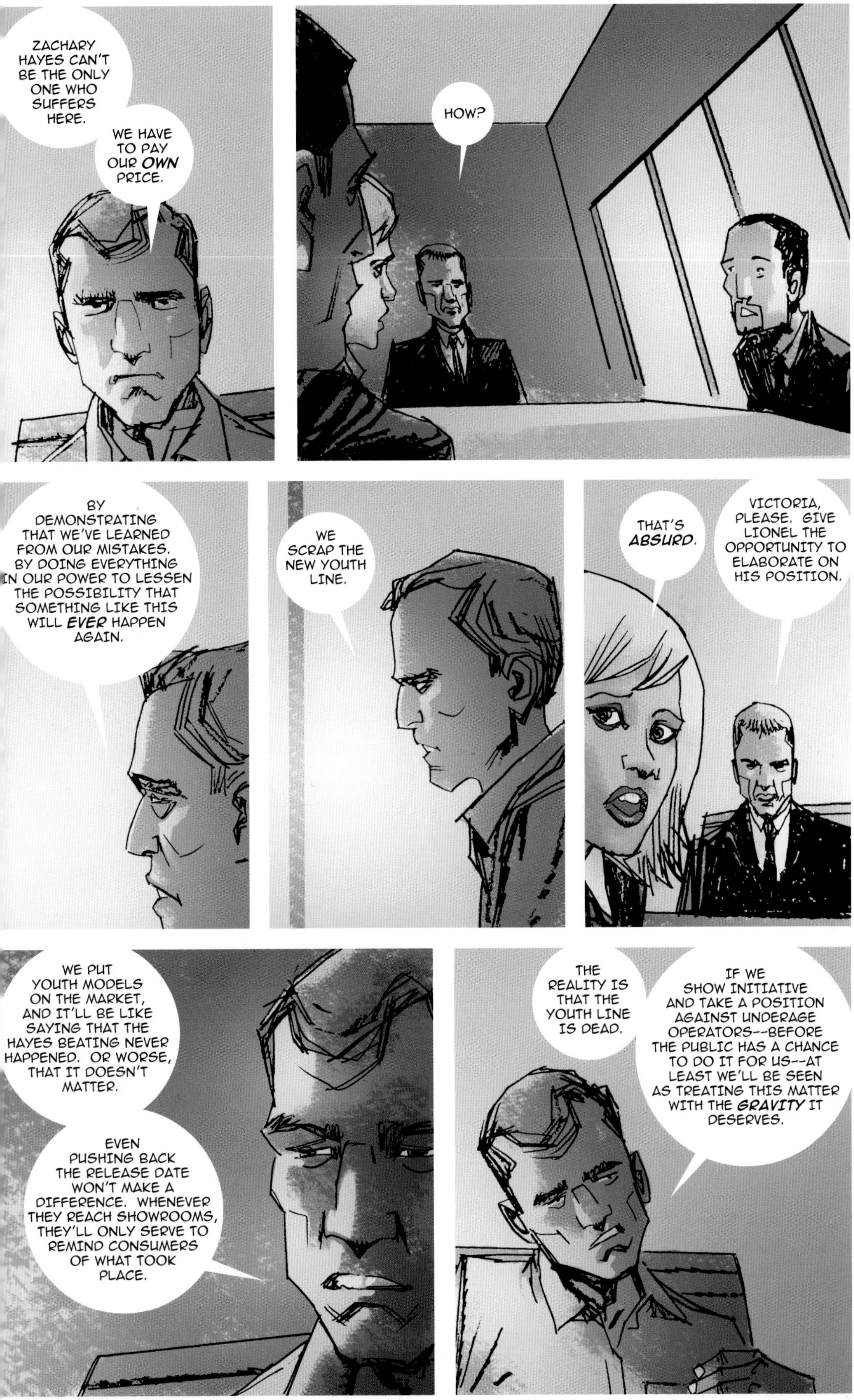
ZACHARY HAYES CAN'T BE THE ONLY ONE WHO SUFFERS HERE.
WE HAVE TO PAY OUR OWN PRICE.
HOW?
BY DEMONSTRATING THAT WE'VE LEARNED FROM OUR MISTAKES. BY DOING EVERYTHING IN OUR POWER TO LESSEN THE POSSIBILITY THAT SOMETHING LIKE THIS WILL EVER HAPPEN AGAIN.
WE SCRAP THE NEW YOUTH LINE.
THAT'S ABSURD.
VICTORIA, PLEASE. GIVE LIONEL THE OPPORTUNITY TO ELABORATE ON HIS POSITION.
WE PUT YOUTH MODELS ON THE MARKET, AND IT'LL BE LIKE SAYING THAT THE HAYES BEATING NEVER HAPPENED. OR WORSE, THAT IT DOESN'T MATTER.
EVEN PUSHING BACK THE RELEASE DATE WON'T MAKE A DIFFERENCE. WHENEVER THEY REACH SHOWROOMS, THEY'LL ONLY SERVE TO REMIND CONSUMERS OF WHAT TOOK PLACE.
THE REALITY IS THAT THE YOUTH LINE IS DEAD.
IF WE SHOW INITIATIVE AND TAKE A POSITION AGAINST UNDERAGE OPERATORS--BEFORE THE PUBLIC HAS A CHANCE TO DO IT FOR US--AT LEAST WE'LL BE SEEN AS TREATING THIS MATTER WITH THE GRAVITY IT DESERVES.

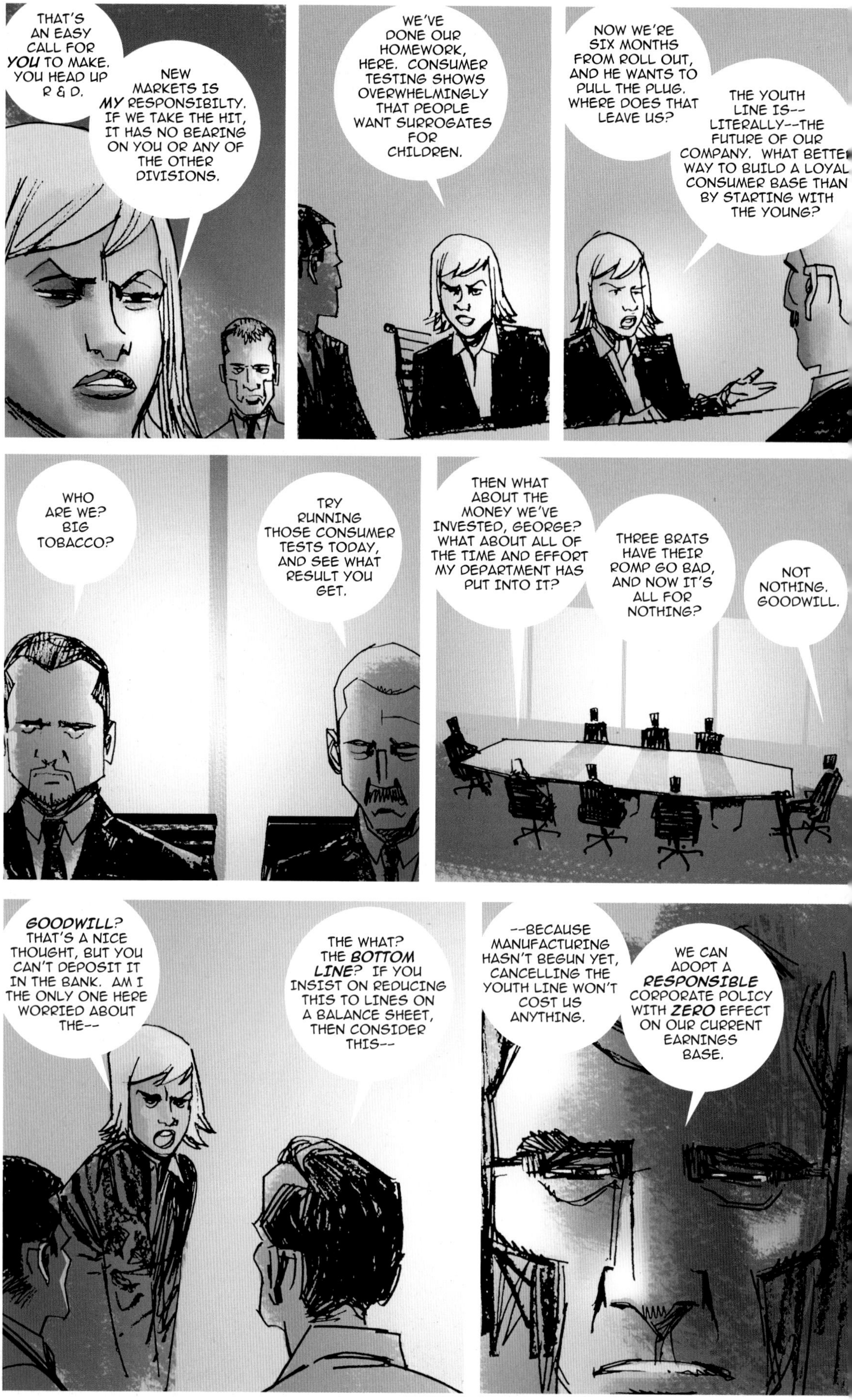
THAT'S AN EASY CALL FOR YOU TO MAKE. YOU HEAD UP R & D.
NEW MARKETS IS MY RESPONSIBILTY. IF WE TAKE THE HIT, IT HAS NO BEARING ON YOU OR ANY OF THE OTHER DIVISIONS.
WE'VE DONE OUR HOMEWORK, HERE. CONSUMER TESTING SHOWS OVERWHELMINGLY THAT PEOPLE WANT SURROGATES FOR CHILDREN.
NOW WE'RE SIX MONTHS FROM ROLL OUT, AND HE WANTS TO PULL THE PLUG. WHERE DOES THAT LEAVE US?
THE YOUTH LINE IS-- LITERALLY--THE FUTURE OF OUR COMPANY. WHAT BETTER WAY TO BUILD A LOYAL CONSUMER BASE THAN BY STARTING WITH THE YOUNG?
WHO ARE WE? BIG TOBACCO?
TRY RUNNING THOSE CONSUMER TESTS TODAY, AND SEE WHAT RESULT YOU GET.
THEN WHAT ABOUT THE MONEY WE'VE INVESTED, GEORGE? WHAT ABOUT ALL OF THE TIME AND EFFORT MY DEPARTMENT HAS PUT INTO IT?
THREE BRATS HAVE THEIR ROMP GO BAD, AND NOW IT'S ALL FOR NOTHING?
NOT NOTHING. GOODWILL.
GOODWILL? THAT'S A NICE THOUGHT, BUT YOU CAN'T DEPOSIT IT IN THE BANK. AM I THE ONLY ONE HERE WORRIED ABOUT THE--
THE WHAT? THE BOTTOM LINE? IF YOU INSIST ON REDUCING THIS TO LINES ON A BALANCE SHEET, THEN CONSIDER THIS--
--BECAUSE MANUFACTURING HASN'T BEGUN YET, CANCELLING THE YOUTH LINE WON'T COST US ANYTHING.
WE CAN ADOPT A RESPONSIBLE CORPORATE POLICY WITH ZERO EFFECT ON OUR CURRENT EARNINGS BASE.

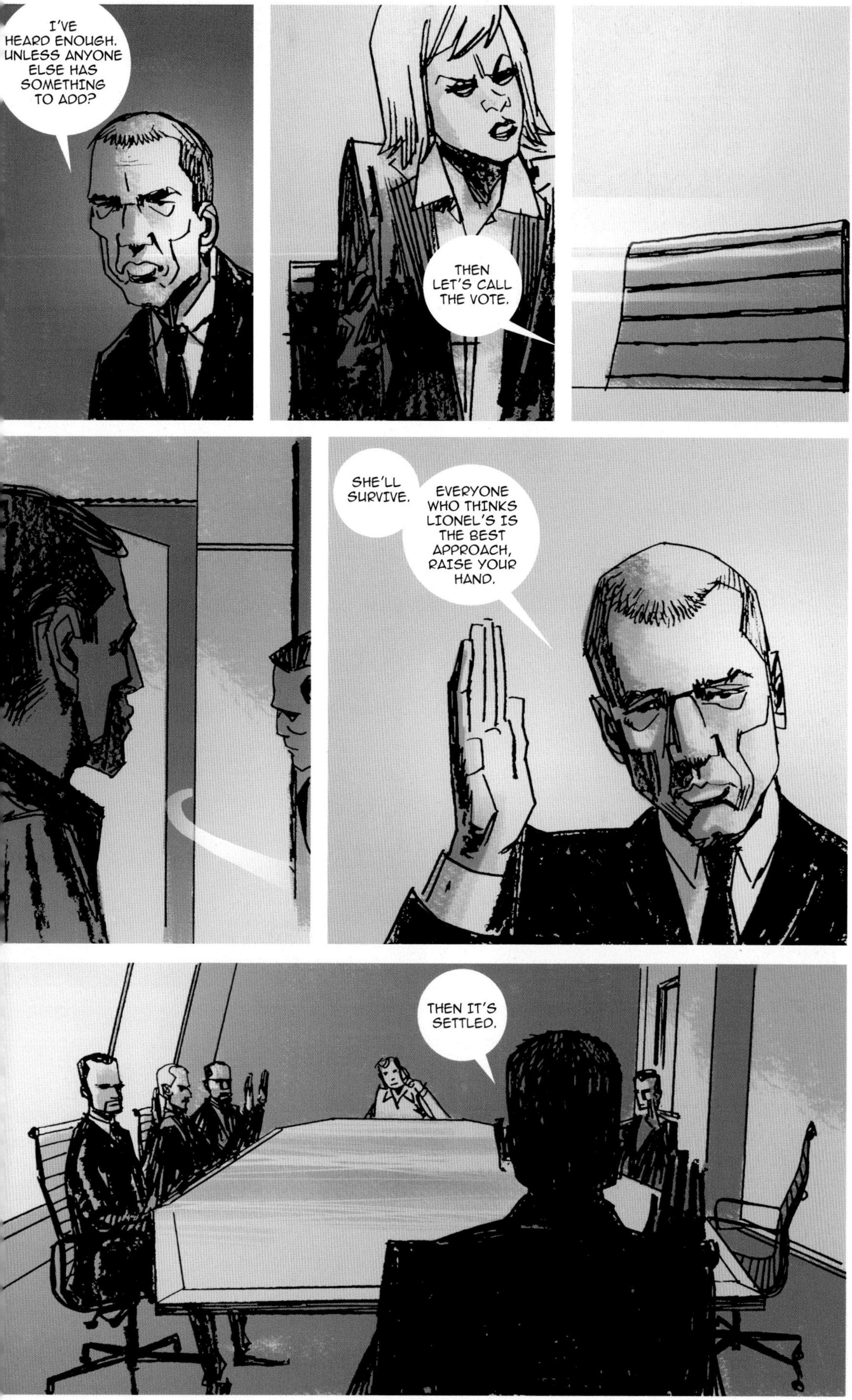
I'VE HEARD ENOUGH. UNLESS ANYONE ELSE HAS SOMETHING TO ADD?
THEN LET'S CALL THE VOTE.
SHE'LL SURVIVE.
EVERYONE WHO THINKS LIONEL'S IS THE BEST APPROACH, RAISE YOUR HAND.
THEN IT'S SETTLED.

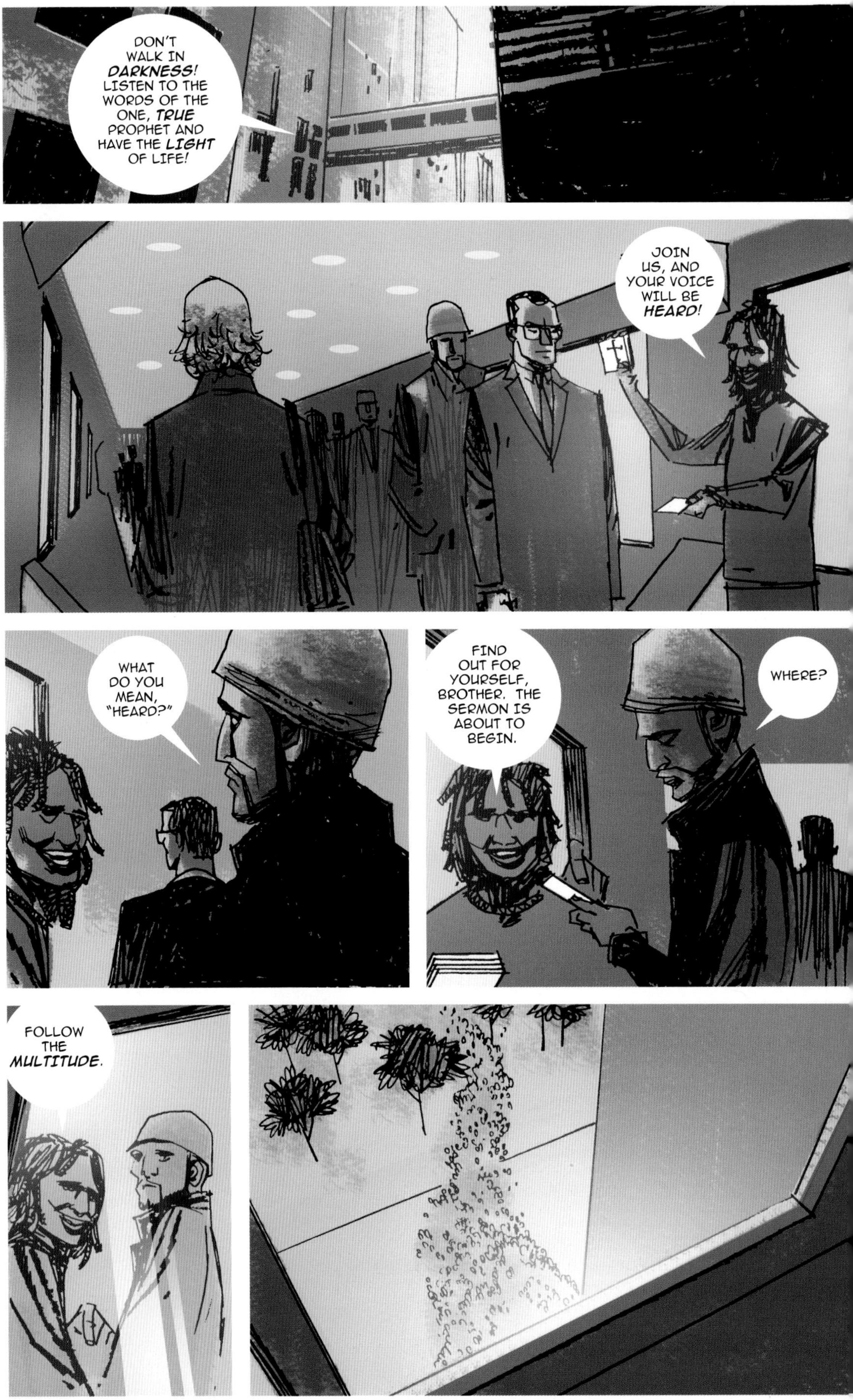

DON'T WALK IN *DARKNESS*! LISTEN TO THE WORDS OF THE ONE, *TRUE* PROPHET AND HAVE THE *LIGHT* OF LIFE!
JOIN US, AND YOUR VOICE WILL BE *HEARD*!
WHAT DO YOU MEAN, "HEARD?"
FIND OUT FOR YOURSELF, BROTHER. THE SERMON IS ABOUT TO BEGIN.
WHERE?
FOLLOW THE *MULTITUDE*.

WE'RE LIVE AT CENTENNIAL PARK, WHERE A CROWD HAS GATHERED FOR AN IMPROMPTU RALLY TO SHOW SOLIDARITY IN THE WAKE OF THE ZACHARY HAYES BEATING.

CENTER STAGE WILL BE A RELIGIOUS LEADER THOSE IN ATTENDANCE ARE REFERRING TO AS "THE PROPHET," WHOSE ANTI-SURROGATE STANCE HAS STRUCK A CHORD AMONG CITIZENS EITHER UNABLE OR UNWILLING TO USE THE INCREASINGLY POPULAR PROXIES.

WHILE HE MAY BE UNFAMILIAR TO MOST IN THIS CITY, THE PROPHET IS *REVERED* BY HIS FOLLOWERS, KNOWN TO EACH OTHER AS "*DREADS*" BECAUSE OF THEIR TRADEMARK DREADLOCKED HAIRSTYLES.

F COVERAG   GNN-TV   LIVE COVERAGE FROM C

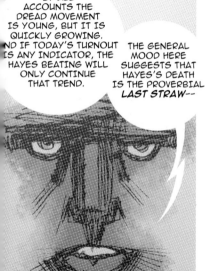

BY ALL ACCOUNTS THE DREAD MOVEMENT IS YOUNG, BUT IT IS QUICKLY GROWING. ND IF TODAY'S TURNOUT IS ANY INDICATOR, THE HAYES BEATING WILL ONLY CONTINUE THAT TREND.

THE GENERAL MOOD HERE SUGGESTS THAT HAYES'S DEATH IS THE PROVERBIAL *LAST STRAW*--

--WITH MANY DREADS DEMANDING THAT PUNISHMENT BE EXACTED ON THE *THREE AREA TEENS* CHARGED WITH COMMITTING THE CRIME.

THAT'S MY *SON* THEIR TALKING ABOUT.

PULL *EVERYONE* OFF OF WHATEVER THEY'RE DOING.

I WANT TO KNOW ALL THERE IS TO KNOW ABOUT THIS "PROPHET." START BY GETTING ME HIS *REAL* NAME, AND FILL IN THE HISTORY FROM THERE.

I UNDERSTAND A THING OR TWO ABOUT WORKING HE PRESS, WYATT, AND I'M TELLING YOU THIS--

--A NETWORK WORKS A TWO-MINUTE SEGMENT INTO THE SIX O'CLOCK NEWS, AND IT'S A SCOOP. THEY ROLL OUT THE TRUCKS FOR LIVE DAYTIME COVERAGE, AND IT'S ORCHESTRATED.

THEN IT SEEMS WE'VE FOUND YOUR OPPORTUNIST.

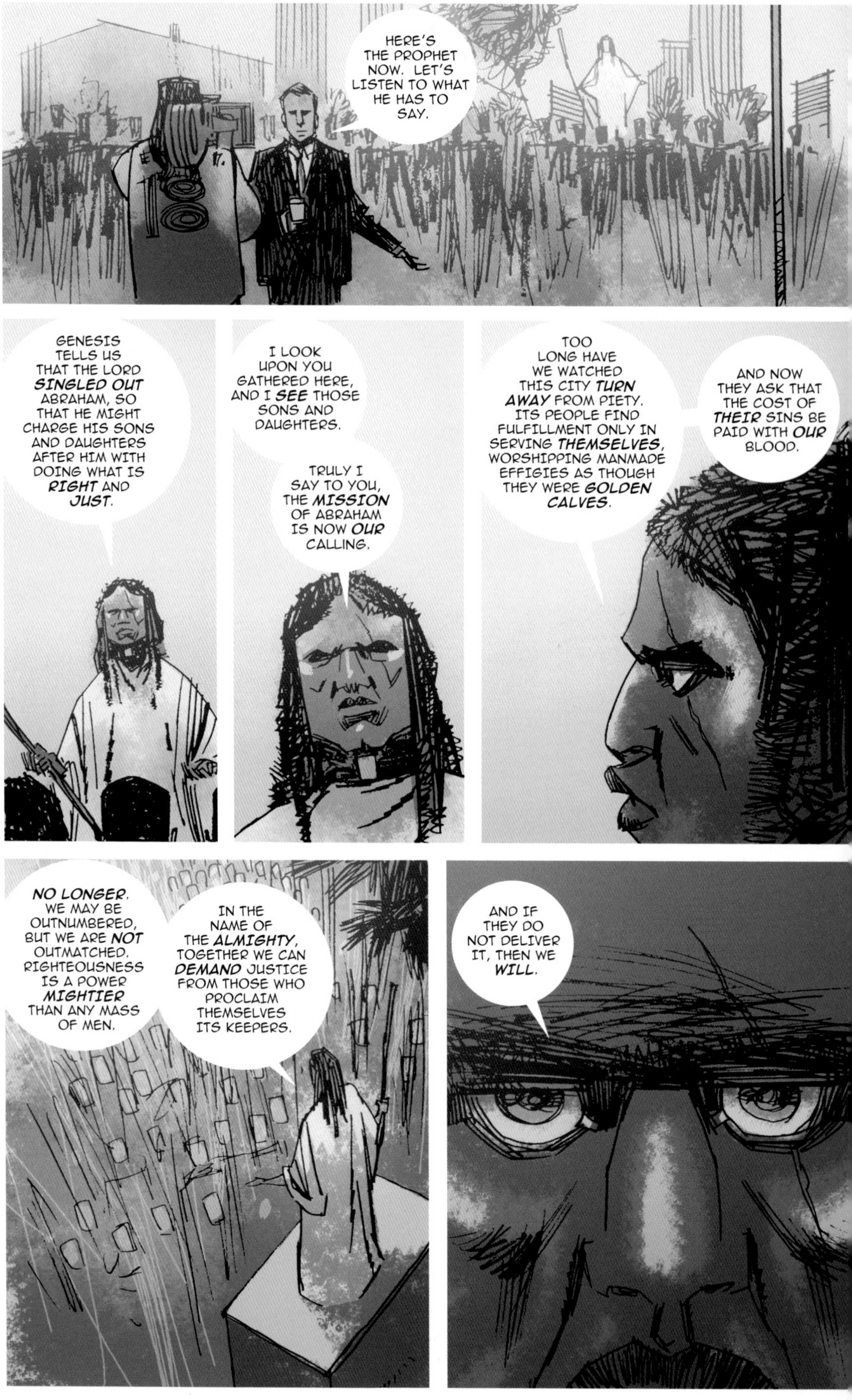
HERE'S THE PROPHET NOW. LET'S LISTEN TO WHAT HE HAS TO SAY.
GENESIS TELLS US THAT THE LORD SINGLED OUT ABRAHAM, SO THAT HE MIGHT CHARGE HIS SONS AND DAUGHTERS AFTER HIM WITH DOING WHAT IS RIGHT AND JUST.
I LOOK UPON YOU GATHERED HERE, AND I SEE THOSE SONS AND DAUGHTERS.
TRULY I SAY TO YOU, THE MISSION OF ABRAHAM IS NOW OUR CALLING.
TOO LONG HAVE WE WATCHED THIS CITY TURN AWAY FROM PIETY. ITS PEOPLE FIND FULFILLMENT ONLY IN SERVING THEMSELVES, WORSHIPPING MANMADE EFFIGIES AS THOUGH THEY WERE GOLDEN CALVES.
AND NOW THEY ASK THAT THE COST OF THEIR SINS BE PAID WITH OUR BLOOD.
NO LONGER. WE MAY BE OUTNUMBERED, BUT WE ARE NOT OUTMATCHED. RIGHTEOUSNESS IS A POWER MIGHTIER THAN ANY MASS OF MEN.
IN THE NAME OF THE ALMIGHTY, TOGETHER WE CAN DEMAND JUSTICE FROM THOSE WHO PROCLAIM THEMSELVES ITS KEEPERS.
AND IF THEY DO NOT DELIVER IT, THEN WE WILL.

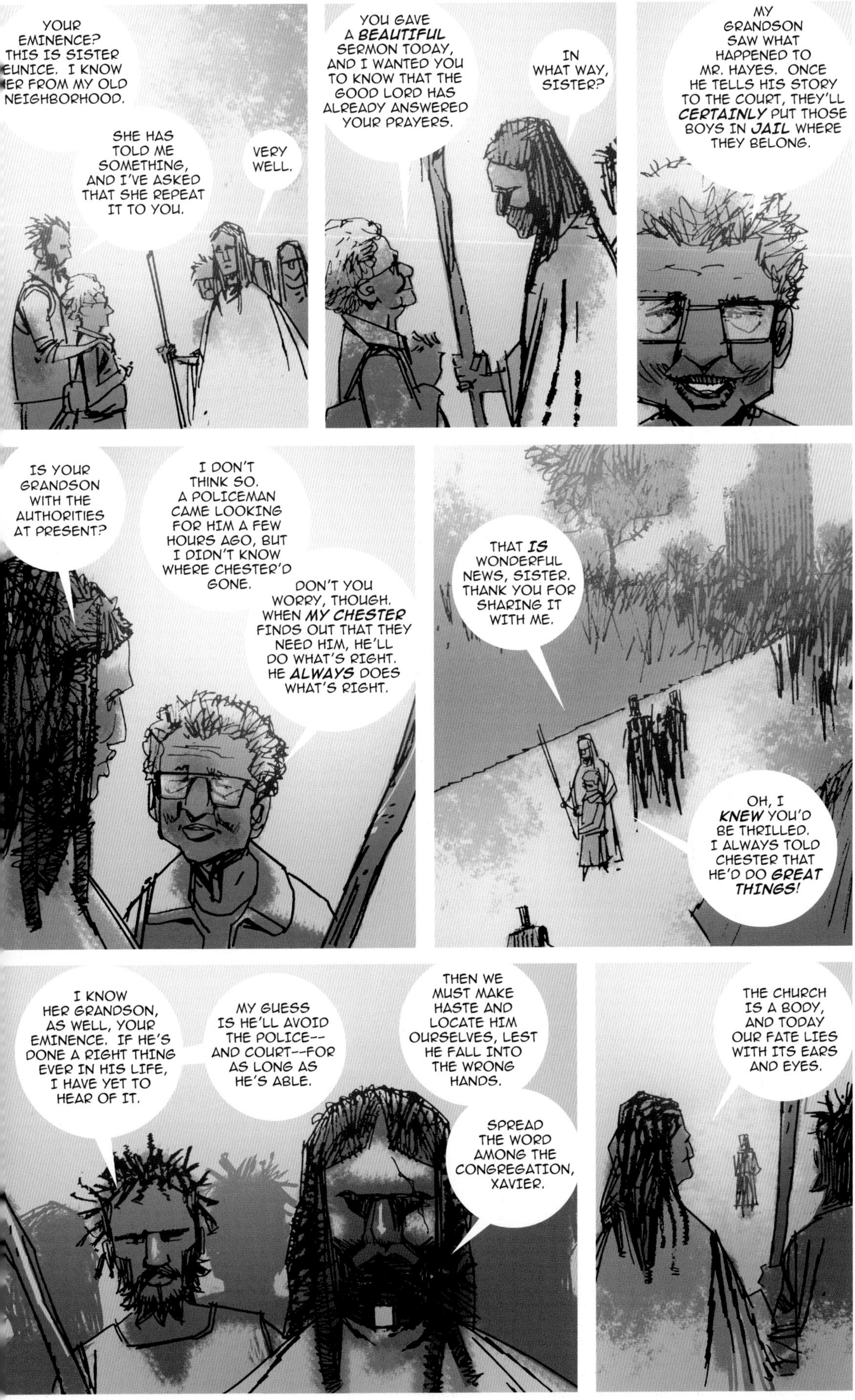

YOUR EMINENCE? THIS IS SISTER EUNICE. I KNOW HER FROM MY OLD NEIGHBORHOOD.
SHE HAS TOLD ME SOMETHING, AND I'VE ASKED THAT SHE REPEAT IT TO YOU.
VERY WELL.
YOU GAVE A BEAUTIFUL SERMON TODAY, AND I WANTED YOU TO KNOW THAT THE GOOD LORD HAS ALREADY ANSWERED YOUR PRAYERS.
IN WHAT WAY, SISTER?
MY GRANDSON SAW WHAT HAPPENED TO MR. HAYES. ONCE HE TELLS HIS STORY TO THE COURT, THEY'LL CERTAINLY PUT THOSE BOYS IN JAIL WHERE THEY BELONG.
IS YOUR GRANDSON WITH THE AUTHORITIES AT PRESENT?
I DON'T THINK SO. A POLICEMAN CAME LOOKING FOR HIM A FEW HOURS AGO, BUT I DIDN'T KNOW WHERE CHESTER'D GONE.
DON'T YOU WORRY, THOUGH. WHEN MY CHESTER FINDS OUT THAT THEY NEED HIM, HE'LL DO WHAT'S RIGHT. HE ALWAYS DOES WHAT'S RIGHT.
THAT IS WONDERFUL NEWS, SISTER. THANK YOU FOR SHARING IT WITH ME.
OH, I KNEW YOU'D BE THRILLED. I ALWAYS TOLD CHESTER THAT HE'D DO GREAT THINGS!
I KNOW HER GRANDSON, AS WELL, YOUR EMINENCE. IF HE'S DONE A RIGHT THING EVER IN HIS LIFE, I HAVE YET TO HEAR OF IT.
MY GUESS IS HE'LL AVOID THE POLICE-- AND COURT--FOR AS LONG AS HE'S ABLE.
THEN WE MUST MAKE HASTE AND LOCATE HIM OURSELVES, LEST HE FALL INTO THE WRONG HANDS.
SPREAD THE WORD AMONG THE CONGREGATION, XAVIER.
THE CHURCH IS A BODY, AND TODAY OUR FATE LIES WITH ITS EARS AND EYES.

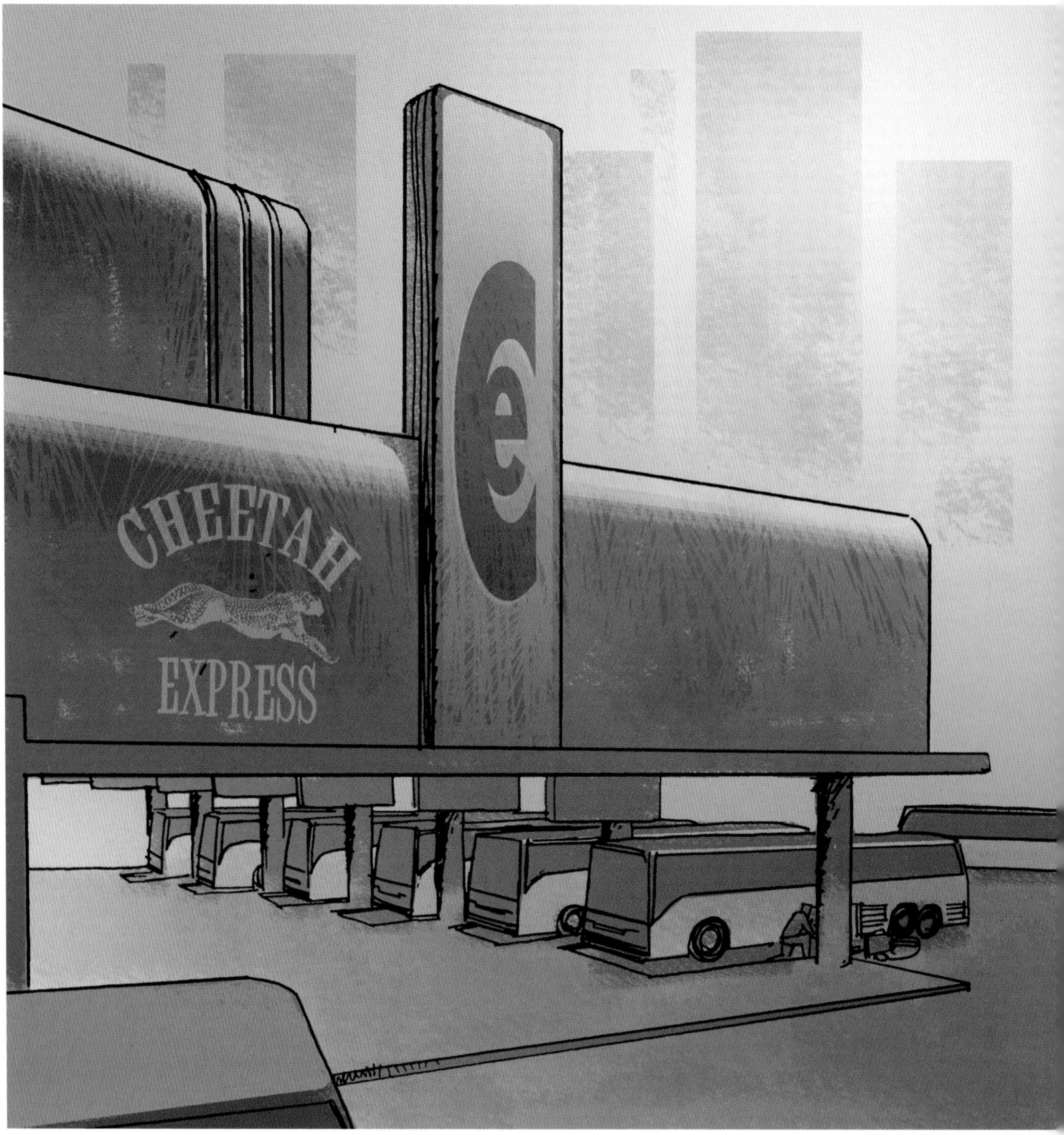
CHEETAH
EXPRESS

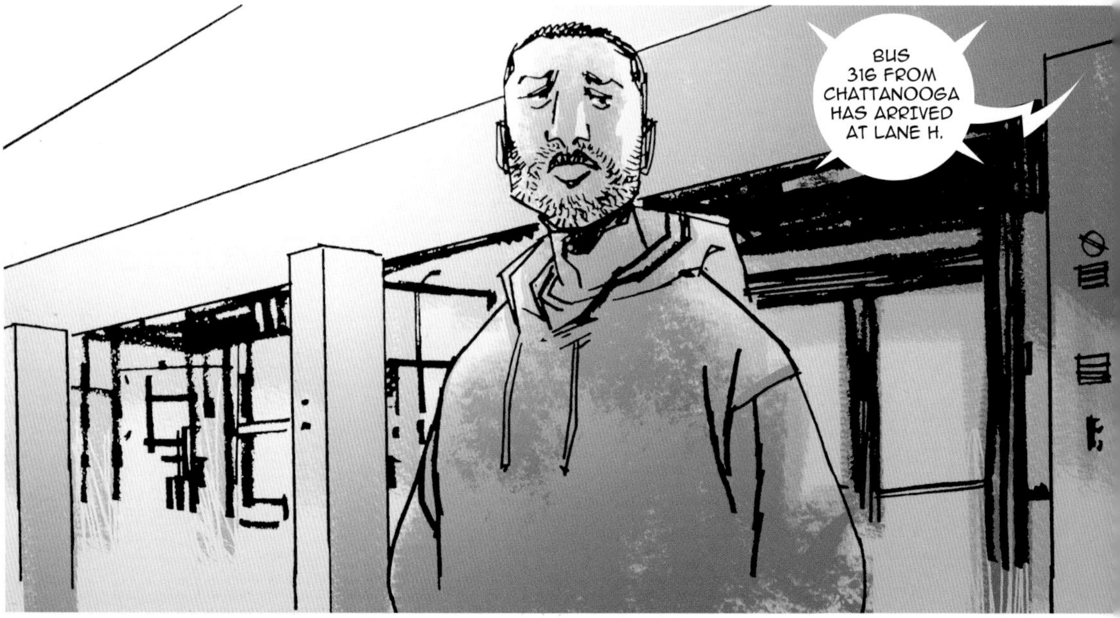
BUS 316 FROM CHATTANOOGA HAS ARRIVED AT LANE H.

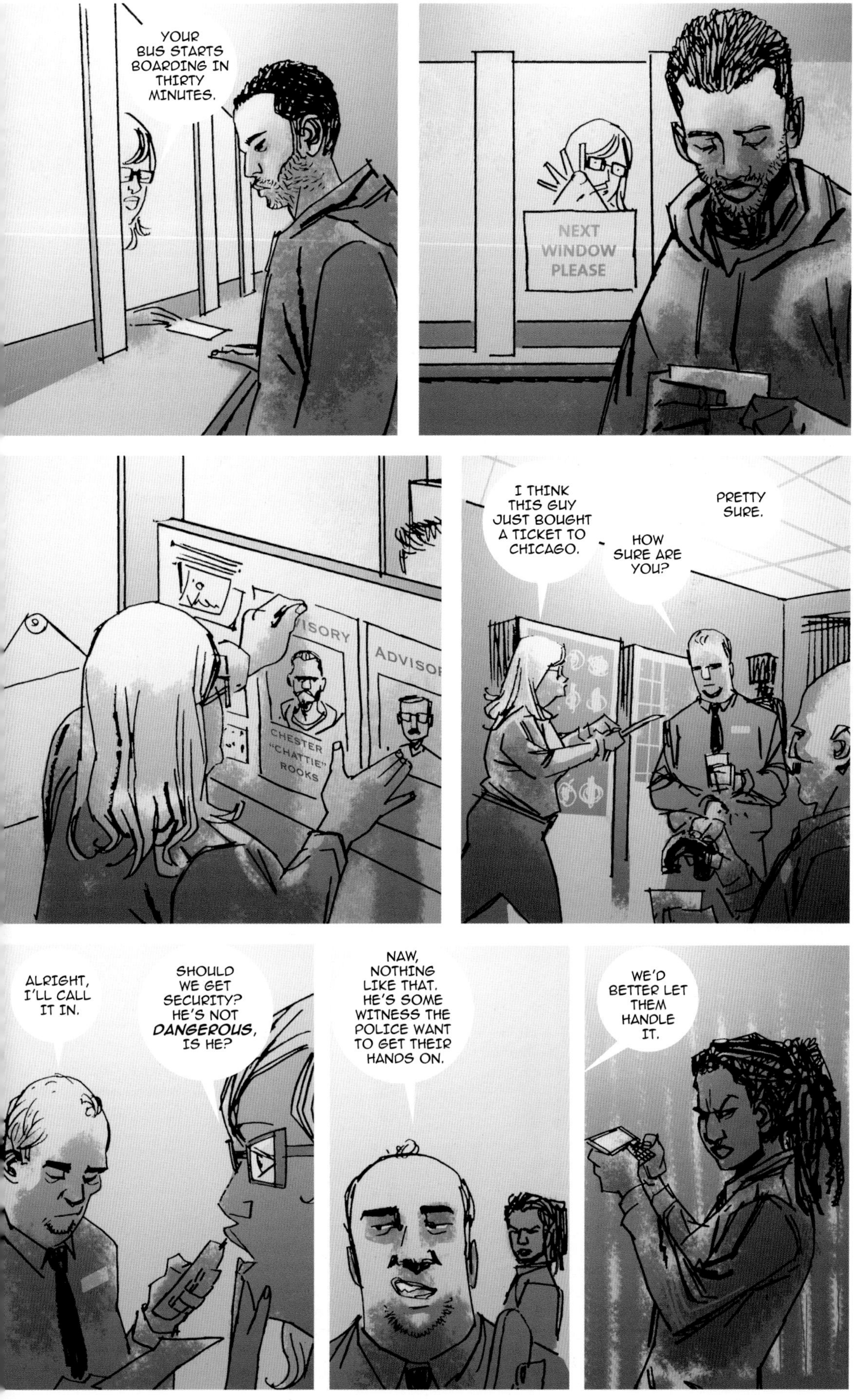
YOUR BUS STARTS BOARDING IN THIRTY MINUTES.
NEXT WINDOW PLEASE
ADVISORY
ADVISOR
CHESTER "CHATTIE" ROOKS
I THINK THIS GUY JUST BOUGHT A TICKET TO CHICAGO.
HOW SURE ARE YOU?
PRETTY SURE.
ALRIGHT, I'LL CALL IT IN.
SHOULD WE GET SECURITY? HE'S NOT *DANGEROUS*, IS HE?
NAW, NOTHING LIKE THAT. HE'S SOME WITNESS THE POLICE WANT TO GET THEIR HANDS ON.
WE'D BETTER LET THEM HANDLE IT.

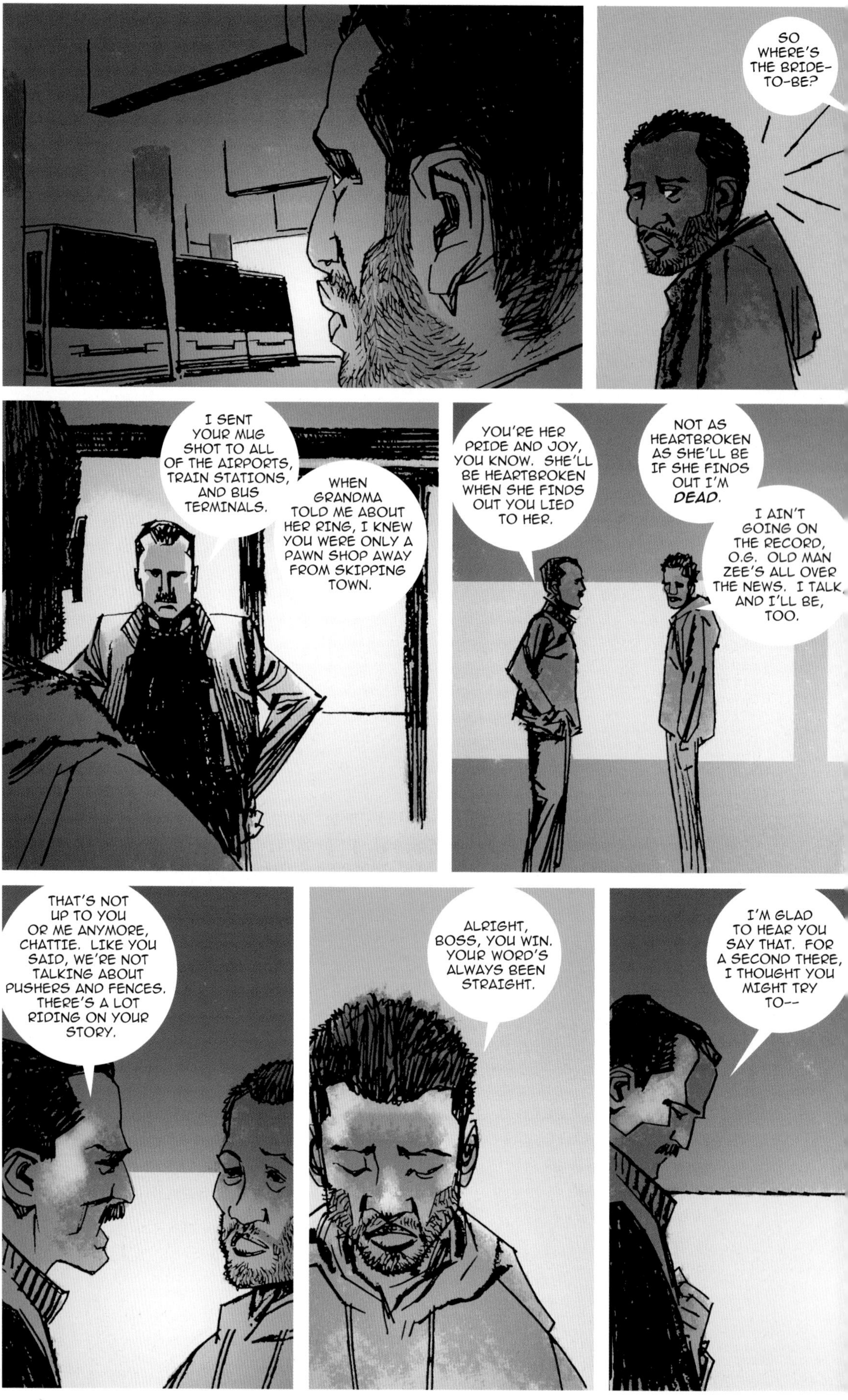
SO WHERE'S THE BRIDE-TO-BE?
I SENT YOUR MUG SHOT TO ALL OF THE AIRPORTS, TRAIN STATIONS, AND BUS TERMINALS.
WHEN GRANDMA TOLD ME ABOUT HER RING, I KNEW YOU WERE ONLY A PAWN SHOP AWAY FROM SKIPPING TOWN.
YOU'RE HER PRIDE AND JOY, YOU KNOW. SHE'LL BE HEARTBROKEN WHEN SHE FINDS OUT YOU LIED TO HER.
NOT AS HEARTBROKEN AS SHE'LL BE IF SHE FINDS OUT I'M DEAD.
I AIN'T GOING ON THE RECORD, O.G. OLD MAN ZEE'S ALL OVER THE NEWS. I TALK AND I'LL BE, TOO.
THAT'S NOT UP TO YOU OR ME ANYMORE, CHATTIE. LIKE YOU SAID, WE'RE NOT TALKING ABOUT PUSHERS AND FENCES. THERE'S A LOT RIDING ON YOUR STORY.
ALRIGHT, BOSS, YOU WIN. YOUR WORD'S ALWAYS BEEN STRAIGHT.
I'M GLAD TO HEAR YOU SAY THAT. FOR A SECOND THERE, I THOUGHT YOU MIGHT TRY TO--

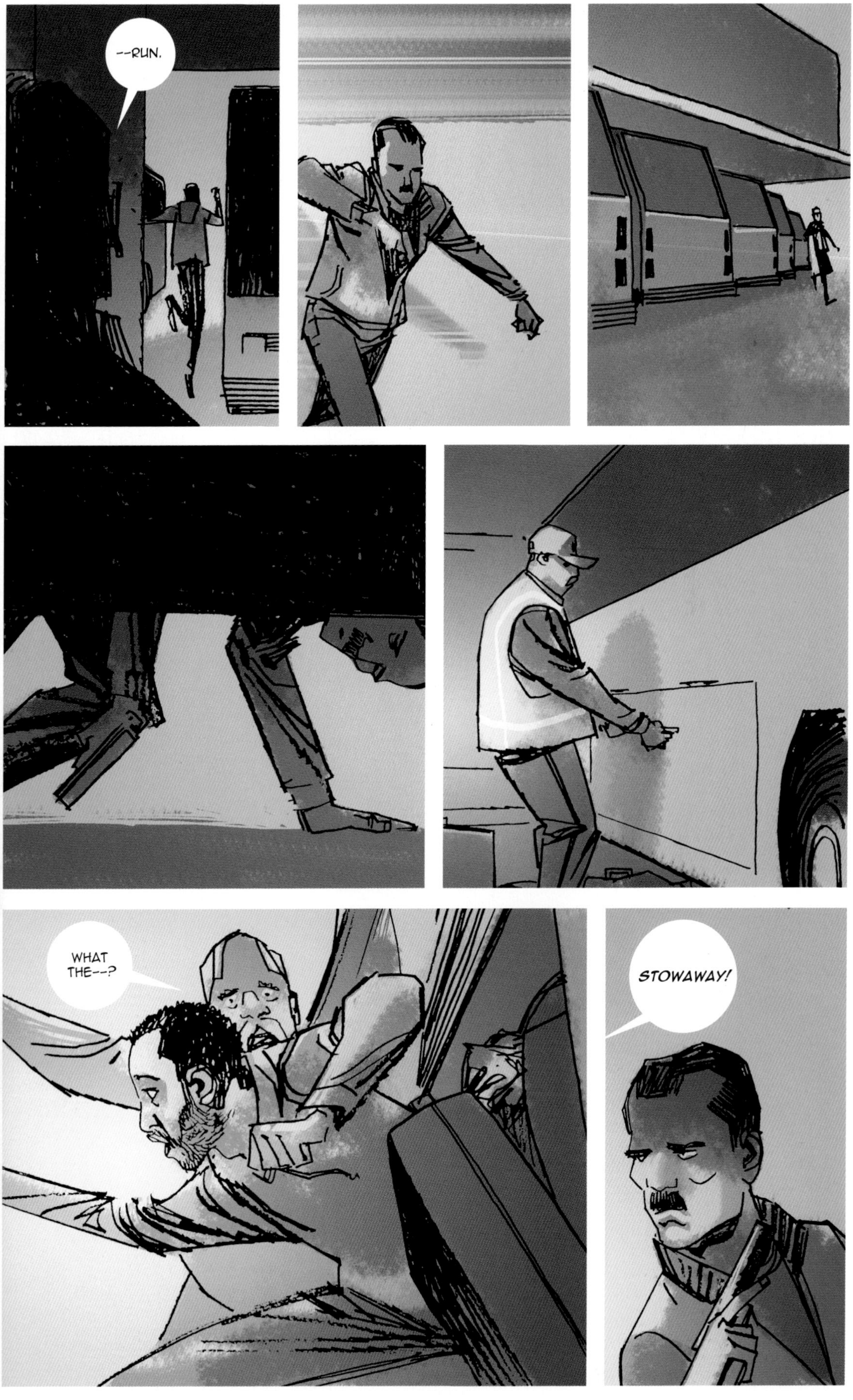
--RUN.
WHAT THE--?
STOWAWAY!

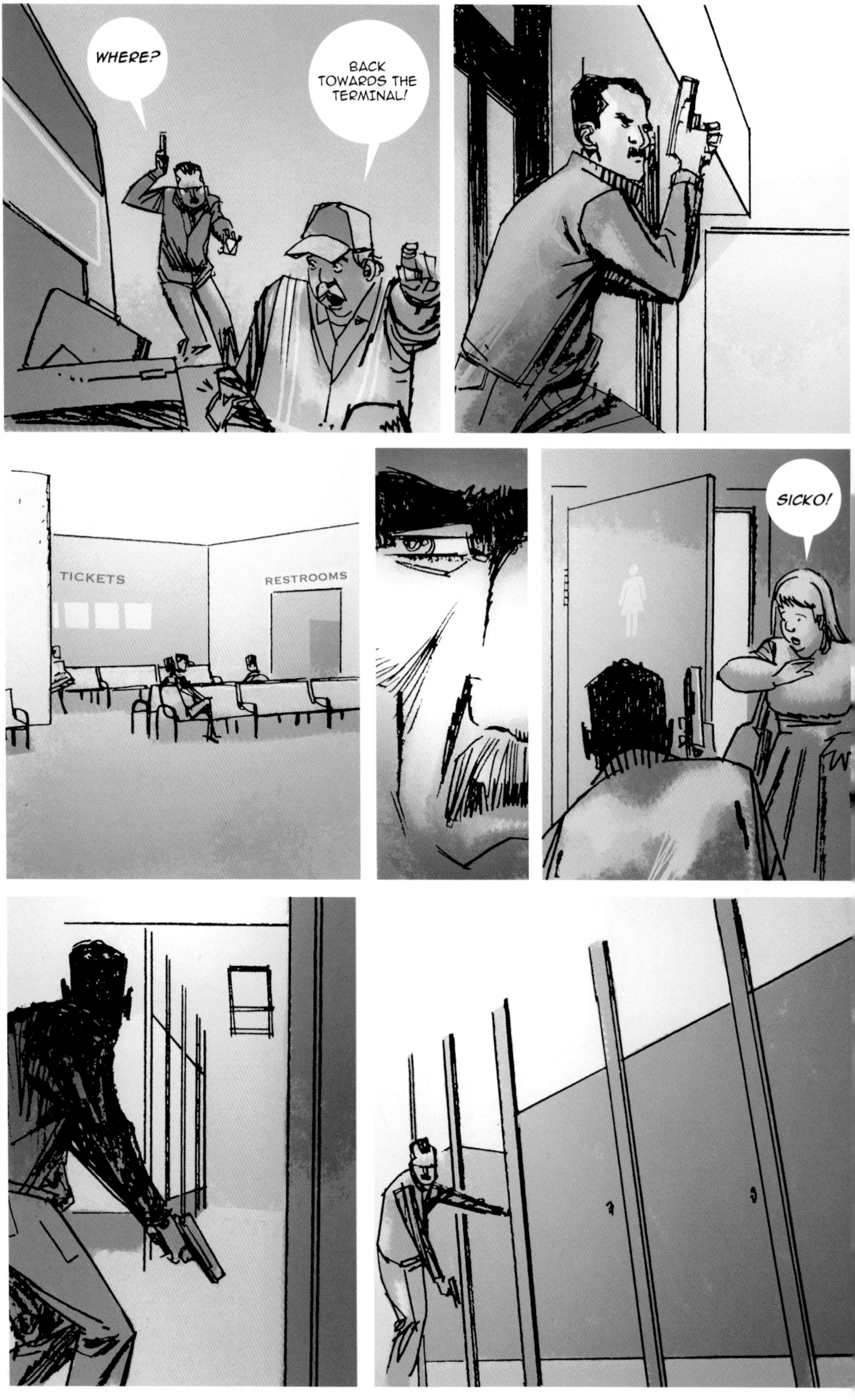
WHERE?
BACK TOWARDS THE TERMINAL!
TICKETS
RESTROOMS
SICKO!

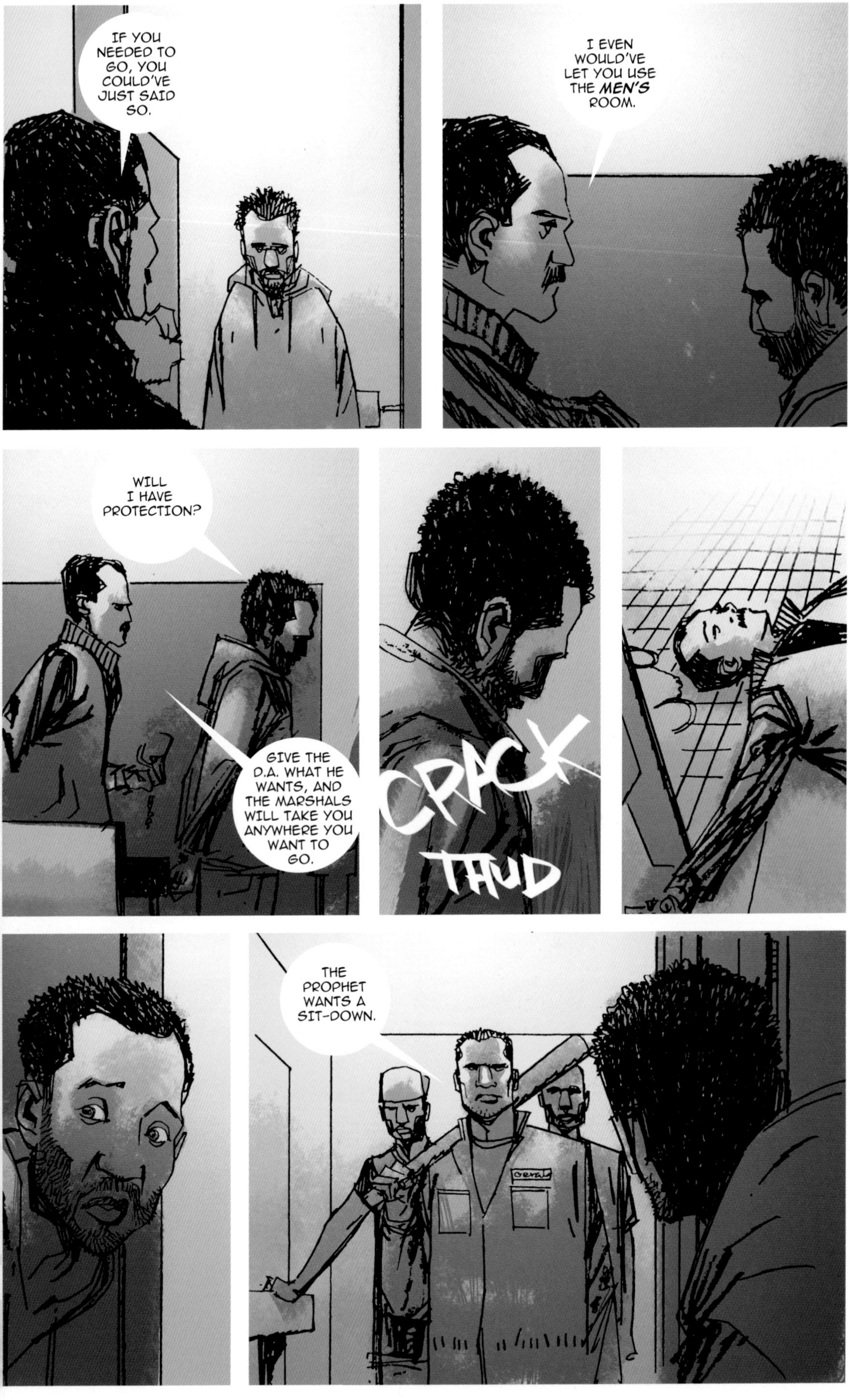
IF YOU NEEDED TO GO, YOU COULD'VE JUST SAID SO.
I EVEN WOULD'VE LET YOU USE THE MEN'S ROOM.
WILL I HAVE PROTECTION?
GIVE THE D.A. WHAT HE WANTS, AND THE MARSHALS WILL TAKE YOU ANYWHERE YOU WANT TO GO.
CRACK
THUD
THE PROPHET WANTS A SIT-DOWN.

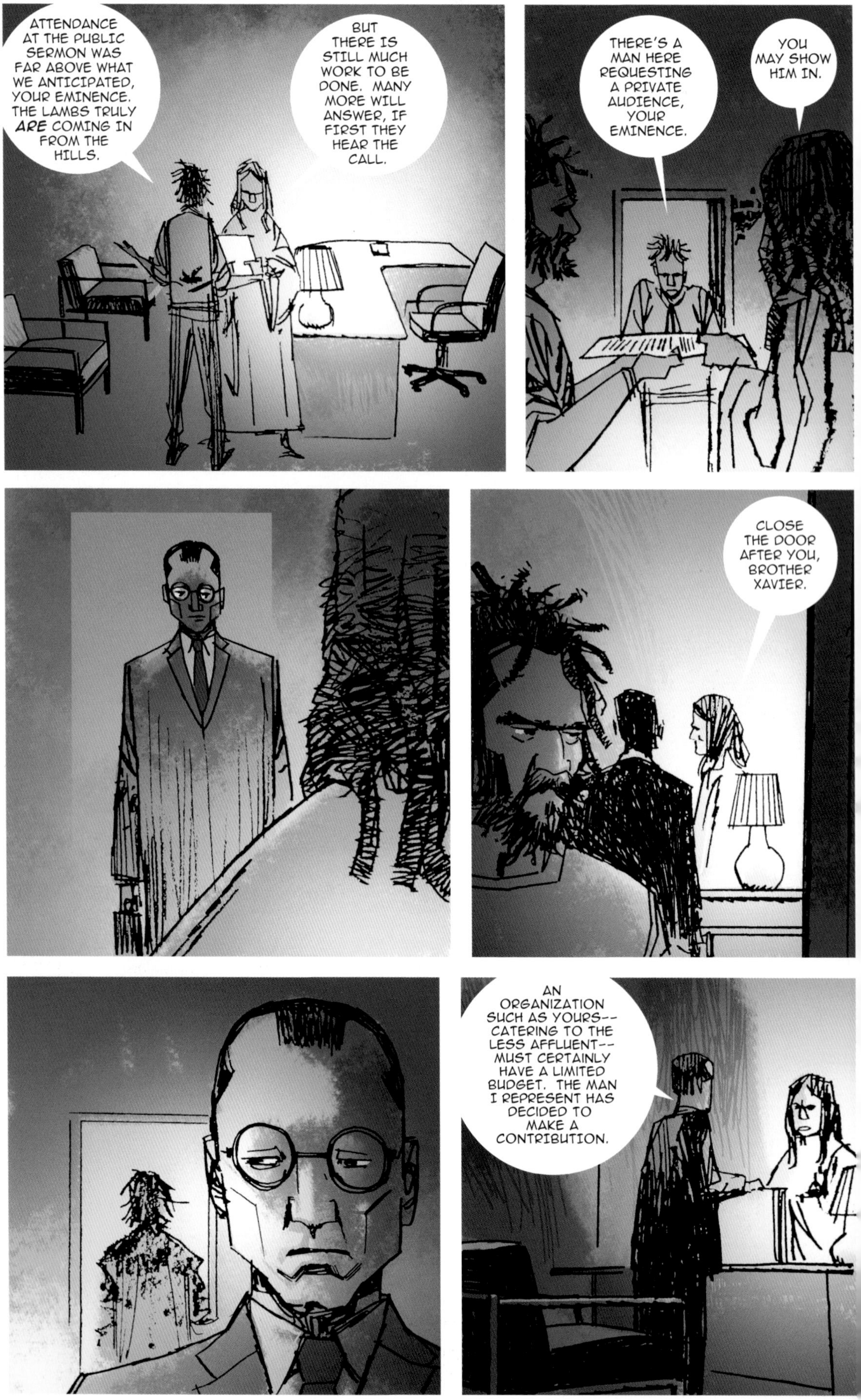

ATTENDANCE AT THE PUBLIC SERMON WAS FAR ABOVE WHAT WE ANTICIPATED, YOUR EMINENCE. THE LAMBS TRULY *ARE* COMING IN FROM THE HILLS.
BUT THERE IS STILL MUCH WORK TO BE DONE. MANY MORE WILL ANSWER, IF FIRST THEY HEAR THE CALL.
THERE'S A MAN HERE REQUESTING A PRIVATE AUDIENCE, YOUR EMINENCE.
YOU MAY SHOW HIM IN.
CLOSE THE DOOR AFTER YOU, BROTHER XAVIER.
AN ORGANIZATION SUCH AS YOURS--CATERING TO THE LESS AFFLUENT--MUST CERTAINLY HAVE A LIMITED BUDGET. THE MAN I REPRESENT HAS DECIDED TO MAKE A CONTRIBUTION.

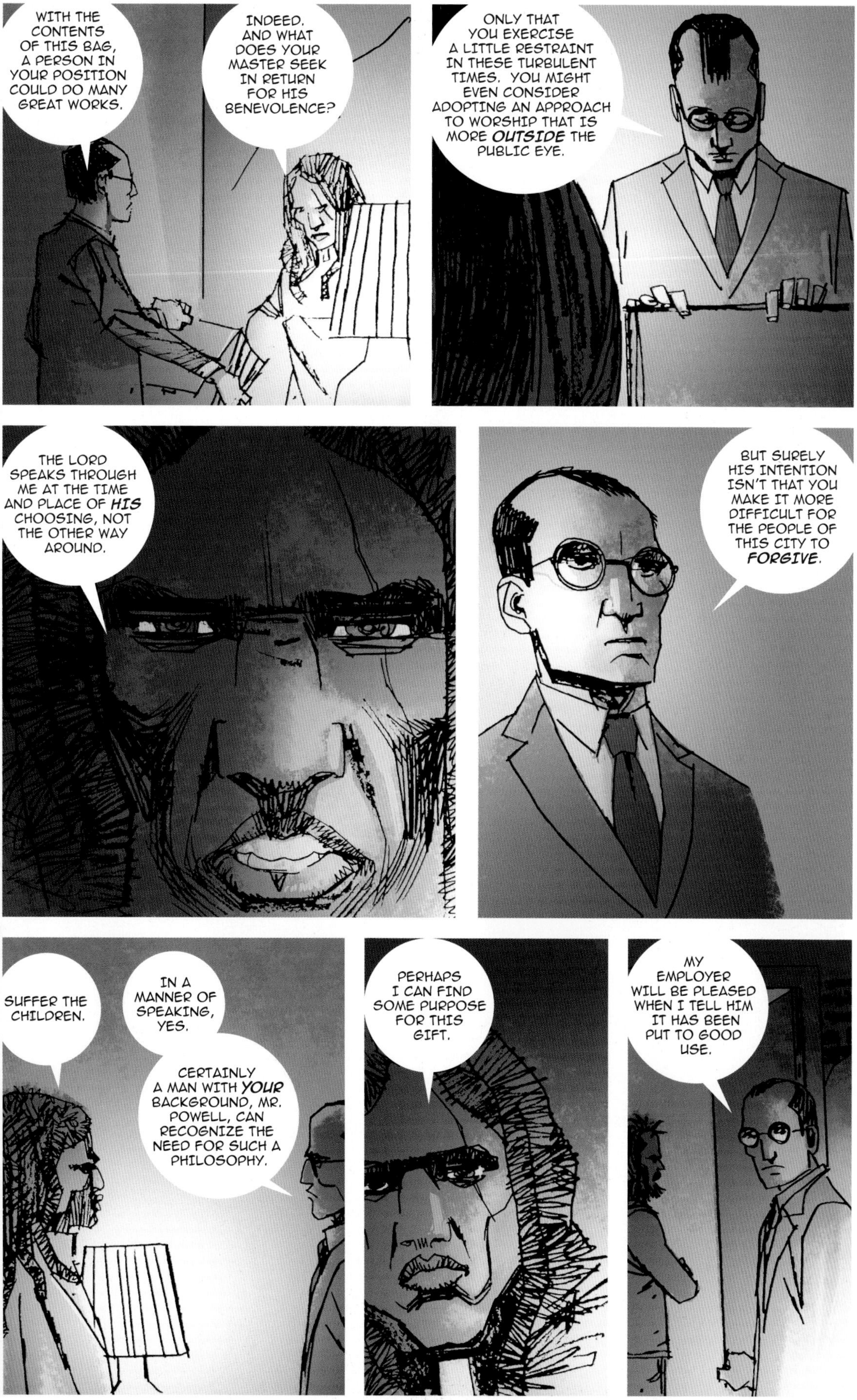
WITH THE CONTENTS OF THIS BAG, A PERSON IN YOUR POSITION COULD DO MANY GREAT WORKS.
INDEED. AND WHAT DOES YOUR MASTER SEEK IN RETURN FOR HIS BENEVOLENCE?
ONLY THAT YOU EXERCISE A LITTLE RESTRAINT IN THESE TURBULENT TIMES. YOU MIGHT EVEN CONSIDER ADOPTING AN APPROACH TO WORSHIP THAT IS MORE ***OUTSIDE*** THE PUBLIC EYE.
THE LORD SPEAKS THROUGH ME AT THE TIME AND PLACE OF ***HIS*** CHOOSING, NOT THE OTHER WAY AROUND.
BUT SURELY HIS INTENTION ISN'T THAT YOU MAKE IT MORE DIFFICULT FOR THE PEOPLE OF THIS CITY TO ***FORGIVE***.
SUFFER THE CHILDREN.
IN A MANNER OF SPEAKING, YES.
CERTAINLY A MAN WITH ***YOUR*** BACKGROUND, MR. POWELL, CAN RECOGNIZE THE NEED FOR SUCH A PHILOSOPHY.
PERHAPS I CAN FIND SOME PURPOSE FOR THIS GIFT.
MY EMPLOYER WILL BE PLEASED WHEN I TELL HIM IT HAS BEEN PUT TO GOOD USE.

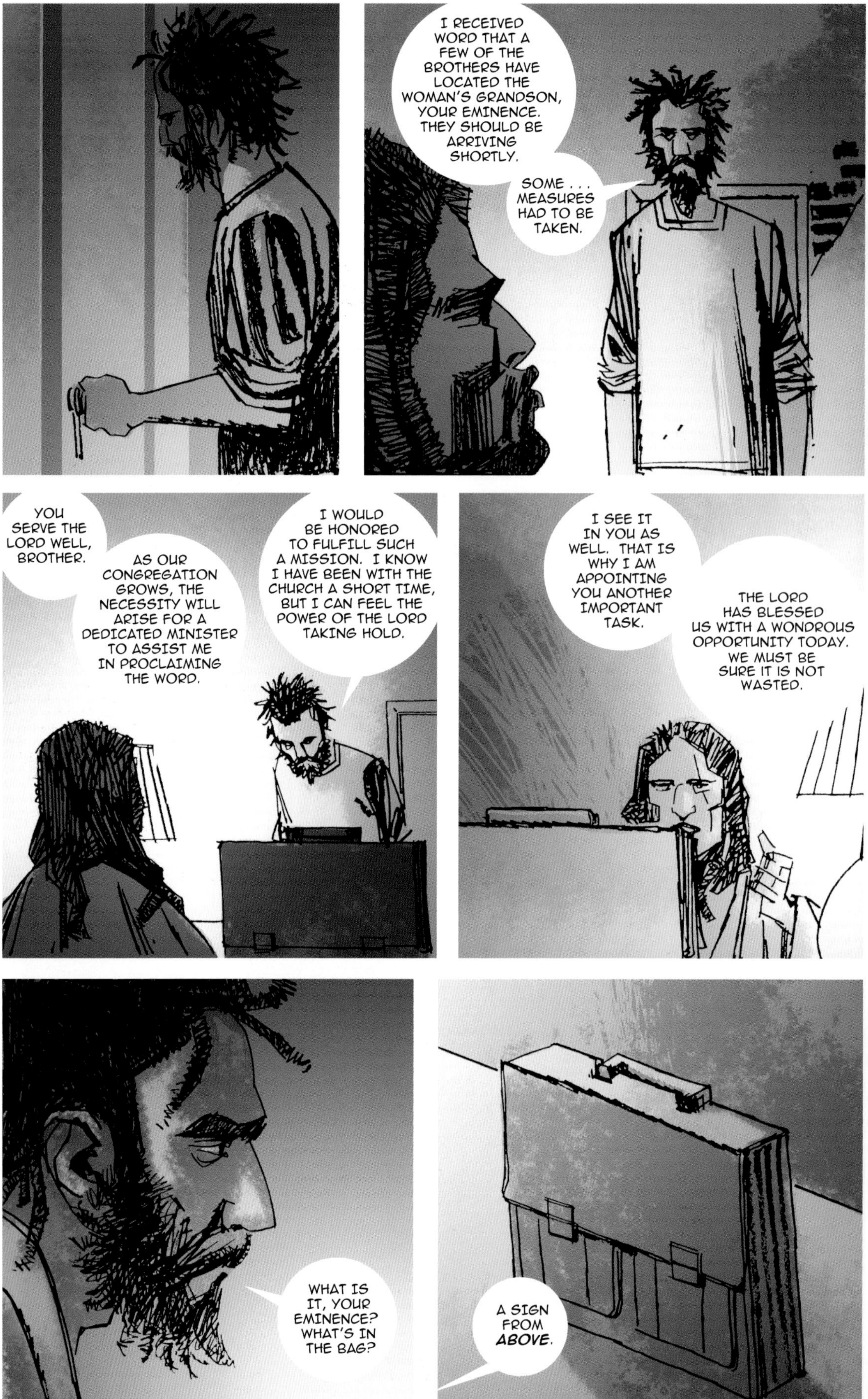

I RECEIVED WORD THAT A FEW OF THE BROTHERS HAVE LOCATED THE WOMAN'S GRANDSON, YOUR EMINENCE. THEY SHOULD BE ARRIVING SHORTLY.
SOME . . . MEASURES HAD TO BE TAKEN.
YOU SERVE THE LORD WELL, BROTHER.
AS OUR CONGREGATION GROWS, THE NECESSITY WILL ARISE FOR A DEDICATED MINISTER TO ASSIST ME IN PROCLAIMING THE WORD.
I WOULD BE HONORED TO FULFILL SUCH A MISSION. I KNOW I HAVE BEEN WITH THE CHURCH A SHORT TIME, BUT I CAN FEEL THE POWER OF THE LORD TAKING HOLD.
I SEE IT IN YOU AS WELL. THAT IS WHY I AM APPOINTING YOU ANOTHER IMPORTANT TASK.
THE LORD HAS BLESSED US WITH A WONDROUS OPPORTUNITY TODAY. WE MUST BE SURE IT IS NOT WASTED.
WHAT IS IT, YOUR EMINENCE? WHAT'S IN THE BAG?
A SIGN FROM ***ABOVE***.

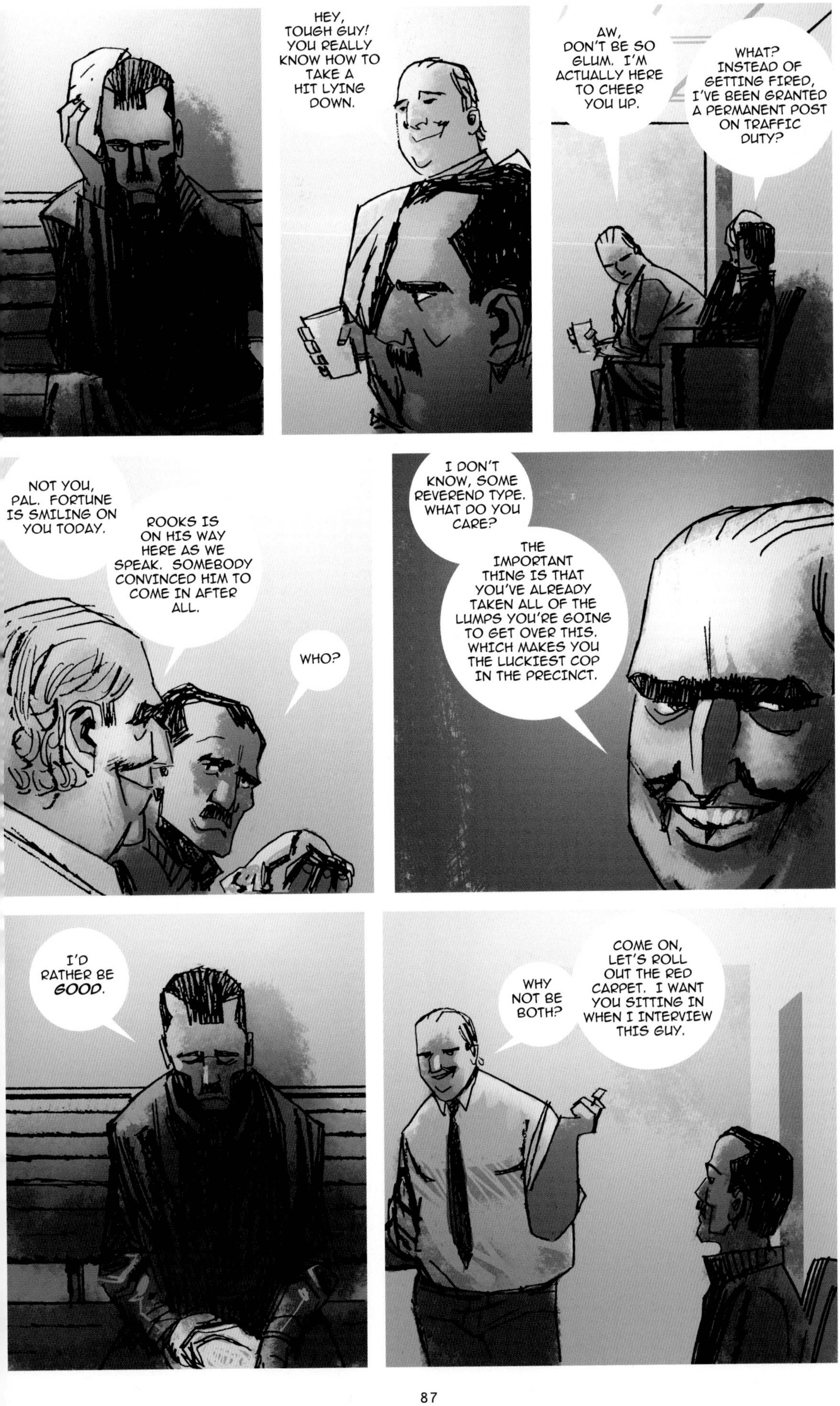
HEY, TOUGH GUY! YOU REALLY KNOW HOW TO TAKE A HIT LYING DOWN.
AW, DON'T BE SO GLUM. I'M ACTUALLY HERE TO CHEER YOU UP.
WHAT? INSTEAD OF GETTING FIRED, I'VE BEEN GRANTED A PERMANENT POST ON TRAFFIC DUTY?
NOT YOU, PAL. FORTUNE IS SMILING ON YOU TODAY.
ROOKS IS ON HIS WAY HERE AS WE SPEAK. SOMEBODY CONVINCED HIM TO COME IN AFTER ALL.
WHO?
I DON'T KNOW, SOME REVEREND TYPE. WHAT DO YOU CARE?
THE IMPORTANT THING IS THAT YOU'VE ALREADY TAKEN ALL OF THE LUMPS YOU'RE GOING TO GET OVER THIS. WHICH MAKES YOU THE LUCKIEST COP IN THE PRECINCT.
I'D RATHER BE *GOOD*.
WHY NOT BE BOTH?
COME ON, LET'S ROLL OUT THE RED CARPET. I WANT YOU SITTING IN WHEN I INTERVIEW THIS GUY.

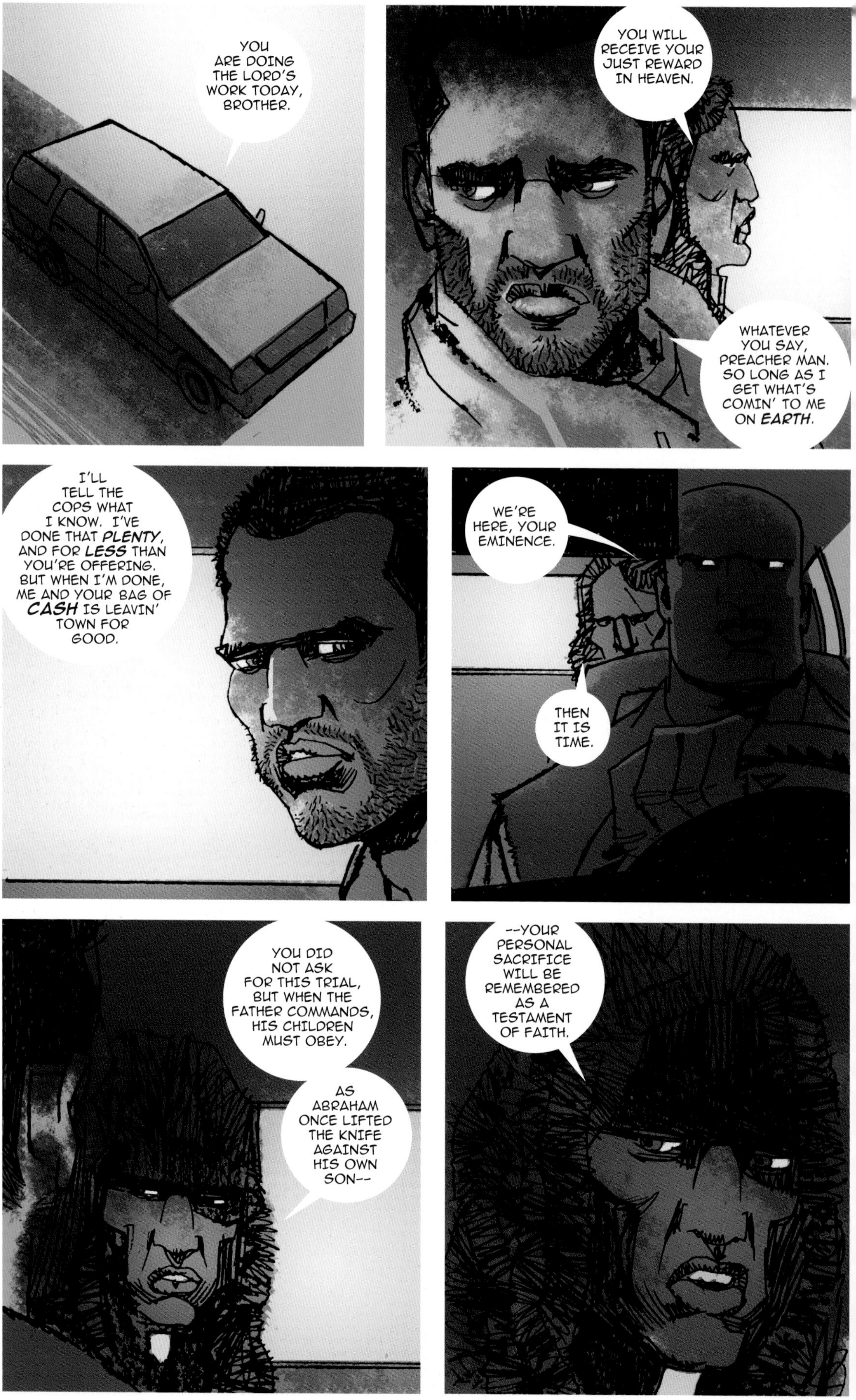
YOU ARE DOING THE LORD'S WORK TODAY, BROTHER.
YOU WILL RECEIVE YOUR JUST REWARD IN HEAVEN.
WHATEVER YOU SAY, PREACHER MAN. SO LONG AS I GET WHAT'S COMIN' TO ME ON *EARTH*.
I'LL TELL THE COPS WHAT I KNOW. I'VE DONE THAT *PLENTY*, AND FOR *LESS* THAN YOU'RE OFFERING. BUT WHEN I'M DONE, ME AND YOUR BAG OF **CASH** IS LEAVIN' TOWN FOR GOOD.
WE'RE HERE, YOUR EMINENCE.
THEN IT IS TIME.
YOU DID NOT ASK FOR THIS TRIAL, BUT WHEN THE FATHER COMMANDS, HIS CHILDREN MUST OBEY.
AS ABRAHAM ONCE LIFTED THE KNIFE AGAINST HIS OWN SON--
--YOUR PERSONAL SACRIFICE WILL BE REMEMBERED AS A TESTAMENT OF FAITH.

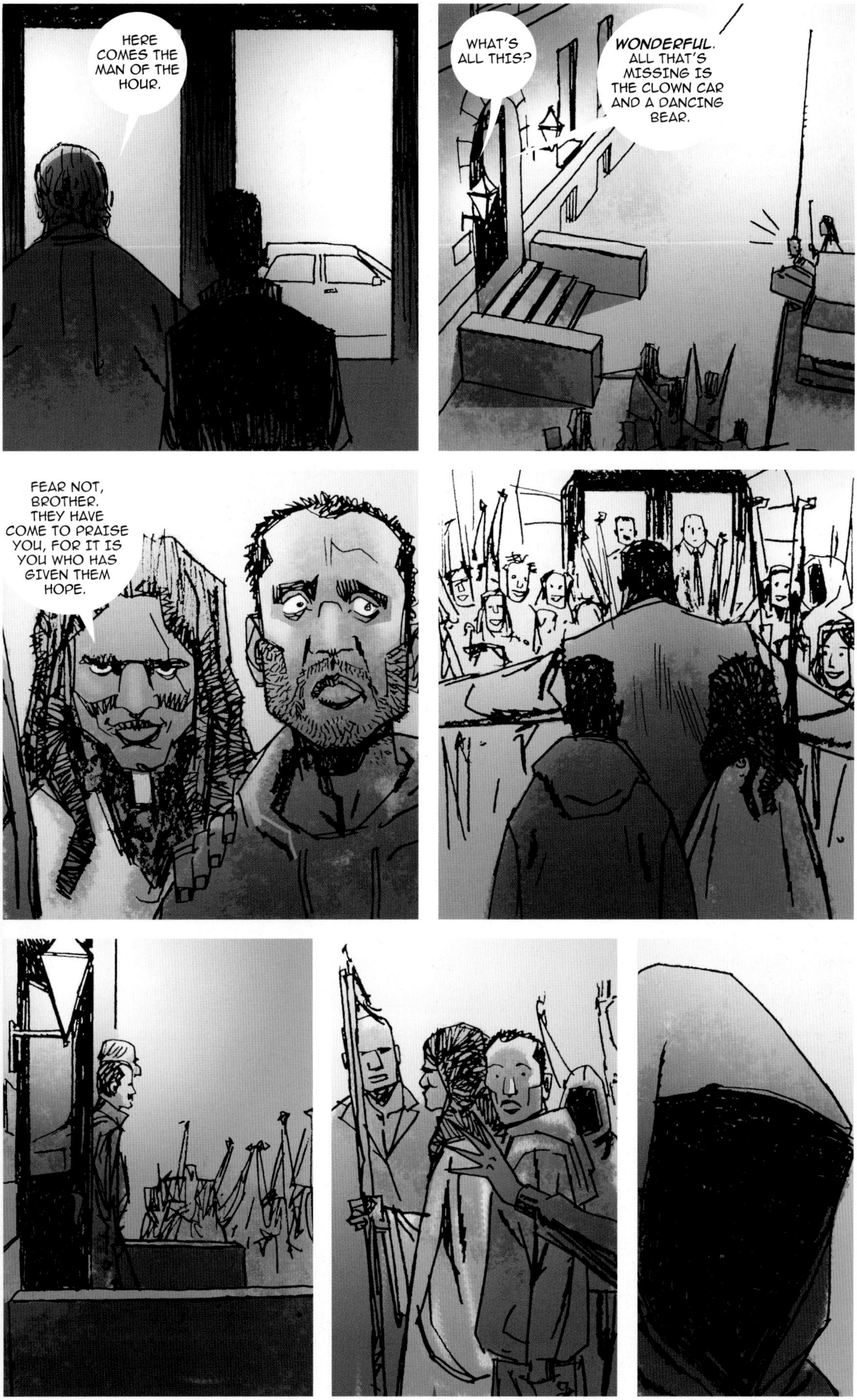
HERE COMES THE MAN OF THE HOUR.
WHAT'S ALL THIS?
WONDERFUL. ALL THAT'S MISSING IS THE CLOWN CAR AND A DANCING BEAR.
FEAR NOT, BROTHER. THEY HAVE COME TO PRAISE YOU, FOR IT IS YOU WHO HAS GIVEN THEM HOPE.

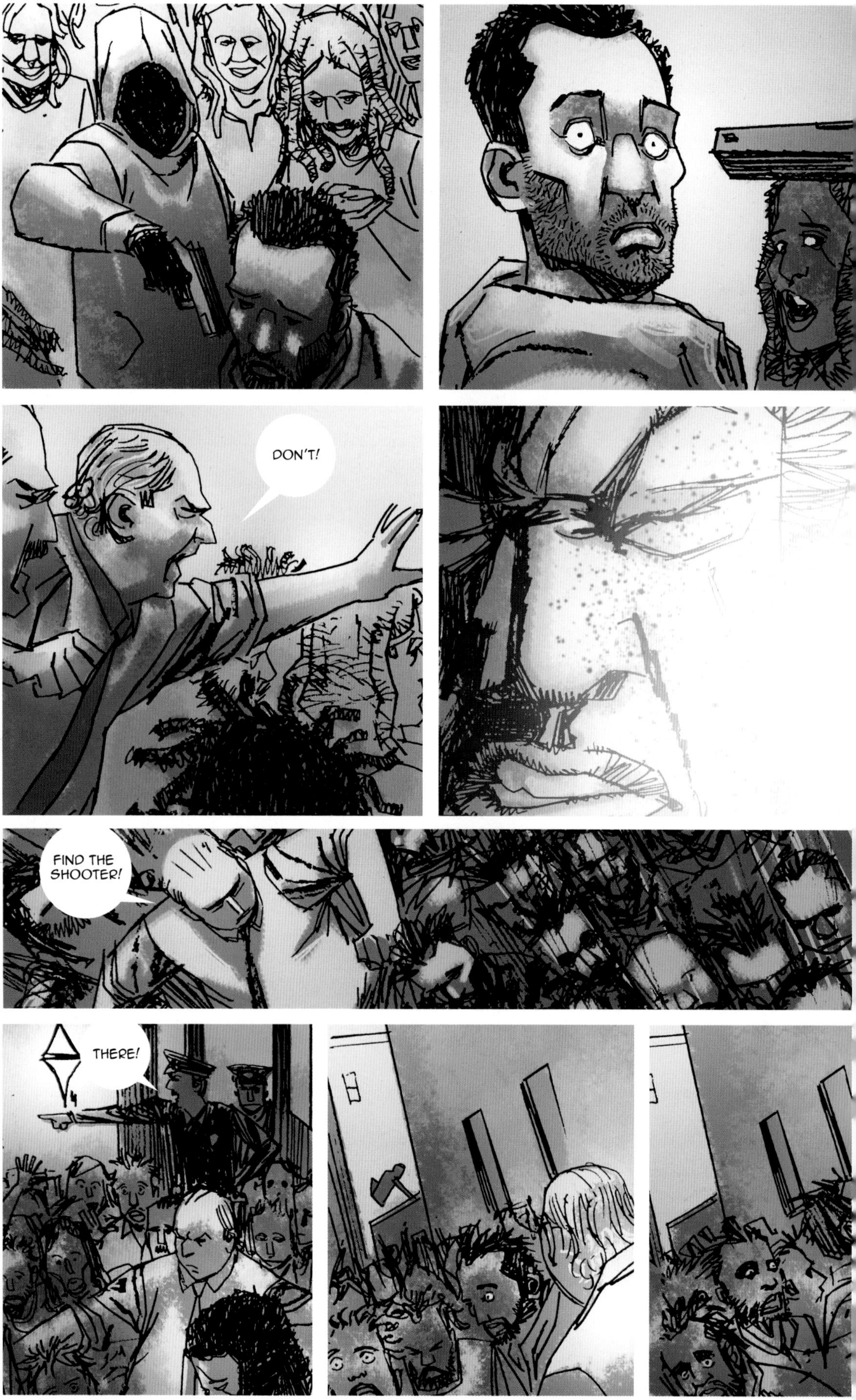
DON'T!
FIND THE SHOOTER!
THERE!

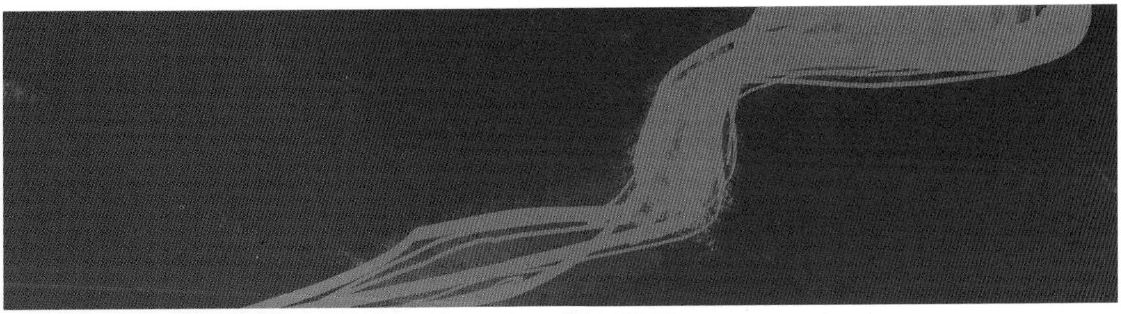

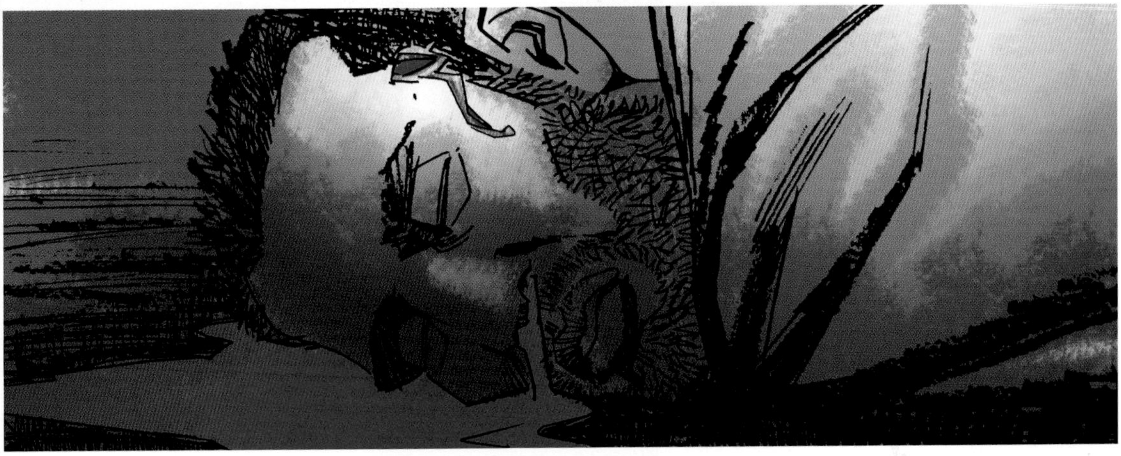

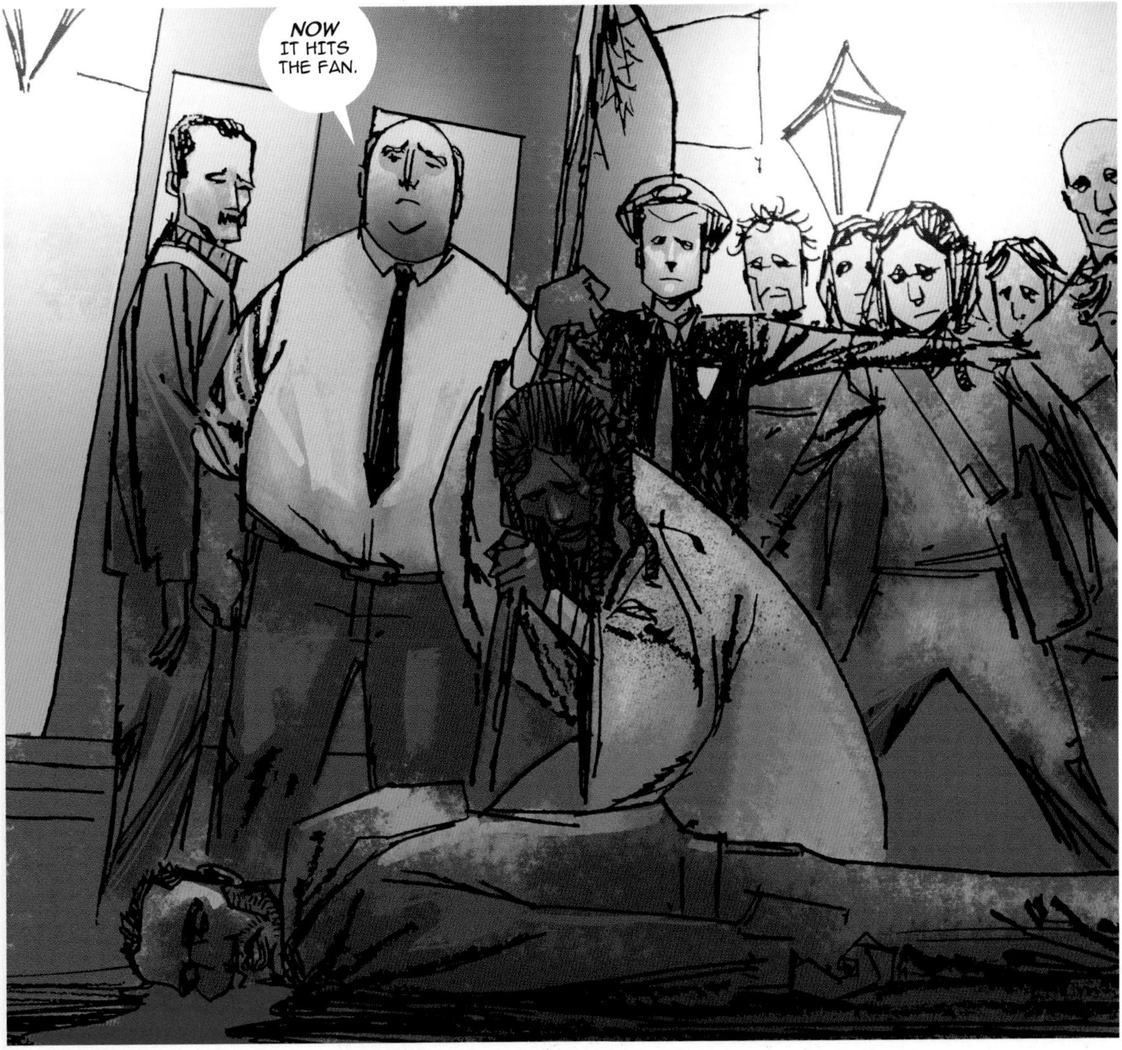
NOW IT HITS THE FAN.

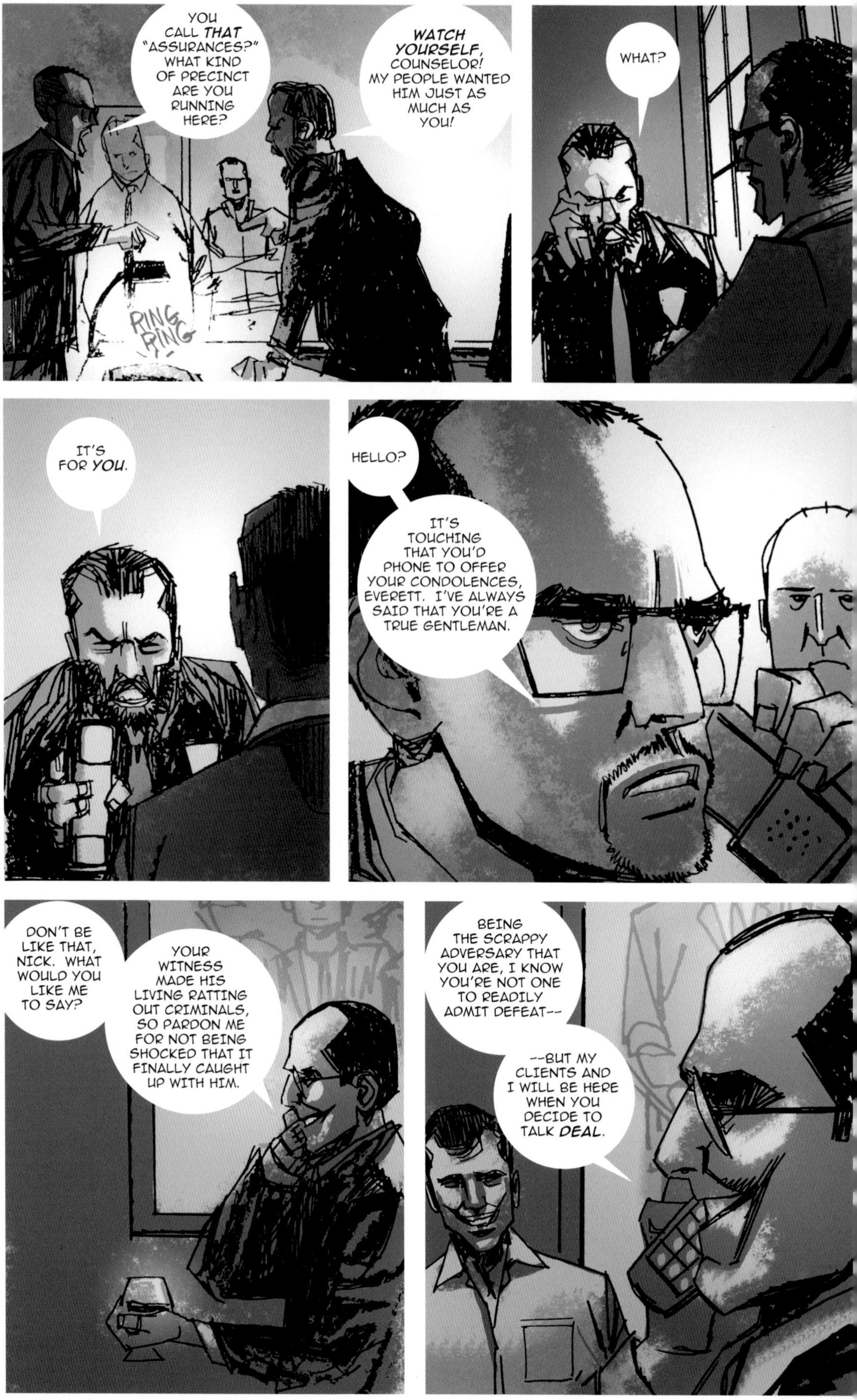
YOU CALL *THAT* "ASSURANCES?" WHAT KIND OF PRECINCT ARE YOU RUNNING HERE?
WATCH YOURSELF, COUNSELOR! MY PEOPLE WANTED HIM JUST AS MUCH AS YOU!
RING RING!
WHAT?
IT'S FOR *YOU*.
HELLO?
IT'S TOUCHING THAT YOU'D PHONE TO OFFER YOUR CONDOLENCES, EVERETT. I'VE ALWAYS SAID THAT YOU'RE A TRUE GENTLEMAN.
DON'T BE LIKE THAT, NICK. WHAT WOULD YOU LIKE ME TO SAY?
YOUR WITNESS MADE HIS LIVING RATTING OUT CRIMINALS, SO PARDON ME FOR NOT BEING SHOCKED THAT IT FINALLY CAUGHT UP WITH HIM.
BEING THE SCRAPPY ADVERSARY THAT YOU ARE, I KNOW YOU'RE NOT ONE TO READILY ADMIT DEFEAT--
--BUT MY CLIENTS AND I WILL BE HERE WHEN YOU DECIDE TO TALK *DEAL*.

CONSUMER QUESTIONNAIRE
YOUTH MODELS

VIRTUALSELF

Survey Site: _____

Date: _____

Instructions: Please answer in black ink only. Read each question carefully, as for some questions there is only one answer, but for others there may be more than one. The accuracy of this survey is dependent upon the truthfulness of the respondents, so be as honest as possible. All answers will remain confidential. If you wish to change your response to a question, mark through your initial answer with an X and then indicate your new answer. You must be 18 years or older and be parent or legal guardian to at least one minor child to participate in this survey.

Personal Information:

1) Age _____

2) Gender _____

3) Race _____

4) Marital status *(choose one)*
___ Married
___ Single *(never married)*
___ Divorced
___ Widowed

5) Income *(if married, please answer according to combined household income)*
___ less than $25,000
___ $25,000 – $50,000
___ $50,000 – $100,000
___ $100,000 – $200,000
___ more than $200,000

6) Education *(indicate highest level graduated)*
___ Primary School
___ High School
___ College *(2–year)*
___ College *(4–year)*
___ Graduate School
___ Vocational/Technical

Experience:

7) Do you own a surrogate unit? *(yes/no)*

If yes, on average how many hours do you operate it each day? _____

8) Have you ever been, or do you know anyone who has been, the victim of a violent crime? *(yes/no)*

9) Have you ever been, or do you know anyone who has been, the victim of discrimination as a result of age, gender, or race? *(yes/no)*

10) Do you suffer from, or do you know anyone who suffers from, a physical disability or injury that affects quality of life? *(yes/no)*

Habits:

11) Do you use tobacco products? *(frequently/occasionally/never)*

12) Do you drink alcohol? *(frequently/occasionally/never)*

13) Do you use drugs? *(frequently/occasionally/never)*

14) How many sexual partners have you had in your lifetime? _____

15) On a scale from 1 to 5, with 1 being the lowest likelihood and 5 being the highest, how likely are you to operate a surrogate unit for the following reasons?

____ Recreation   ____ Safety
____ Injury/Physical disability   ____ Self-improvement
____ Health   ____ Job/Professional
____ Convenience   ____ Social
____ Privacy   ____ Other *(please specify)* _____
                                   _____

16) On a scale from 1 to 10, with 1 being the least important and 10 being the most, rank the following reasons for operating a surrogate unit in their order of importance to you:

____ Recreation   ____ Safety
____ Injury/Physical disability   ____ Self-improvement
____ Health   ____ Job/Professional
____ Convenience   ____ Social
____ Privacy   ____ Other *(please specify)* _____
                                   _____

17) On a scale from 1 to 5, with 1 indicating that you strongly disagree and 5 indicating that you strongly agree, rate the following statements:

____ I am pleased with my body image.
____ I feel secure when outside my home.
____ I find my job fulfilling.
____ My lifestyle is limited by my physical condition.
____ I am comfortable in social settings.
____ I have a spontaneous personality.
____ I enjoy outdoor activities.
____ Others find me attractive.
____ I never indulge in things that I know are bad for my health.

Children:

18) Indicate the age and gender of each of your children in order from oldest to youngest. *(ex: girl 13, boy 9, girl 6)*

_____

19) Do you plan to have more children -- either through conception, adoption, or remarriage to someone who is already a parent or legal guardian? *(yes/no)*

20) To the best of your knowledge, does one or more of your children:
Use alcohol or drugs *(yes/no)*
Engage in underage sex *(yes/no)*
Suffer from poor self-image *(yes/no)*
Been diagnosed with a condition triggered by their surroundings
    or activities, such as allergies, asthma, chronic fatigue *(yes/no)*
Experience bullying *(yes/no)*
Succumb easily to peer pressure *(yes/no)*
Been the victim of physical or sexual abuse *(yes/no)*
Have difficulty making friends *(yes/no)*
Exhibit symptoms of eating disorder *(yes/no)*
Require prescription eyeglasses and/or hearing aid *(yes/no)*
Suffer from physical handicap and/or debilitating illness, such as
    cystic fibrosis, multiple sclerosis, shrunken limb *(yes/no)*
Experience bouts of anxiety triggered by fear or phobia *(yes/no)*

21) For each of the following risk factors, indicate whether you believe that children today are more at risk, less at risk, or at the same level of risk than they were **10 years ago**:
Contractible illness, such as influenza, rotavirus, or staph infection *(more/less/same)*
Physical and/or sexual abuse *(more/less/same)*
Injury requiring physician's care, such as broken bone,
    concussion, or deep laceration *(more/less/same)*
Pregnancy *(more/less/same)*
School violence *(more/less/same)*
Depression *(more/less/same)*
Abduction *(more/less/same)*
Sexually transmitted disease *(more/less/same)*
Drug and/or alcohol addiction *(more/less/same)*
Injury due to car accident, as either driver or passenger *(more/less/same)*

22) For the same risk factors, indicate whether you believe that children today are more at risk, less at risk, or at the same level of risk than they will be **10 years from now**:
Contractible illness, such as influenza, rotavirus, or staph infection *(more/less/same)*
Physical and/or sexual abuse *(more/less/same)*
Injury requiring physician's care, such as broken bone,
    concussion, or deep laceration *(more/less/same)*
Pregnancy *(more/less/same)*
School violence *(more/less/same)*
Depression *(more/less/same)*
Abduction *(more/less/same)*
Sexually transmitted disease *(more/less/same)*
Drug and/or alcohol addiction *(more/less/same)*
Injury due to car accident, as either driver or passenger *(more/less/same)*

23) Now indicate whether you believe that providing a child with a surrogate unit
   would lessen their exposure to the same risk factors:
   Contractible illness, such as influenza, rotavirus, or staph infection *(yes/no)*
   Physical and/or sexual abuse *(yes/no)*
   Injury requiring physician's care, such as broken bone,
      concussion, or deep laceration *(yes/no)*
   Pregnancy *(yes/no)*
   School violence *(yes/no)*
   Depression *(yes/no)*
   Abduction *(yes/no)*
   Sexually transmitted disease *(yes/no)*
   Drug and/or alcohol addiction *(yes/no)*
   Injury due to car accident, as either driver or passenger *(yes/no)*

24) On a scale from 1 to 5, with 1 being no effect and 5 being the highest level of
   effect, rate the extent to which you believe providing a youth model surrogate unit
   for one or more of your children would have a **positive** effect on the following:
   ____ Self-esteem   ____ Acceptance among peers
   ____ Independence   ____ Physical well-being
   ____ Assertiveness   ____ Interactive play
   ____ Personal safety   ____ Confidence
   ____ Psychological development   ____ Social skills

25) On a scale from 1 to 5, with 1 being no effect and 5 being the highest level of
   effect, rate the extent to which you believe providing a youth model surrogate unit
   for one or more of your children would have a **negative** effect on the following:
   ____ Self-esteem   ____ Acceptance among peers
   ____ Independence   ____ Physical well-being
   ____ Assertiveness   ____ Interactive play
   ____ Personal safety   ____ Confidence
   ____ Psychological development   ____ Social skills

26) If youth model surrogates were made available to minors, would you purchase
   a unit for one or more of your children? *(yes/no)*

   If you answered no, please briefly state your reason(s):
   _____
   _____

Contact:

27) Can we contact you with information about our products and services? Your
   contact information will be randomly sorted and not associated with the answers
   you have provided during this survey. *(yes/no)*

   If yes, please provide one or more of the following:
   Email: _____
   Phone: _____
   Mailing address: _____
   _____

The survey has ended. Please return all materials to the surveyor.
Virtual Self thanks you for your time and participation.

chapter
FOUR

Inferno

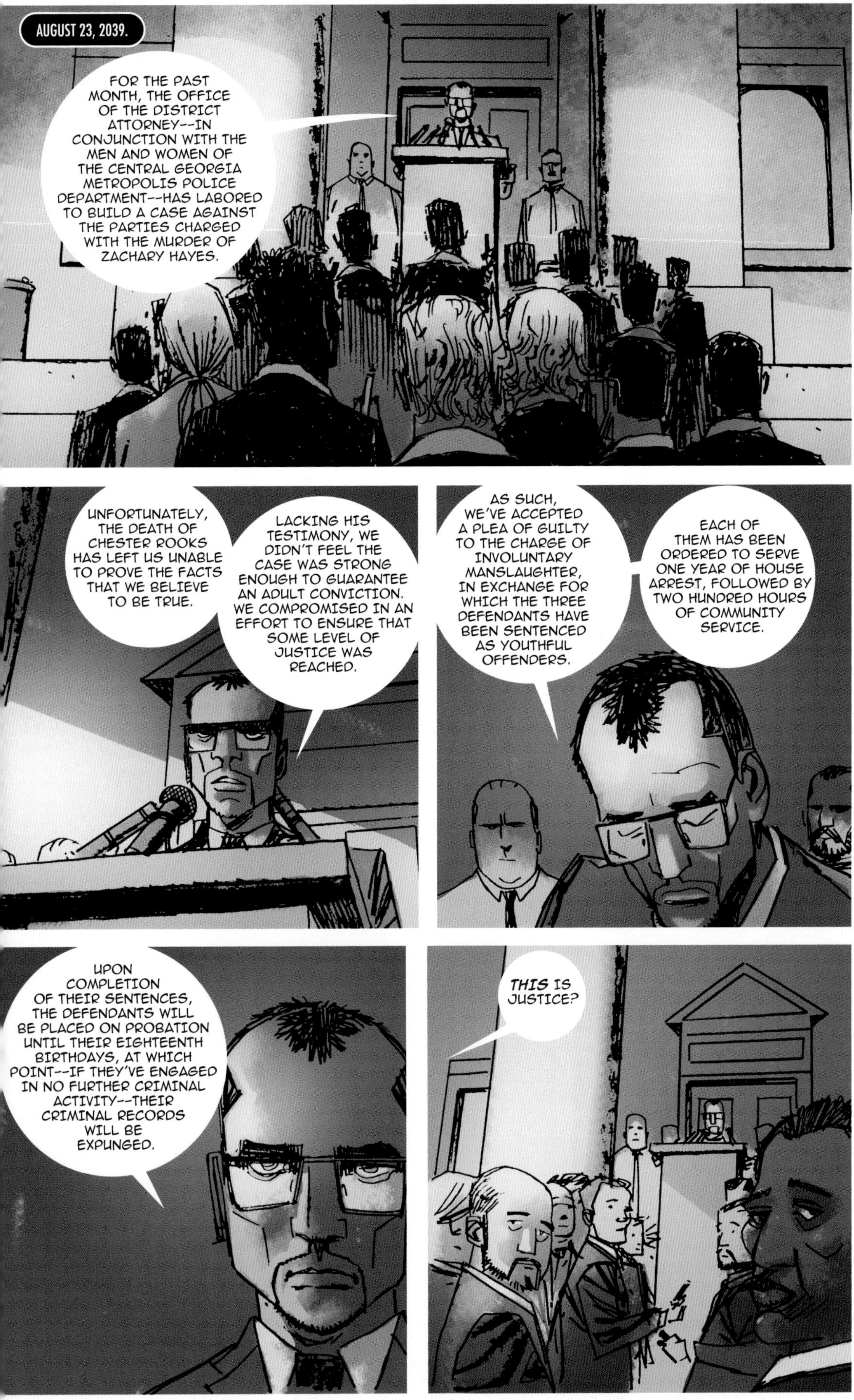
AUGUST 23, 2039.
FOR THE PAST MONTH, THE OFFICE OF THE DISTRICT ATTORNEY--IN CONJUNCTION WITH THE MEN AND WOMEN OF THE CENTRAL GEORGIA METROPOLIS POLICE DEPARTMENT--HAS LABORED TO BUILD A CASE AGAINST THE PARTIES CHARGED WITH THE MURDER OF ZACHARY HAYES.
UNFORTUNATELY, THE DEATH OF CHESTER ROOKS HAS LEFT US UNABLE TO PROVE THE FACTS THAT WE BELIEVE TO BE TRUE.
LACKING HIS TESTIMONY, WE DIDN'T FEEL THE CASE WAS STRONG ENOUGH TO GUARANTEE AN ADULT CONVICTION. WE COMPROMISED IN AN EFFORT TO ENSURE THAT SOME LEVEL OF JUSTICE WAS REACHED.
AS SUCH, WE'VE ACCEPTED A PLEA OF GUILTY TO THE CHARGE OF INVOLUNTARY MANSLAUGHTER, IN EXCHANGE FOR WHICH THE THREE DEFENDANTS HAVE BEEN SENTENCED AS YOUTHFUL OFFENDERS.
EACH OF THEM HAS BEEN ORDERED TO SERVE ONE YEAR OF HOUSE ARREST, FOLLOWED BY TWO HUNDRED HOURS OF COMMUNITY SERVICE.
UPON COMPLETION OF THEIR SENTENCES, THE DEFENDANTS WILL BE PLACED ON PROBATION UNTIL THEIR EIGHTEENTH BIRTHDAYS, AT WHICH POINT--IF THEY'VE ENGAGED IN NO FURTHER CRIMINAL ACTIVITY--THEIR CRIMINAL RECORDS WILL BE EXPUNGED.
THIS IS JUSTICE?

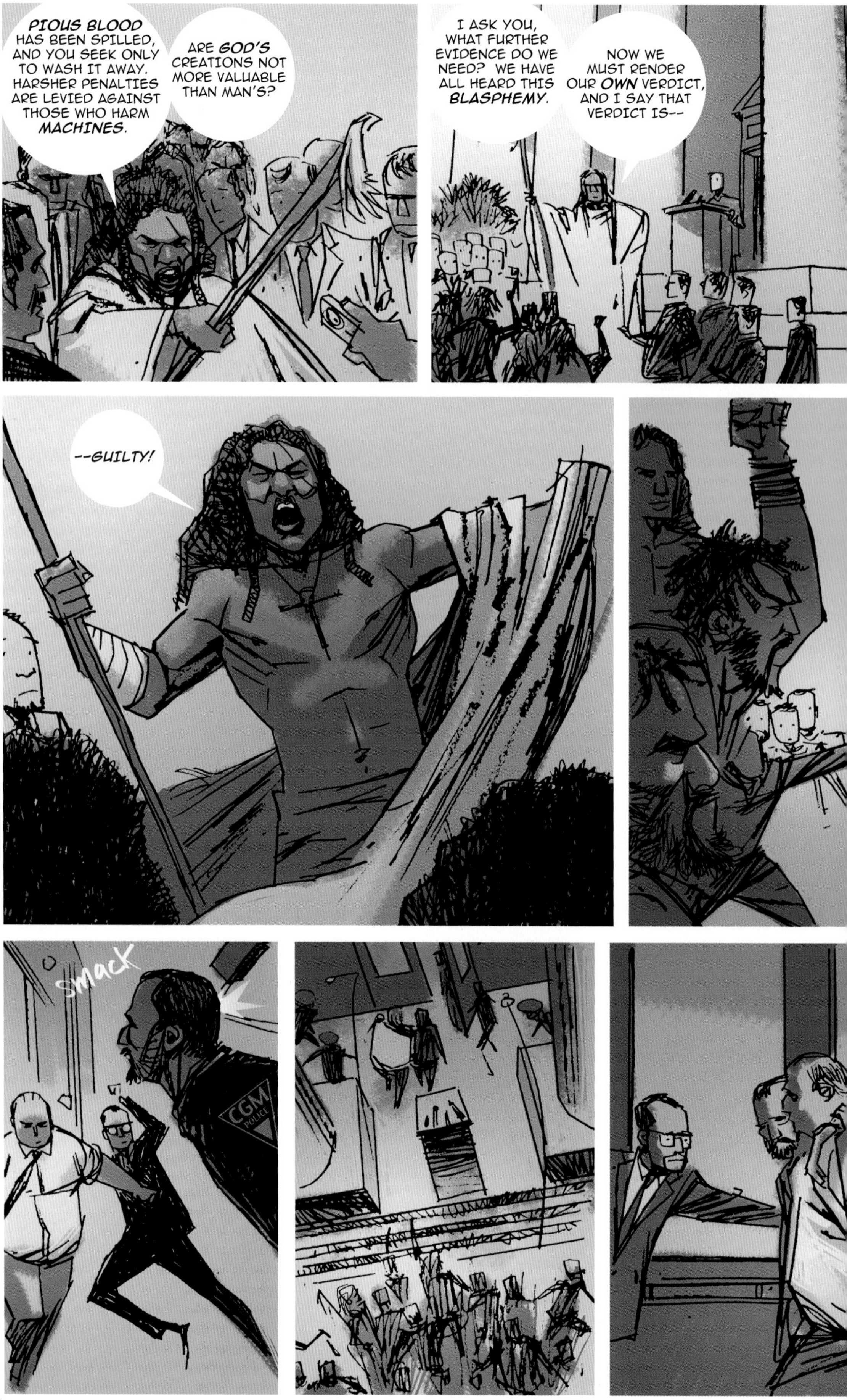
PIOUS BLOOD HAS BEEN SPILLED, AND YOU SEEK ONLY TO WASH IT AWAY. HARSHER PENALTIES ARE LEVIED AGAINST THOSE WHO HARM MACHINES.
ARE GOD'S CREATIONS NOT MORE VALUABLE THAN MAN'S?
I ASK YOU, WHAT FURTHER EVIDENCE DO WE NEED? WE HAVE ALL HEARD THIS BLASPHEMY.
NOW WE MUST RENDER OUR OWN VERDICT, AND I SAY THAT VERDICT IS--
--GUILTY!
smack
CGM POLICE

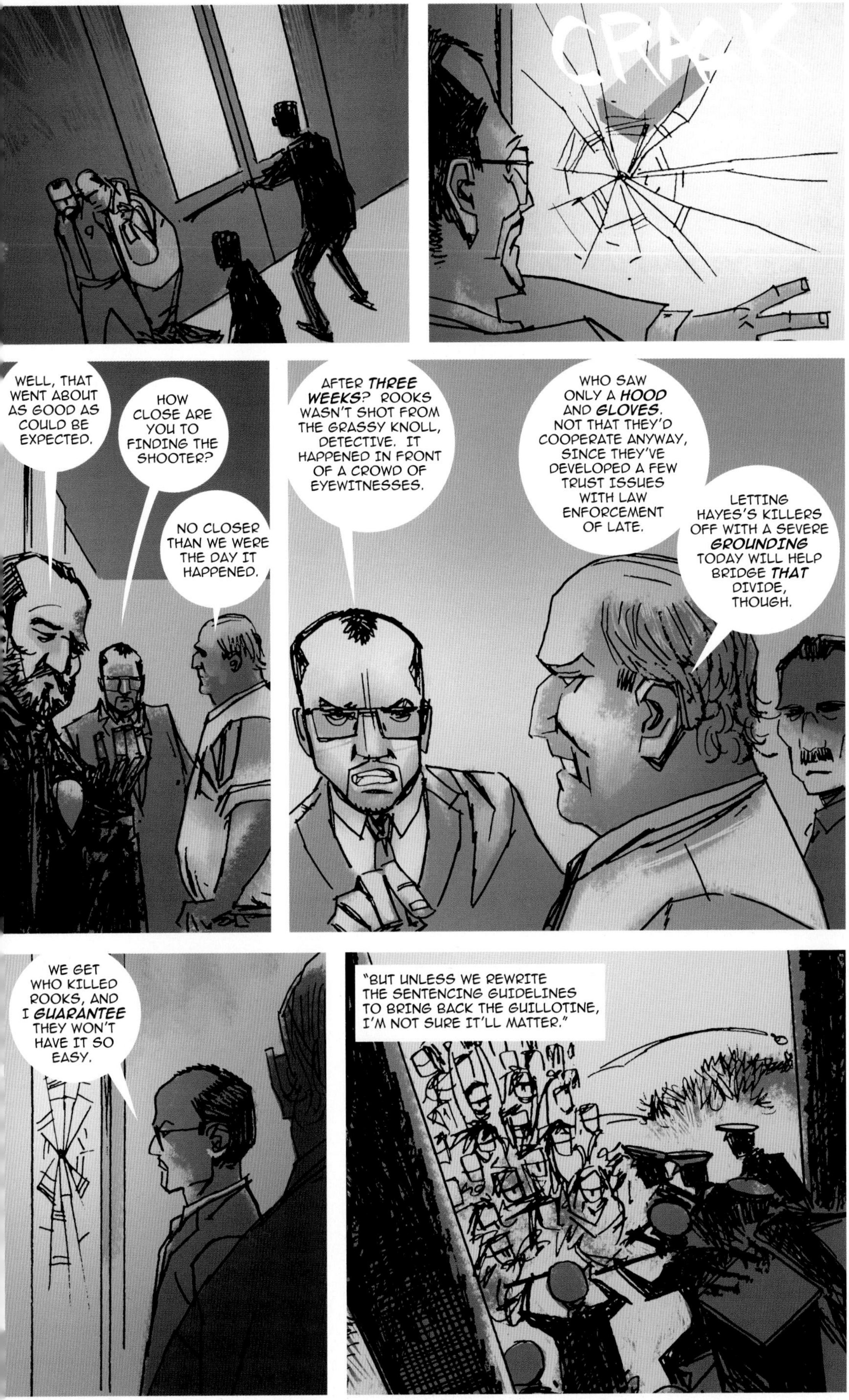

CRACK
WELL, THAT WENT ABOUT AS GOOD AS COULD BE EXPECTED.
HOW CLOSE ARE YOU TO FINDING THE SHOOTER?
NO CLOSER THAN WE WERE THE DAY IT HAPPENED.
AFTER THREE WEEKS? ROOKS WASN'T SHOT FROM THE GRASSY KNOLL, DETECTIVE. IT HAPPENED IN FRONT OF A CROWD OF EYEWITNESSES.
WHO SAW ONLY A HOOD AND GLOVES. NOT THAT THEY'D COOPERATE ANYWAY, SINCE THEY'VE DEVELOPED A FEW TRUST ISSUES WITH LAW ENFORCEMENT OF LATE.
LETTING HAYES'S KILLERS OFF WITH A SEVERE GROUNDING TODAY WILL HELP BRIDGE THAT DIVIDE, THOUGH.
WE GET WHO KILLED ROOKS, AND I GUARANTEE THEY WON'T HAVE IT SO EASY.
"BUT UNLESS WE REWRITE THE SENTENCING GUIDELINES TO BRING BACK THE GUILLOTINE, I'M NOT SURE IT'LL MATTER."

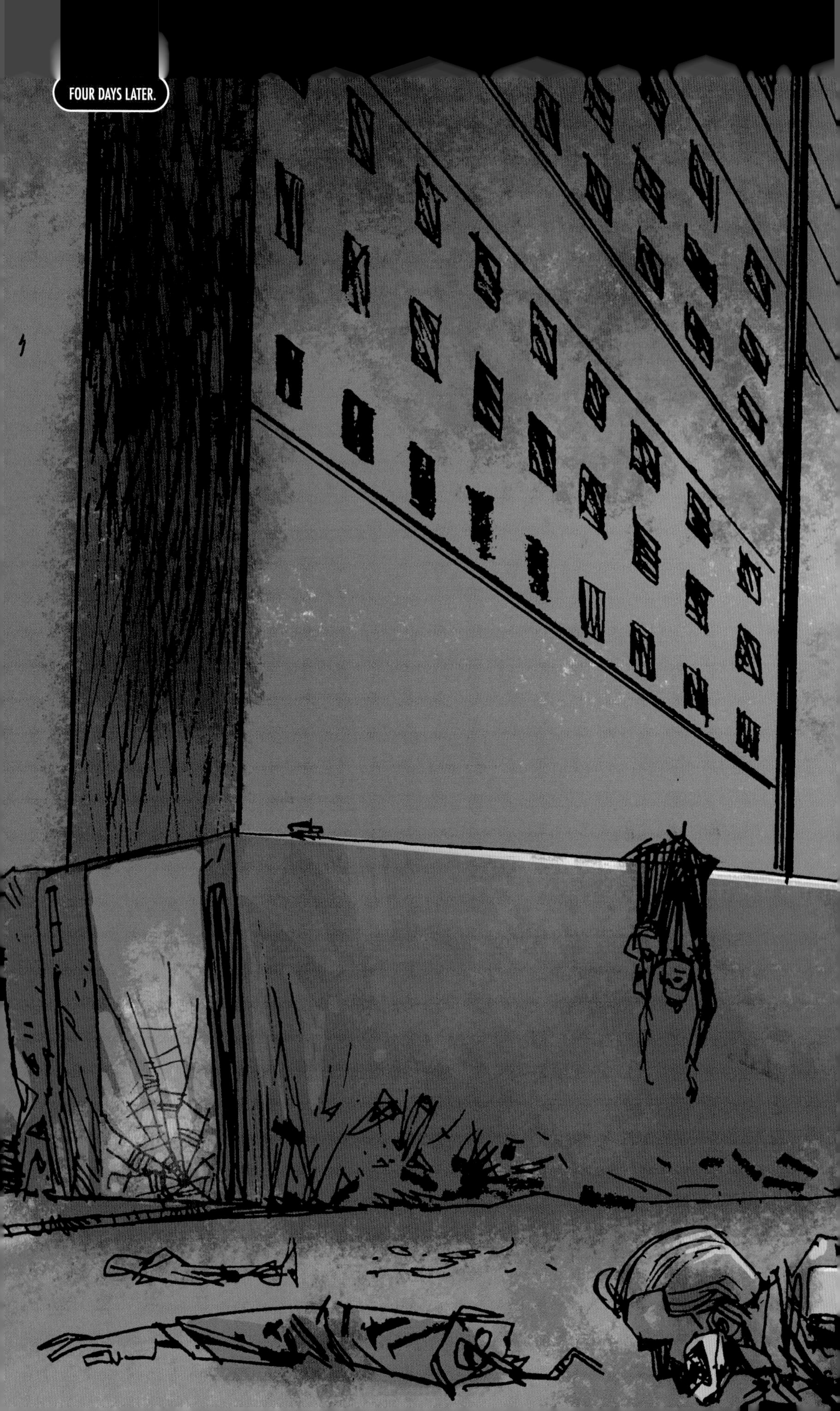
FOUR DAYS LATER.

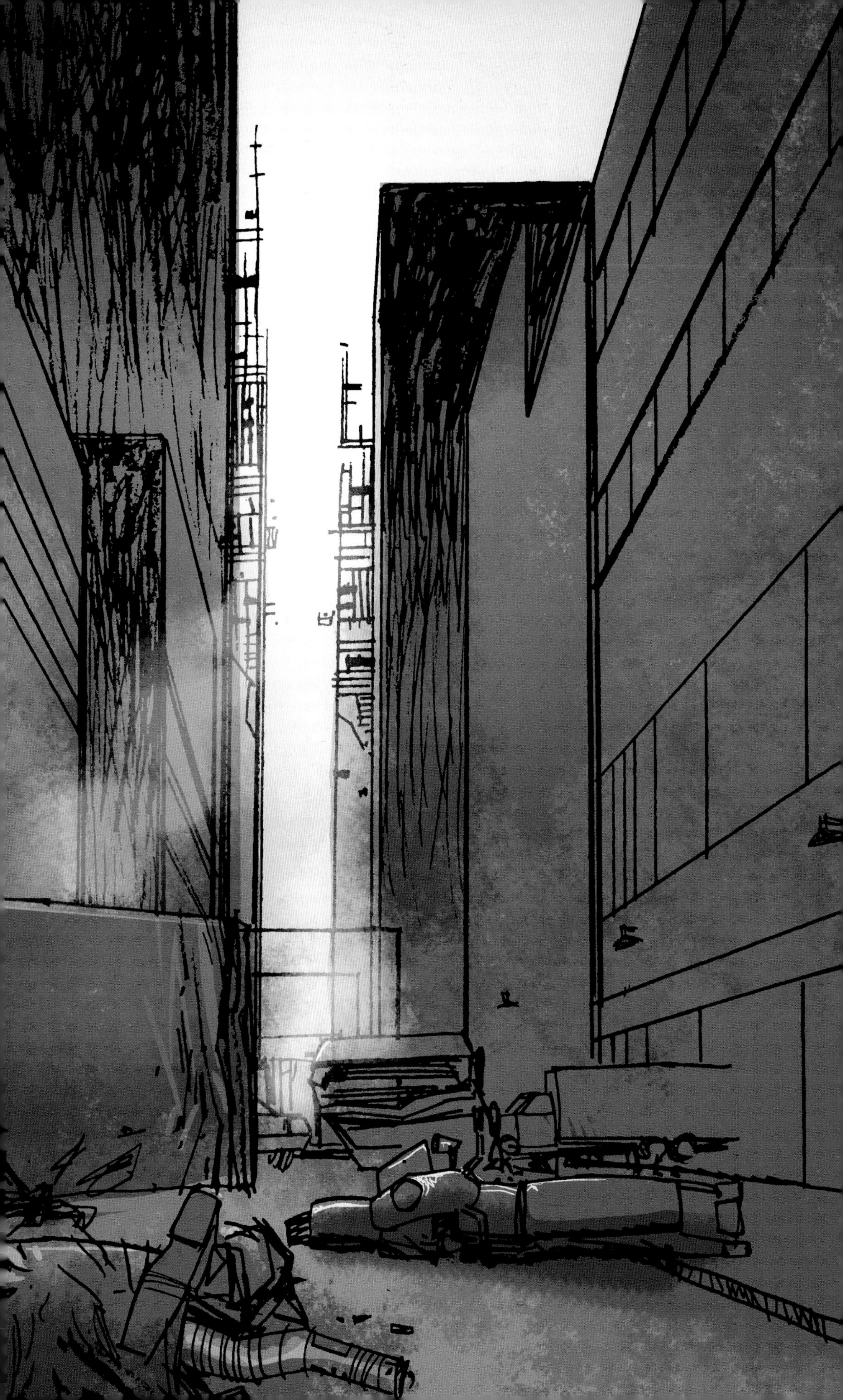

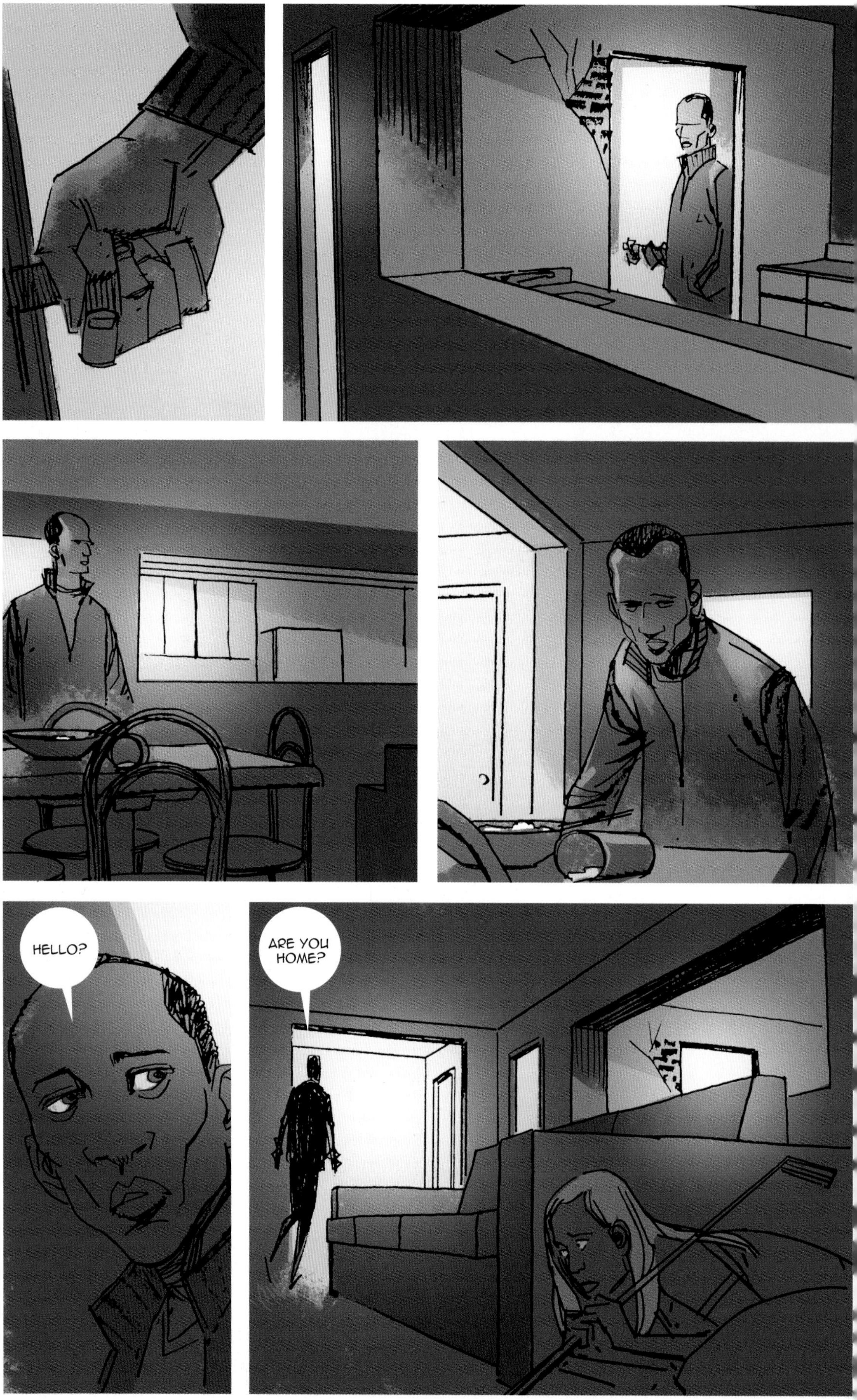
HELLO?
ARE YOU HOME?

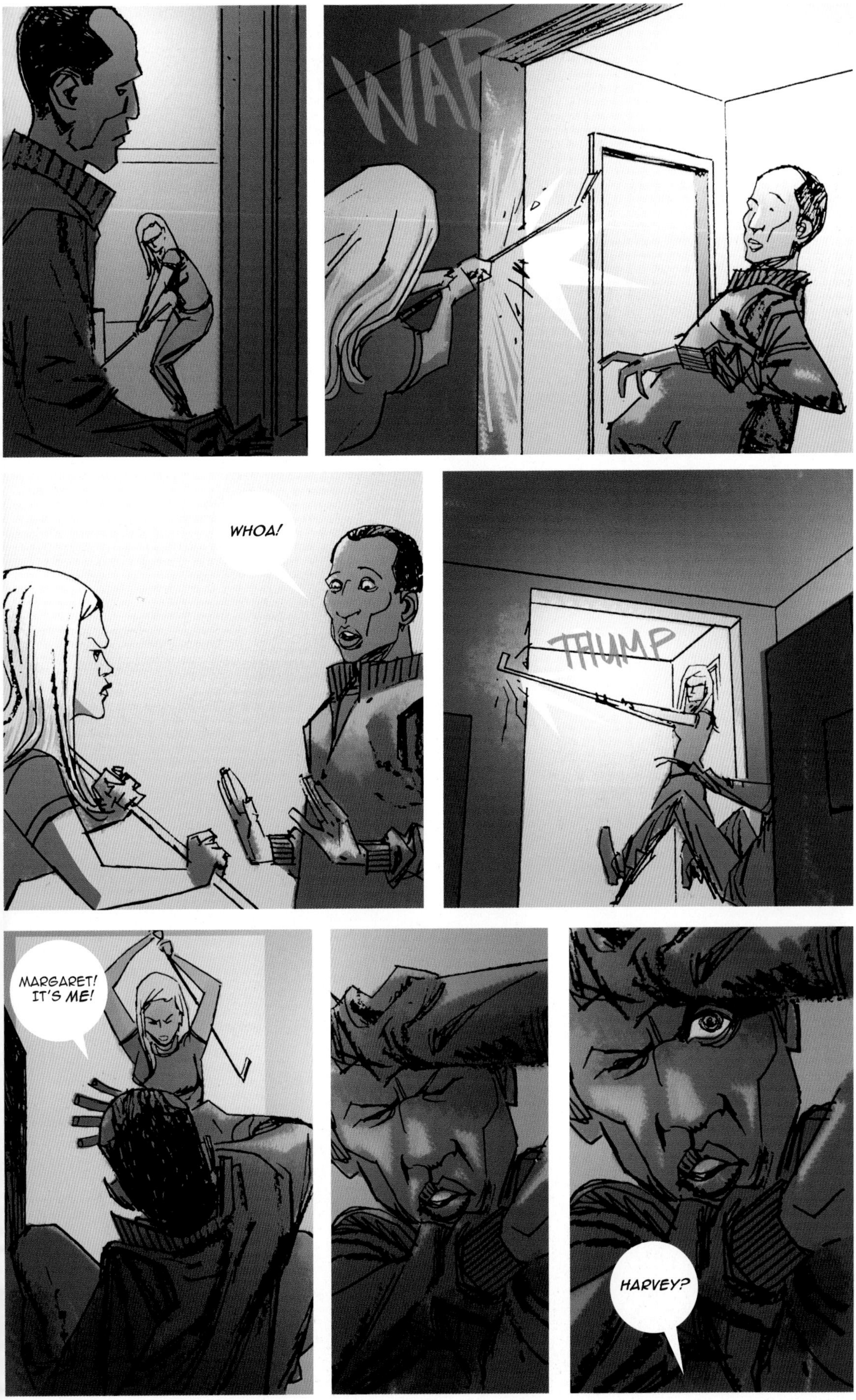
WAP
WHOA!
THUMP
MARGARET! IT'S ME!
HARVEY?

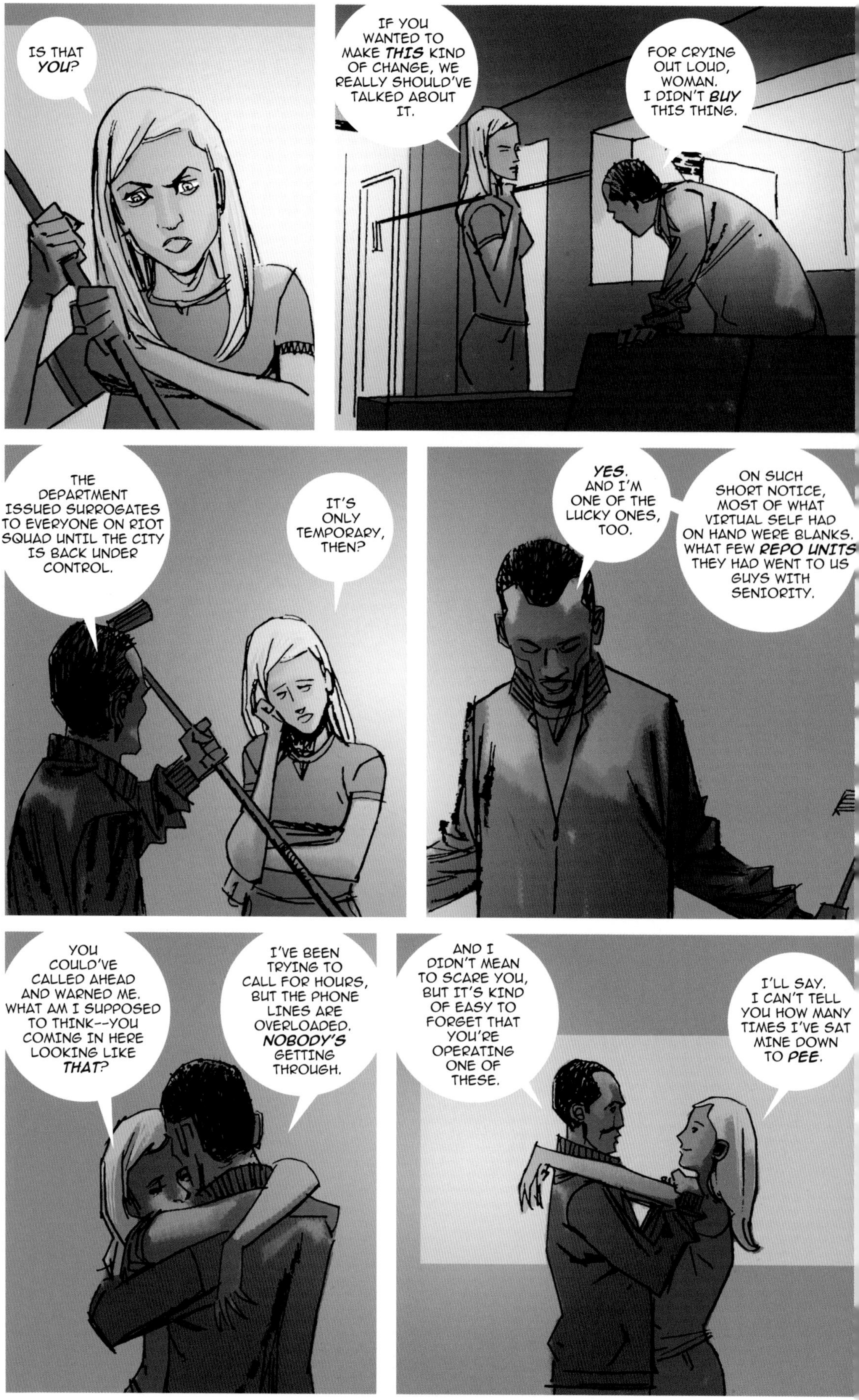
IS THAT *YOU*?
IF YOU WANTED TO MAKE *THIS* KIND OF CHANGE, WE REALLY SHOULD'VE TALKED ABOUT IT.
FOR CRYING OUT LOUD, WOMAN. I DIDN'T *BUY* THIS THING.
THE DEPARTMENT ISSUED SURROGATES TO EVERYONE ON RIOT SQUAD UNTIL THE CITY IS BACK UNDER CONTROL.
IT'S ONLY TEMPORARY, THEN?
YES. AND I'M ONE OF THE LUCKY ONES, TOO.
ON SUCH SHORT NOTICE, MOST OF WHAT VIRTUAL SELF HAD ON HAND WERE BLANKS. WHAT FEW *REPO UNITS* THEY HAD WENT TO US GUYS WITH SENIORITY.
YOU COULD'VE CALLED AHEAD AND WARNED ME. WHAT AM I SUPPOSED TO THINK--YOU COMING IN HERE LOOKING LIKE *THAT*?
I'VE BEEN TRYING TO CALL FOR HOURS, BUT THE PHONE LINES ARE OVERLOADED. *NOBODY'S* GETTING THROUGH.
AND I DIDN'T MEAN TO SCARE YOU, BUT IT'S KIND OF EASY TO FORGET THAT YOU'RE OPERATING ONE OF THESE.
I'LL SAY. I CAN'T TELL YOU HOW MANY TIMES I'VE SAT MINE DOWN TO *PEE*.

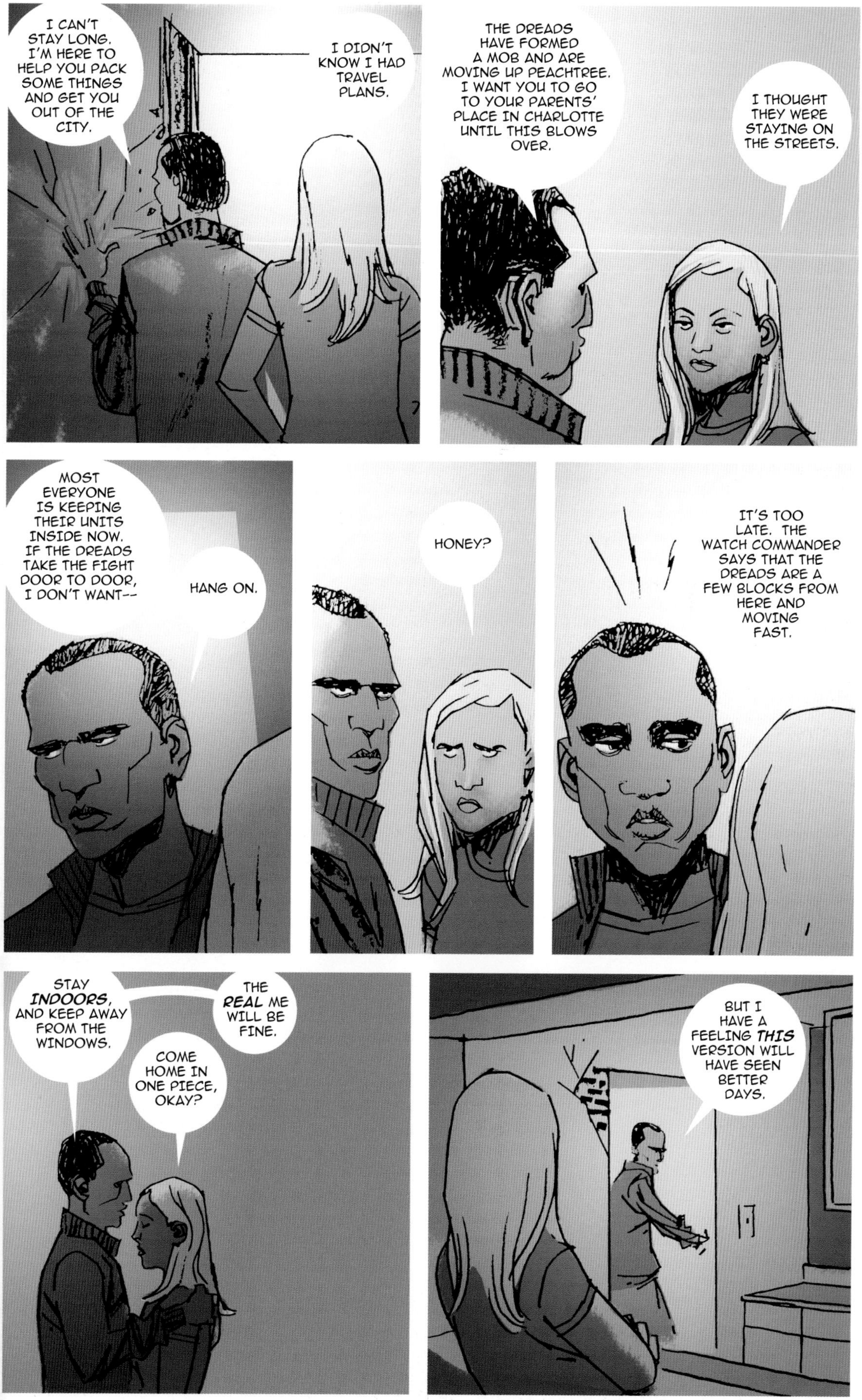

I CAN'T STAY LONG. I'M HERE TO HELP YOU PACK SOME THINGS AND GET YOU OUT OF THE CITY.
I DIDN'T KNOW I HAD TRAVEL PLANS.
THE DREADS HAVE FORMED A MOB AND ARE MOVING UP PEACHTREE. I WANT YOU TO GO TO YOUR PARENTS' PLACE IN CHARLOTTE UNTIL THIS BLOWS OVER.
I THOUGHT THEY WERE STAYING ON THE STREETS.
MOST EVERYONE IS KEEPING THEIR UNITS INSIDE NOW. IF THE DREADS TAKE THE FIGHT DOOR TO DOOR, I DON'T WANT--
HANG ON.
HONEY?
IT'S TOO LATE. THE WATCH COMMANDER SAYS THAT THE DREADS ARE A FEW BLOCKS FROM HERE AND MOVING FAST.
STAY *INDOORS*, AND KEEP AWAY FROM THE WINDOWS.
THE *REAL* ME WILL BE FINE.
COME HOME IN ONE PIECE, OKAY?
BUT I HAVE A FEELING *THIS* VERSION WILL HAVE SEEN BETTER DAYS.

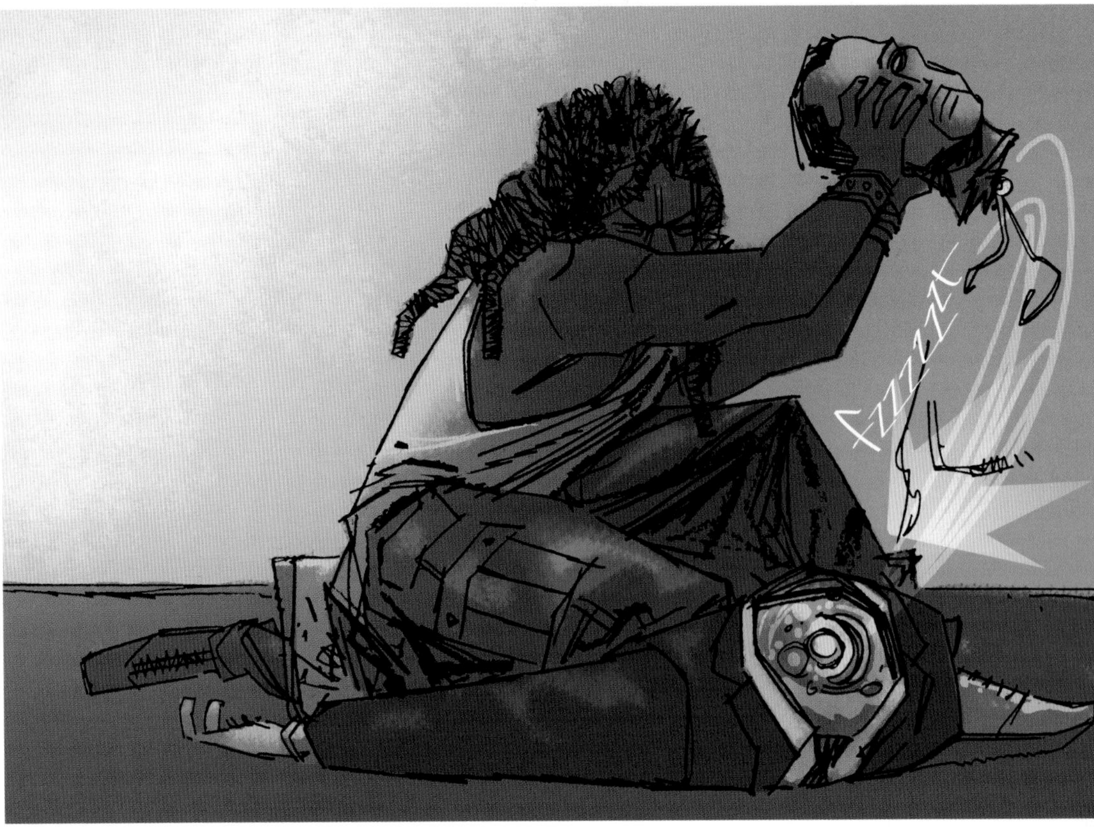
Fzzzzzzt

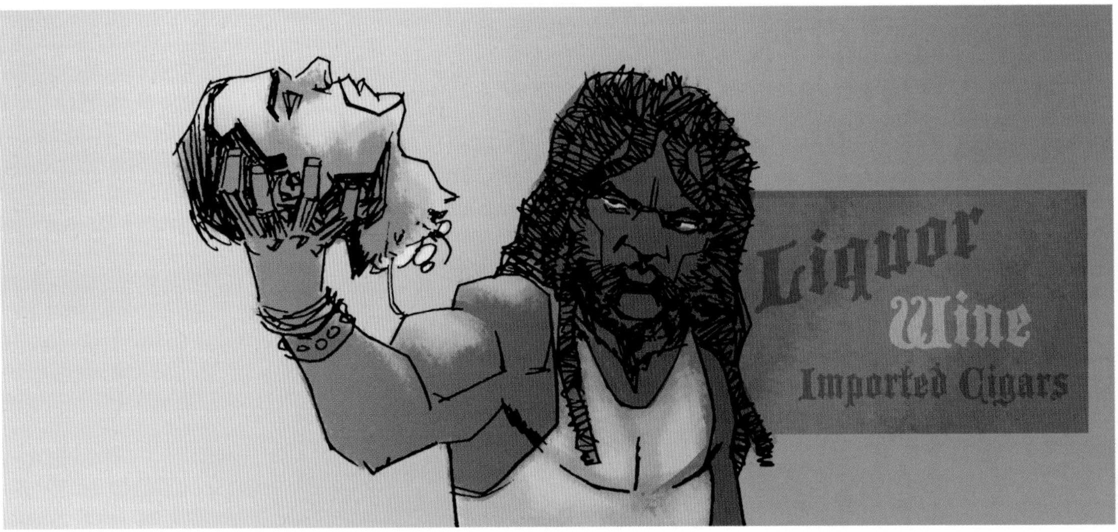
Liquor
Wine
Imported Cigars

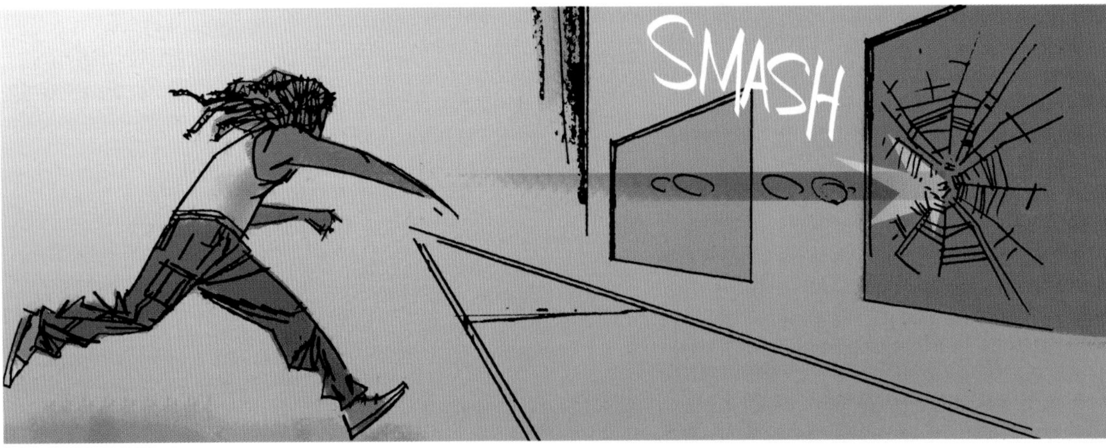
SMASH

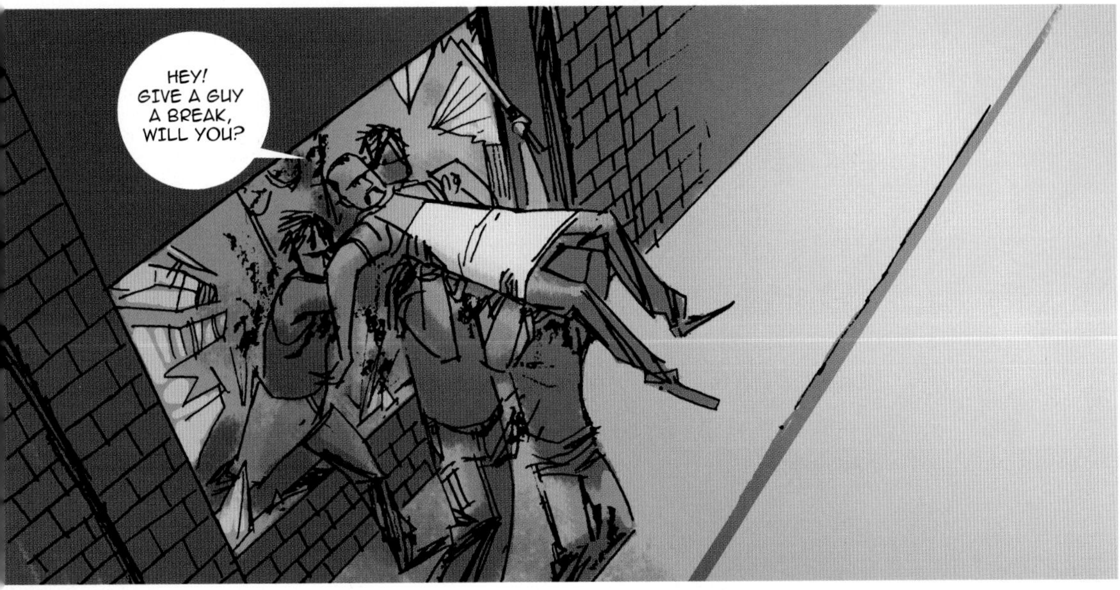
HEY!
GIVE A GUY A BREAK, WILL YOU?

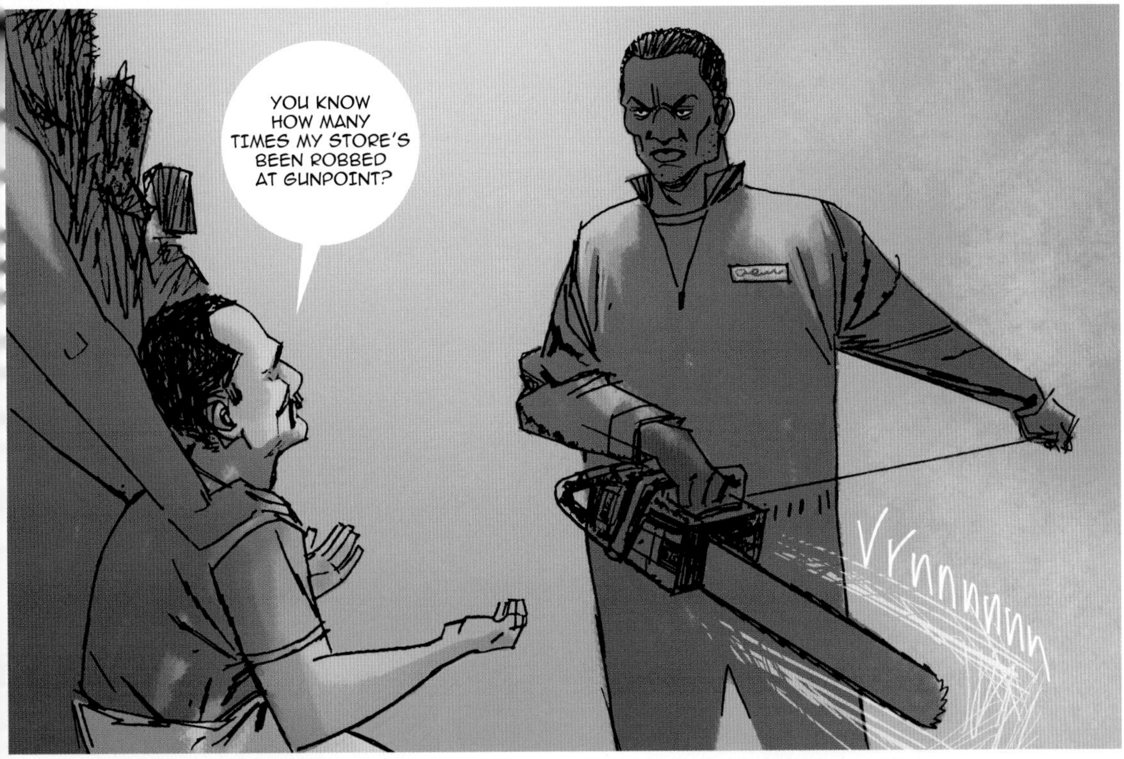
YOU KNOW HOW MANY TIMES MY STORE'S BEEN ROBBED AT GUNPOINT?
Vrnnnnnn

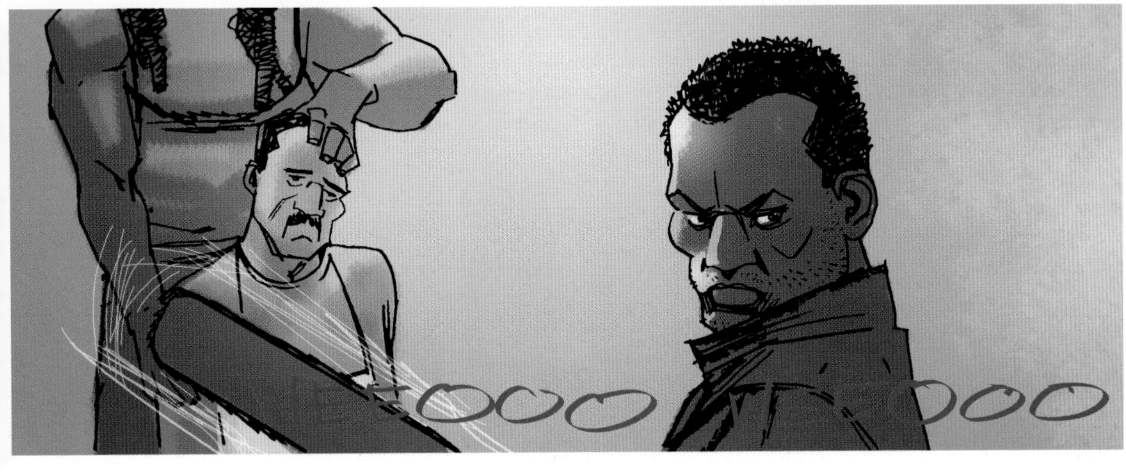

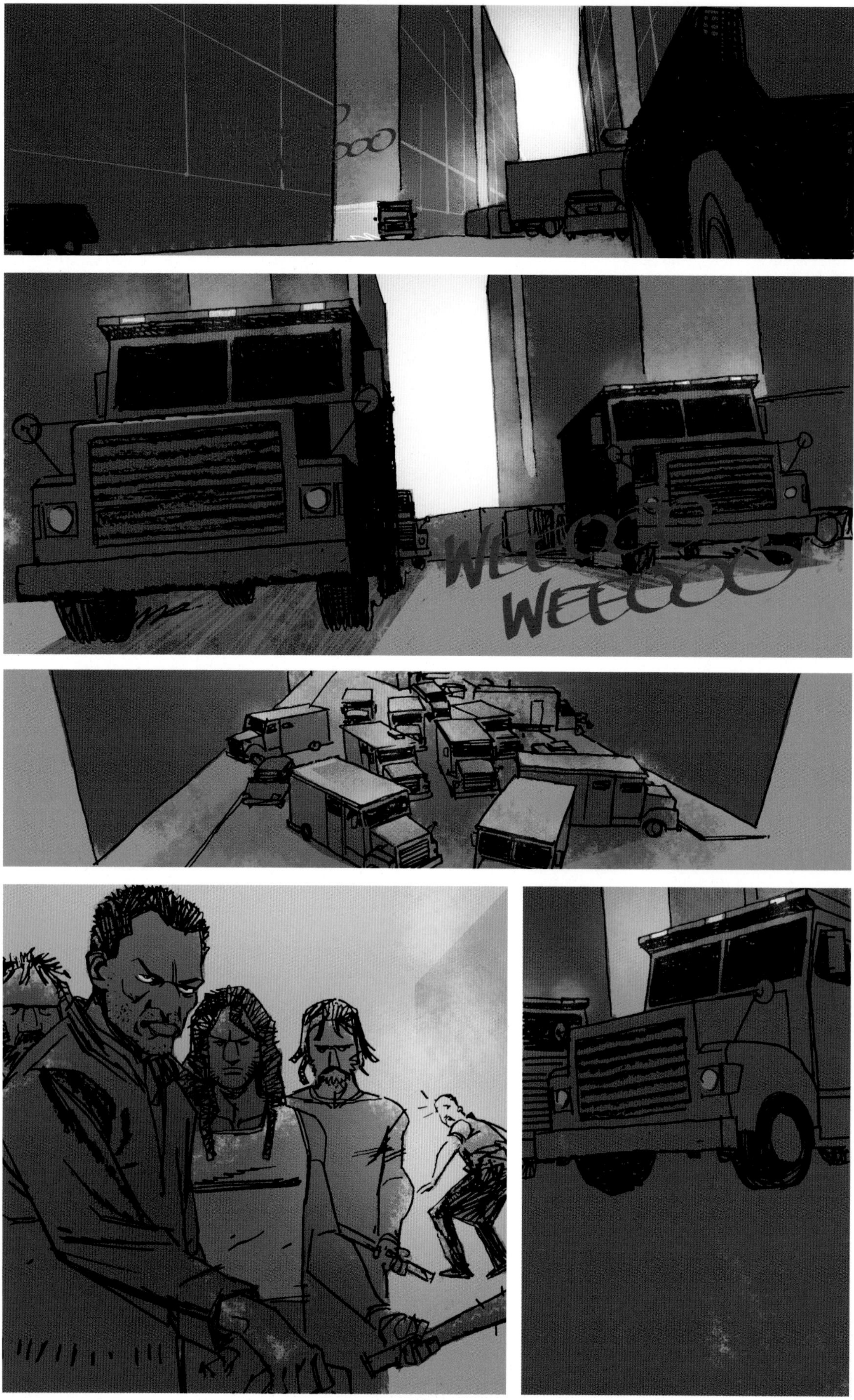

WEEOOO

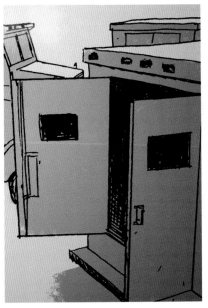

EVERYONE FALL IN!

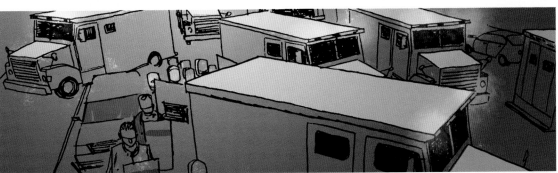

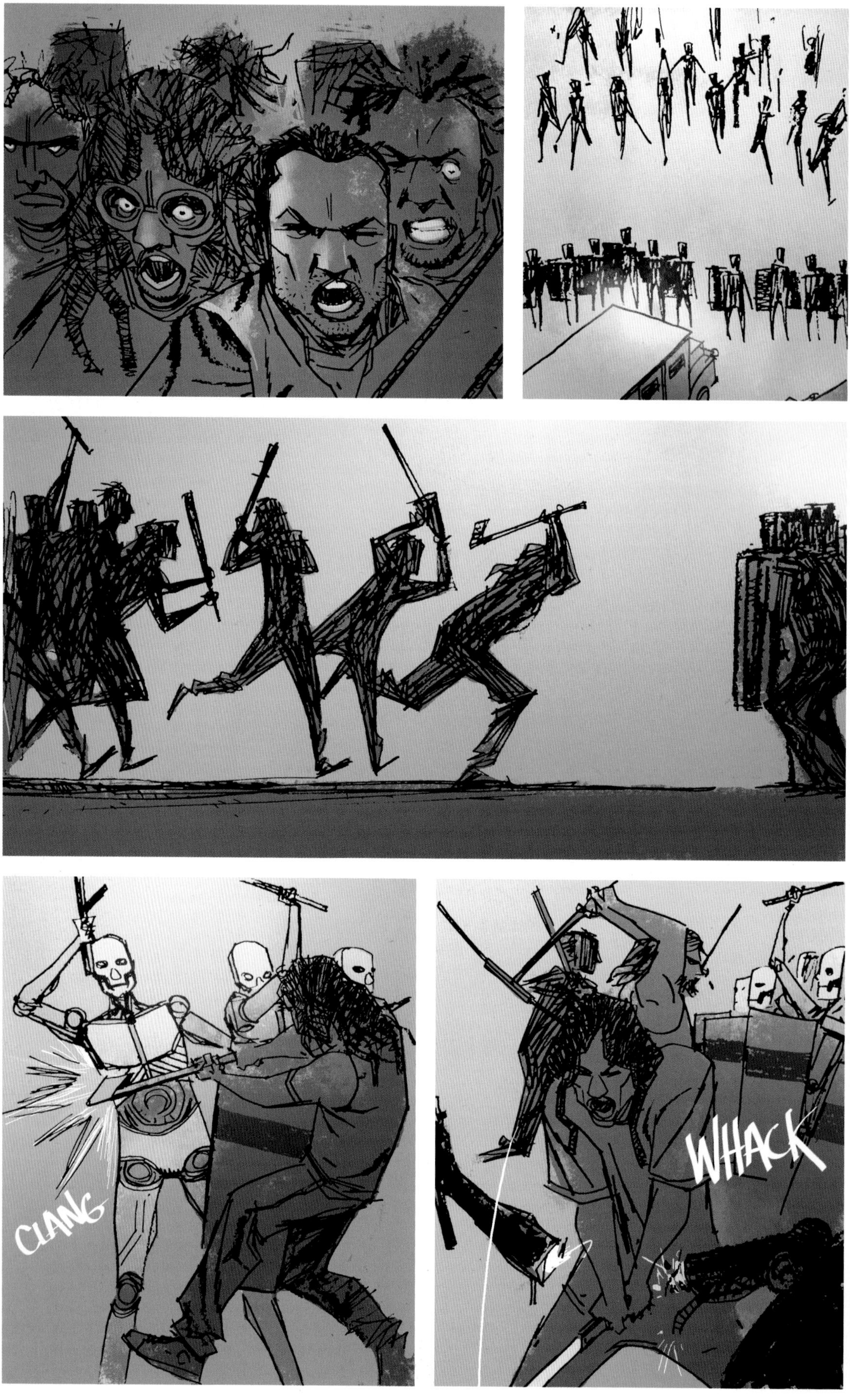
CLANG
WHACK

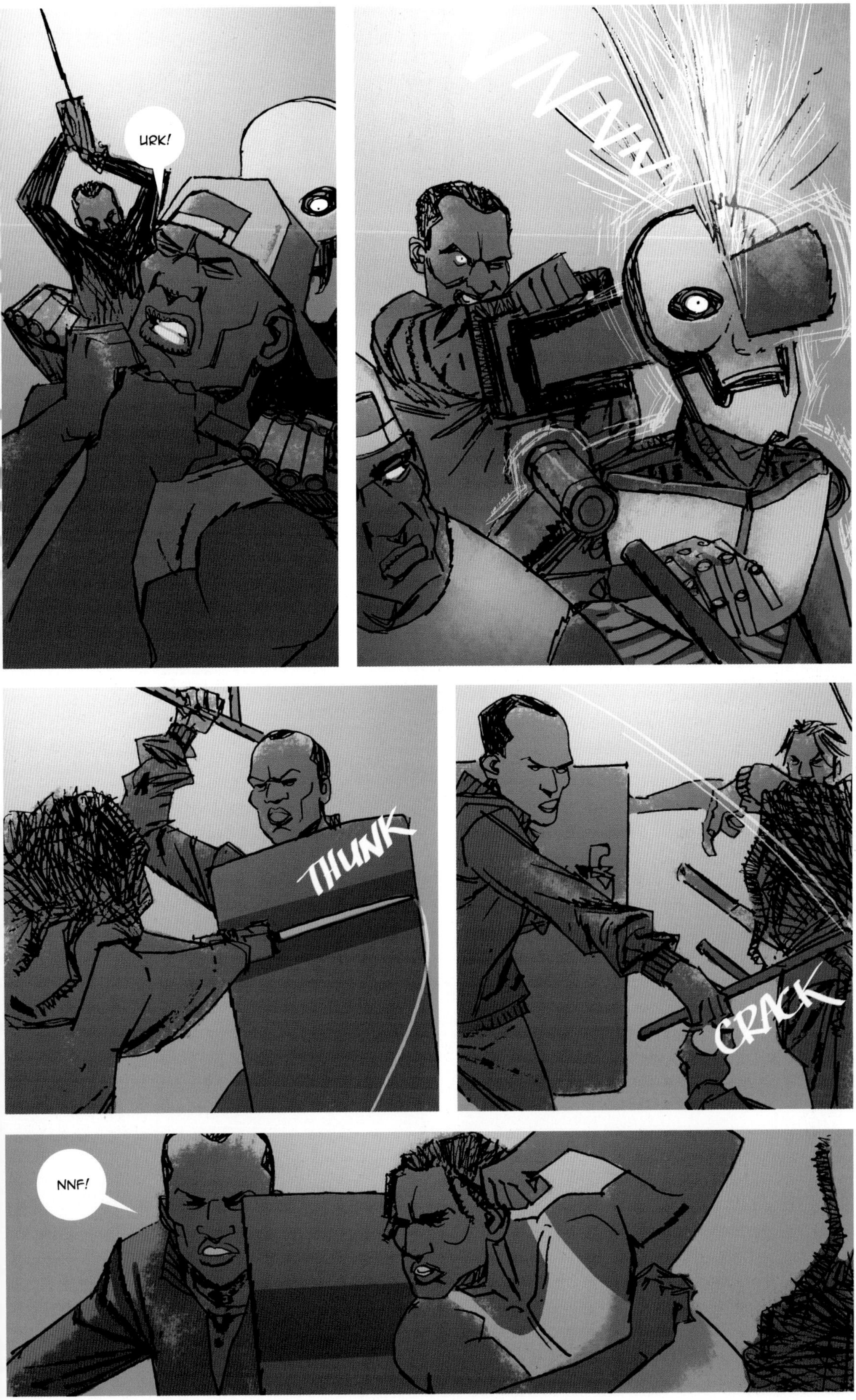
URK!
THUNK
CRACK
NNF!

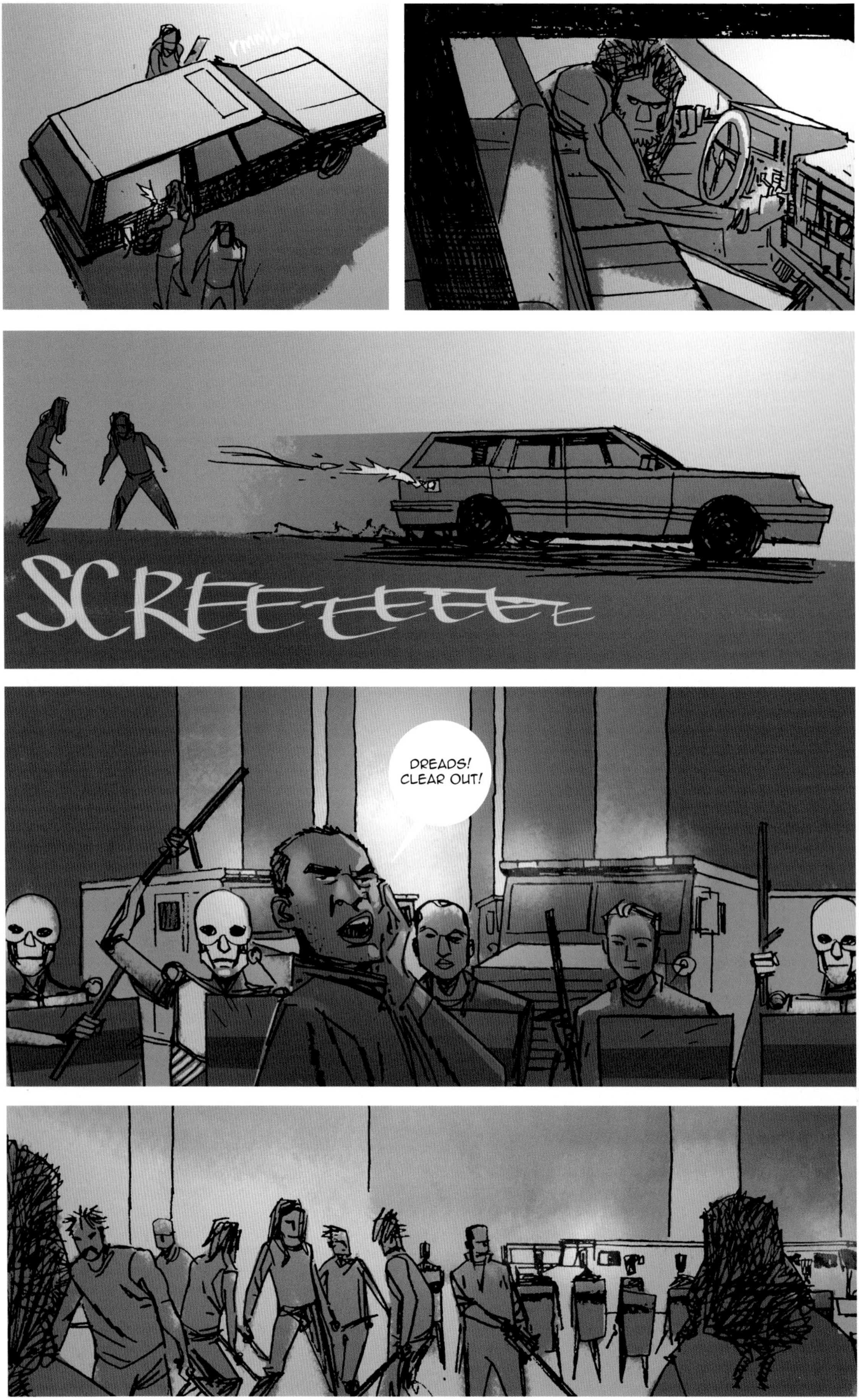
SCREEEEEEEE
DREADS! CLEAR OUT!

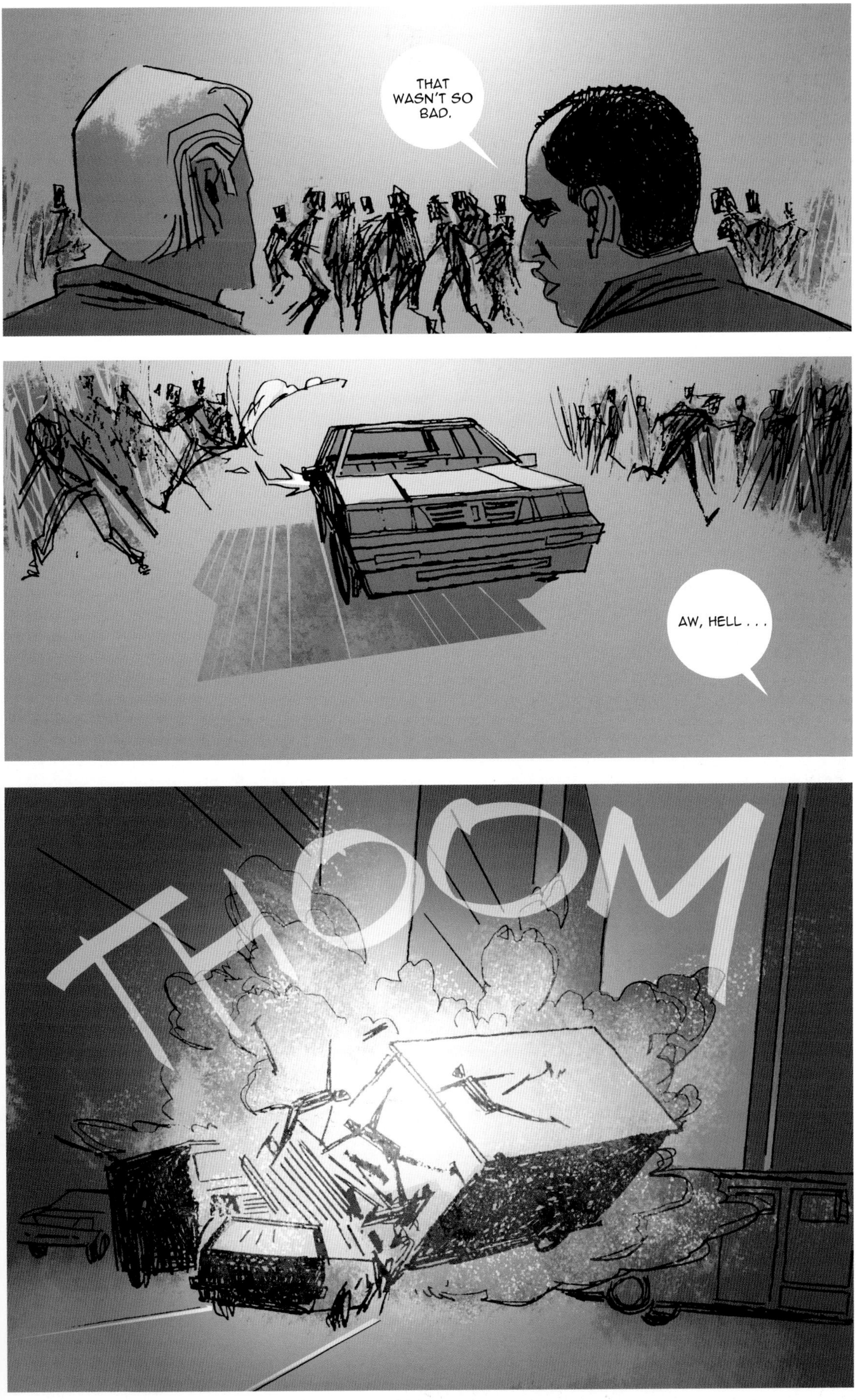
THAT WASN'T SO BAD.
AW, HELL . . .
THOOM

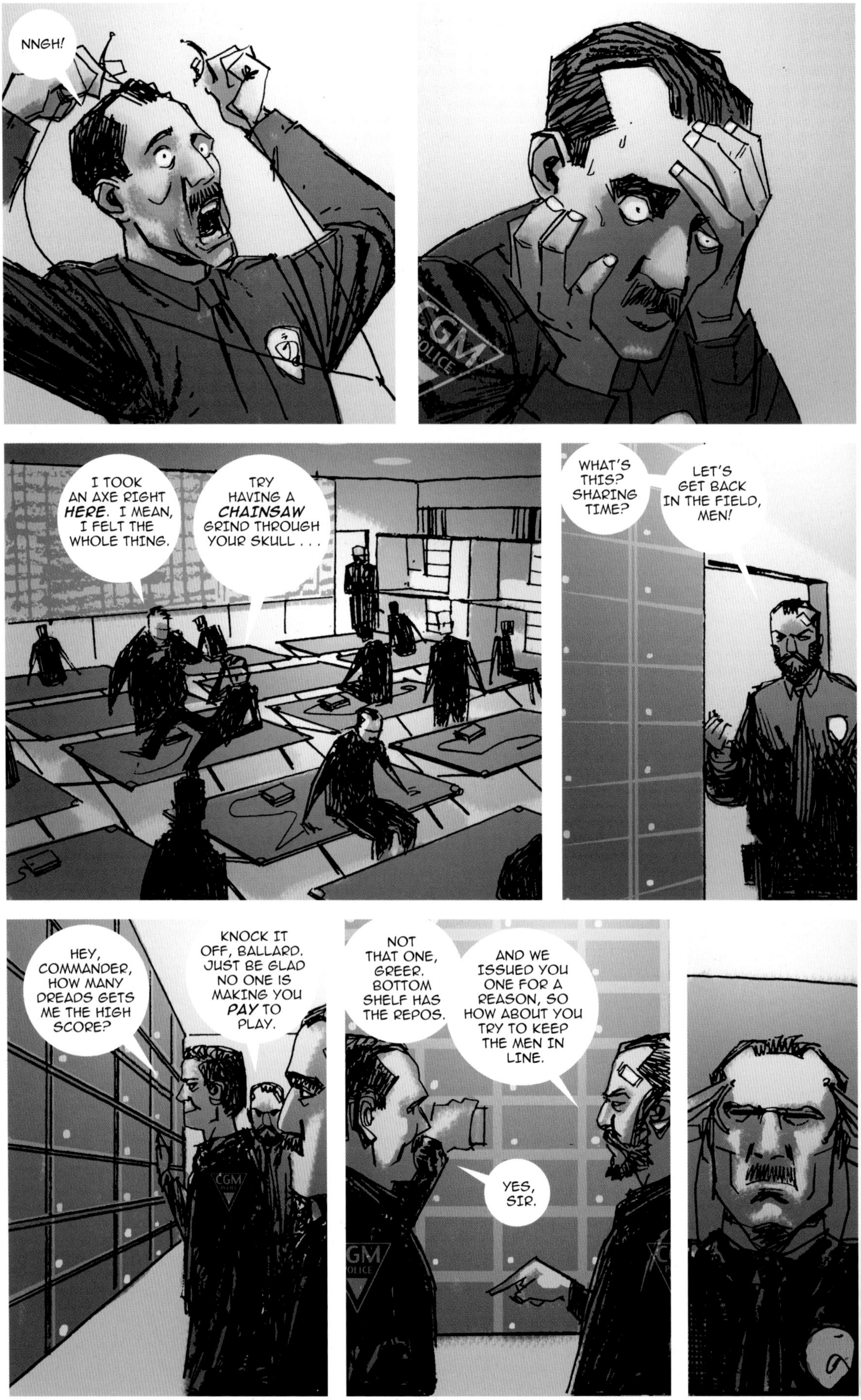
NNGH!
I TOOK AN AXE RIGHT HERE. I MEAN, I FELT THE WHOLE THING.
TRY HAVING A CHAINSAW GRIND THROUGH YOUR SKULL . . .
WHAT'S THIS? SHARING TIME?
LET'S GET BACK IN THE FIELD, MEN!
HEY, COMMANDER, HOW MANY DREADS GETS ME THE HIGH SCORE?
KNOCK IT OFF, BALLARD. JUST BE GLAD NO ONE IS MAKING YOU PAY TO PLAY.
NOT THAT ONE, GREER. BOTTOM SHELF HAS THE REPOS.
AND WE ISSUED YOU ONE FOR A REASON, SO HOW ABOUT YOU TRY TO KEEP THE MEN IN LINE.
YES, SIR.

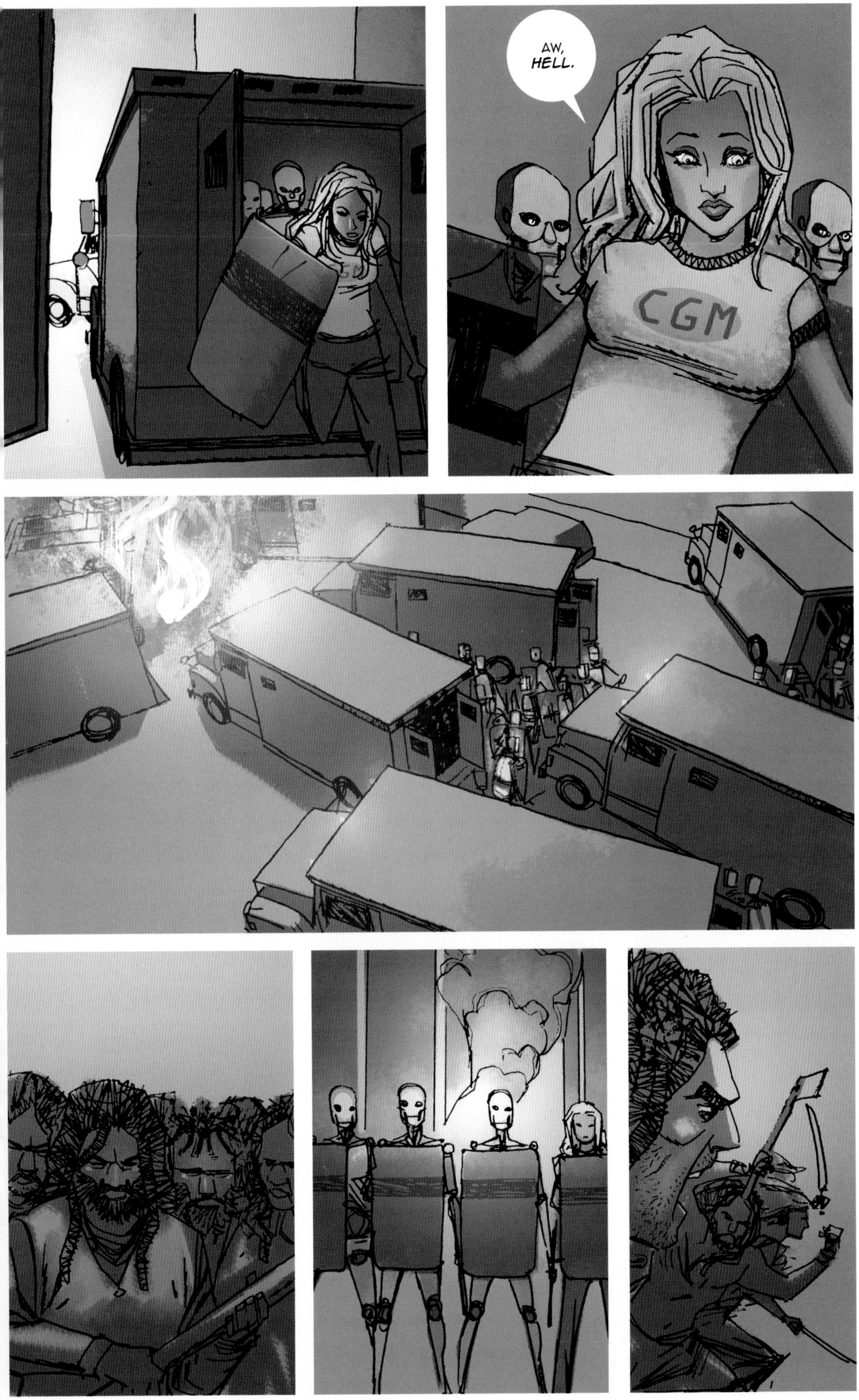
AW, HELL.

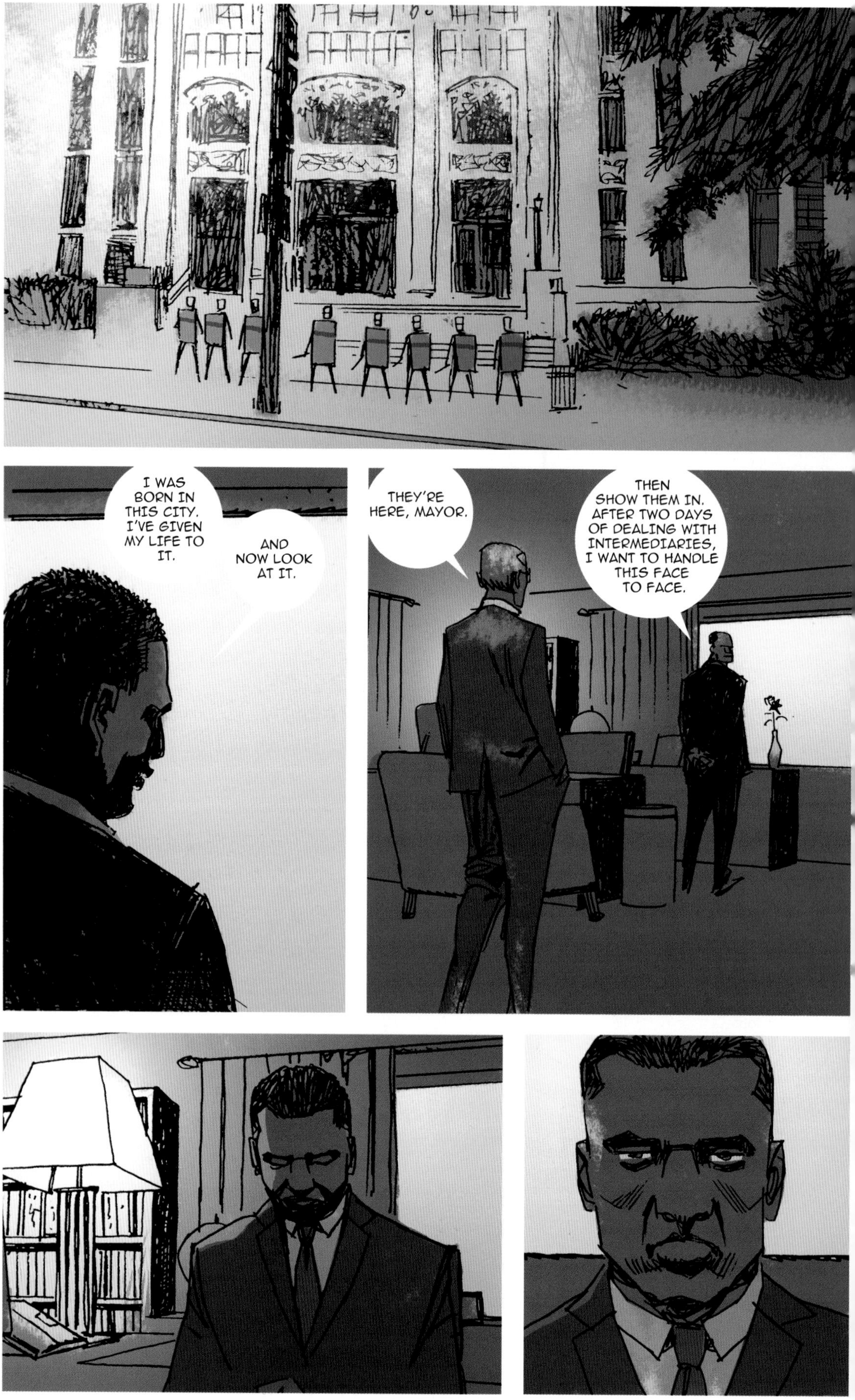

I WAS BORN IN THIS CITY. I'VE GIVEN MY LIFE TO IT.
AND NOW LOOK AT IT.
THEY'RE HERE, MAYOR.
THEN SHOW THEM IN. AFTER TWO DAYS OF DEALING WITH INTERMEDIARIES, I WANT TO HANDLE THIS FACE TO FACE.

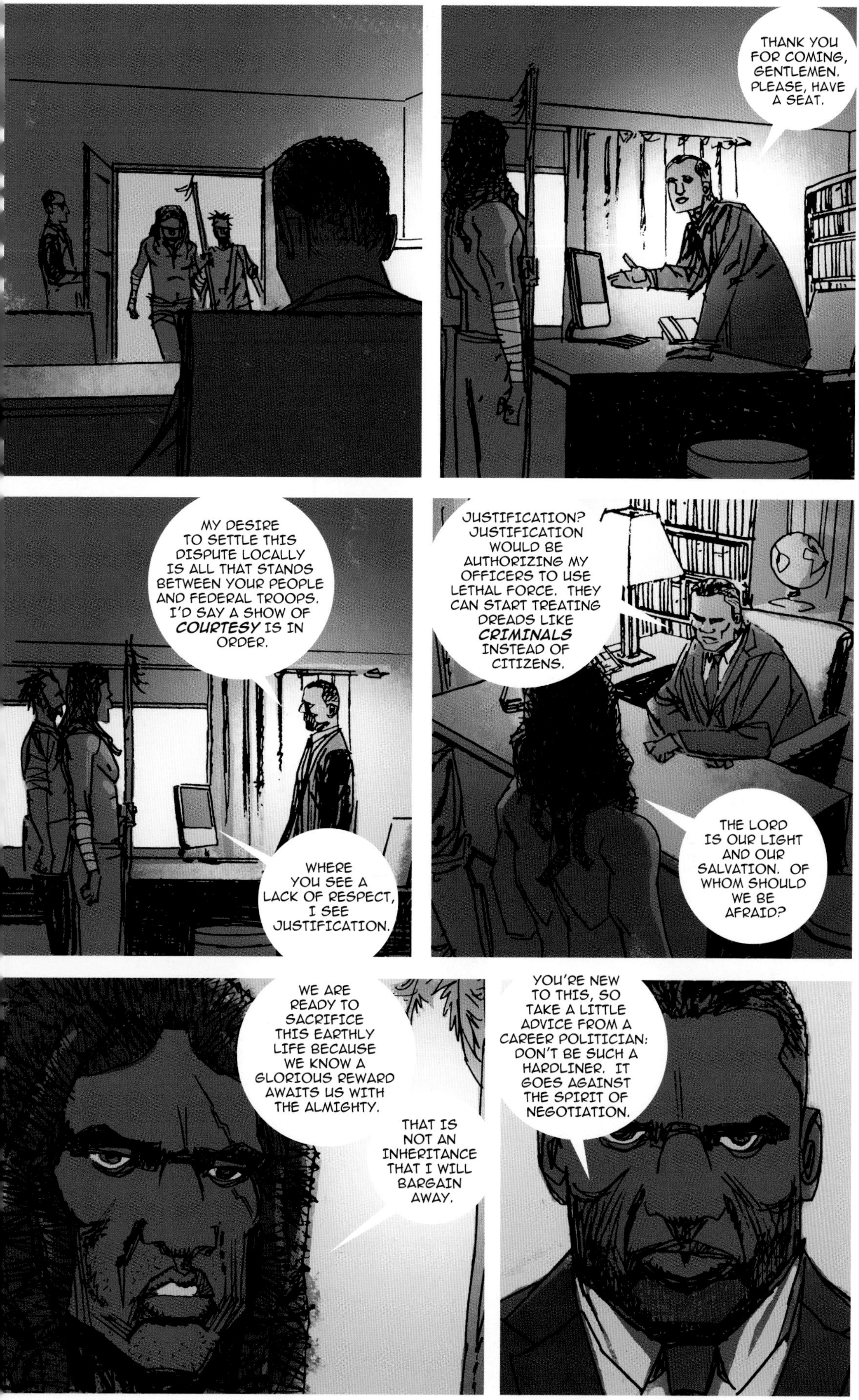
THANK YOU FOR COMING, GENTLEMEN. PLEASE, HAVE A SEAT.
MY DESIRE TO SETTLE THIS DISPUTE LOCALLY IS ALL THAT STANDS BETWEEN YOUR PEOPLE AND FEDERAL TROOPS. I'D SAY A SHOW OF COURTESY IS IN ORDER.
WHERE YOU SEE A LACK OF RESPECT, I SEE JUSTIFICATION.
JUSTIFICATION? JUSTIFICATION WOULD BE AUTHORIZING MY OFFICERS TO USE LETHAL FORCE. THEY CAN START TREATING DREADS LIKE CRIMINALS INSTEAD OF CITIZENS.
THE LORD IS OUR LIGHT AND OUR SALVATION. OF WHOM SHOULD WE BE AFRAID?
WE ARE READY TO SACRIFICE THIS EARTHLY LIFE BECAUSE WE KNOW A GLORIOUS REWARD AWAITS US WITH THE ALMIGHTY.
THAT IS NOT AN INHERITANCE THAT I WILL BARGAIN AWAY.
YOU'RE NEW TO THIS, SO TAKE A LITTLE ADVICE FROM A CAREER POLITICIAN: DON'T BE SUCH A HARDLINER. IT GOES AGAINST THE SPIRIT OF NEGOTIATION.

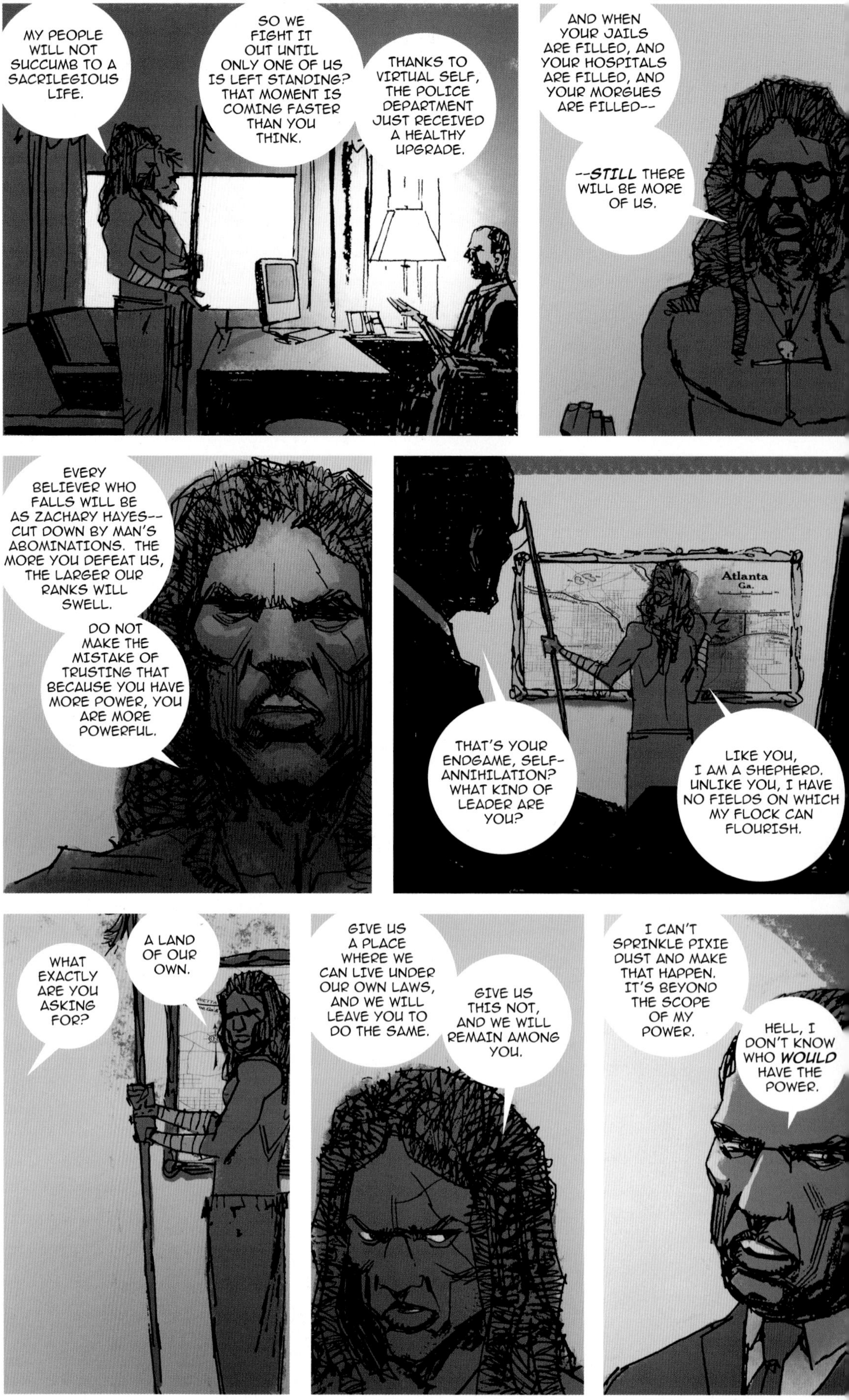
MY PEOPLE WILL NOT SUCCUMB TO A SACRILEGIOUS LIFE.
SO WE FIGHT IT OUT UNTIL ONLY ONE OF US IS LEFT STANDING? THAT MOMENT IS COMING FASTER THAN YOU THINK.
THANKS TO VIRTUAL SELF, THE POLICE DEPARTMENT JUST RECEIVED A HEALTHY UPGRADE.
AND WHEN YOUR JAILS ARE FILLED, AND YOUR HOSPITALS ARE FILLED, AND YOUR MORGUES ARE FILLED--
--*STILL* THERE WILL BE MORE OF US.
EVERY BELIEVER WHO FALLS WILL BE AS ZACHARY HAYES-- CUT DOWN BY MAN'S ABOMINATIONS. THE MORE YOU DEFEAT US, THE LARGER OUR RANKS WILL SWELL.
DO NOT MAKE THE MISTAKE OF TRUSTING THAT BECAUSE YOU HAVE MORE POWER, YOU ARE MORE POWERFUL.
Atlanta
Ga.
THAT'S YOUR ENDGAME, SELF-ANNIHILATION? WHAT KIND OF LEADER ARE YOU?
LIKE YOU, I AM A SHEPHERD. UNLIKE YOU, I HAVE NO FIELDS ON WHICH MY FLOCK CAN FLOURISH.
WHAT EXACTLY ARE YOU ASKING FOR?
A LAND OF OUR OWN.
GIVE US A PLACE WHERE WE CAN LIVE UNDER OUR OWN LAWS, AND WE WILL LEAVE YOU TO DO THE SAME.
GIVE US THIS NOT, AND WE WILL REMAIN AMONG YOU.
I CAN'T SPRINKLE PIXIE DUST AND MAKE THAT HAPPEN. IT'S BEYOND THE SCOPE OF MY POWER.
HELL, I DON'T KNOW WHO *WOULD* HAVE THE POWER.

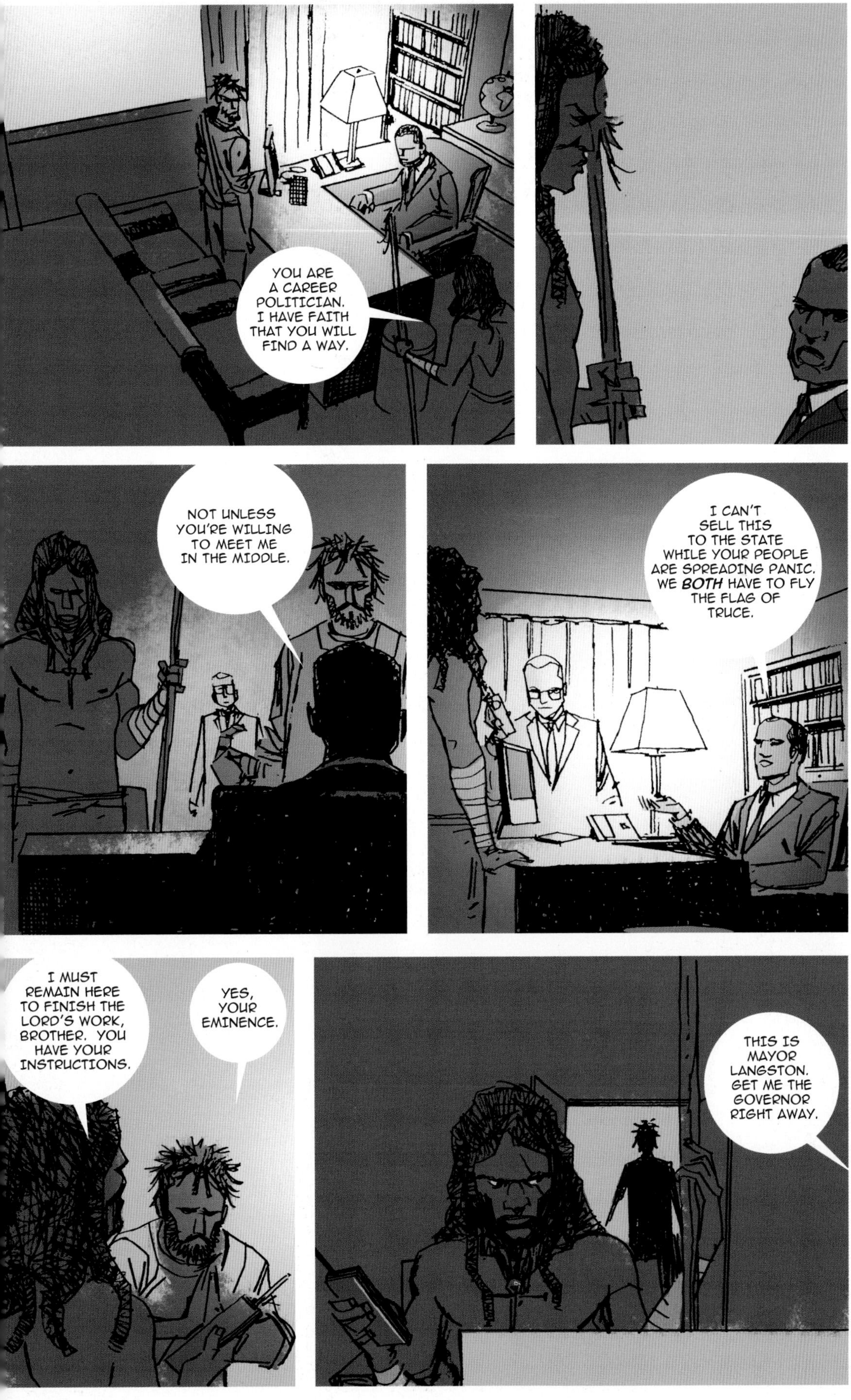
YOU ARE A CAREER POLITICIAN. I HAVE FAITH THAT YOU WILL FIND A WAY.
NOT UNLESS YOU'RE WILLING TO MEET ME IN THE MIDDLE.
I CAN'T SELL THIS TO THE STATE WHILE YOUR PEOPLE ARE SPREADING PANIC. WE *BOTH* HAVE TO FLY THE FLAG OF TRUCE.
I MUST REMAIN HERE TO FINISH THE LORD'S WORK, BROTHER. YOU HAVE YOUR INSTRUCTIONS.
YES, YOUR EMINENCE.
THIS IS MAYOR LANGSTON. GET ME THE GOVERNOR RIGHT AWAY.

KSSHH

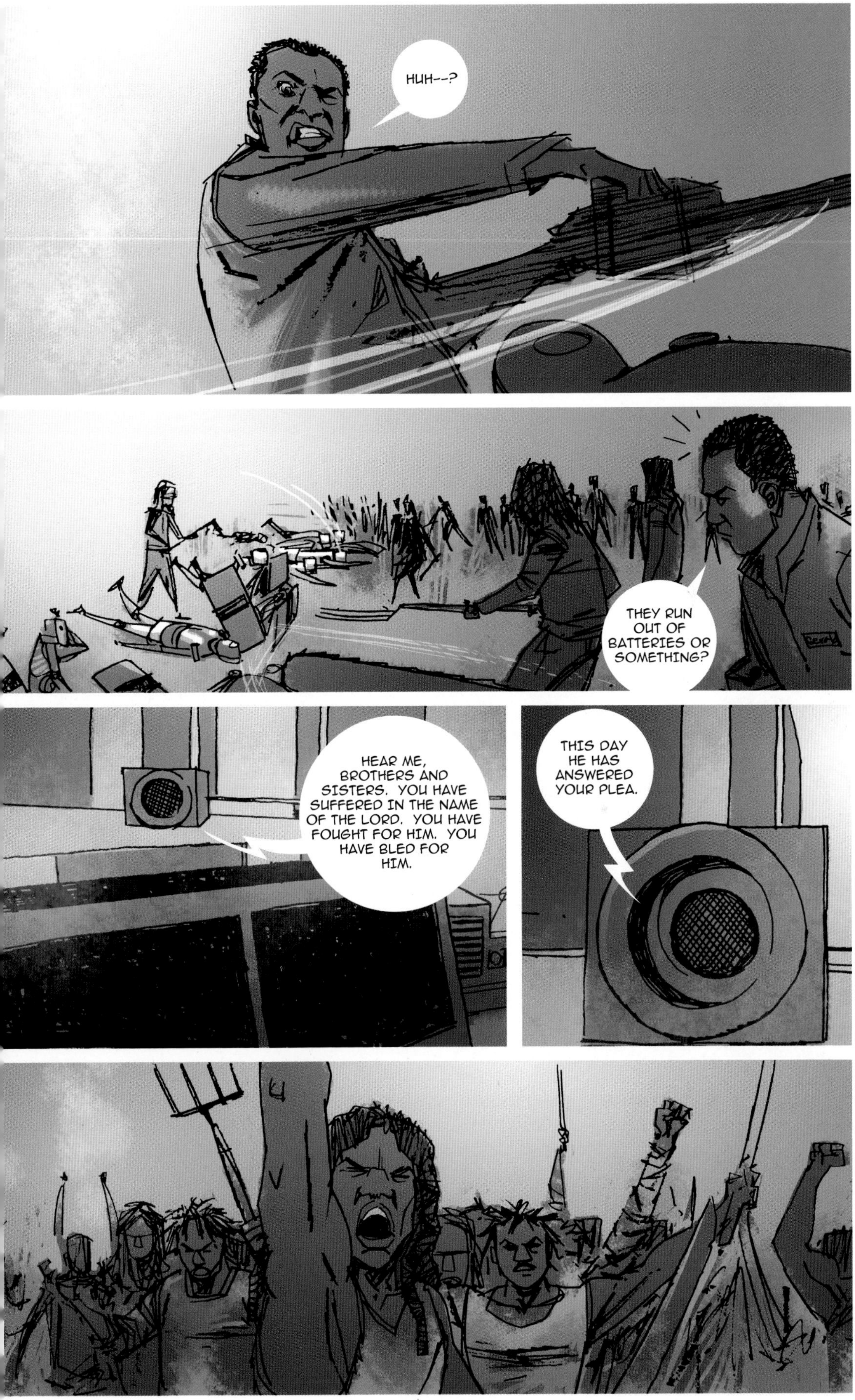
HUH--?
THEY RUN OUT OF BATTERIES OR SOMETHING?
HEAR ME, BROTHERS AND SISTERS. YOU HAVE SUFFERED IN THE NAME OF THE LORD. YOU HAVE FOUGHT FOR HIM. YOU HAVE BLED FOR HIM.
THIS DAY HE HAS ANSWERED YOUR PLEA.

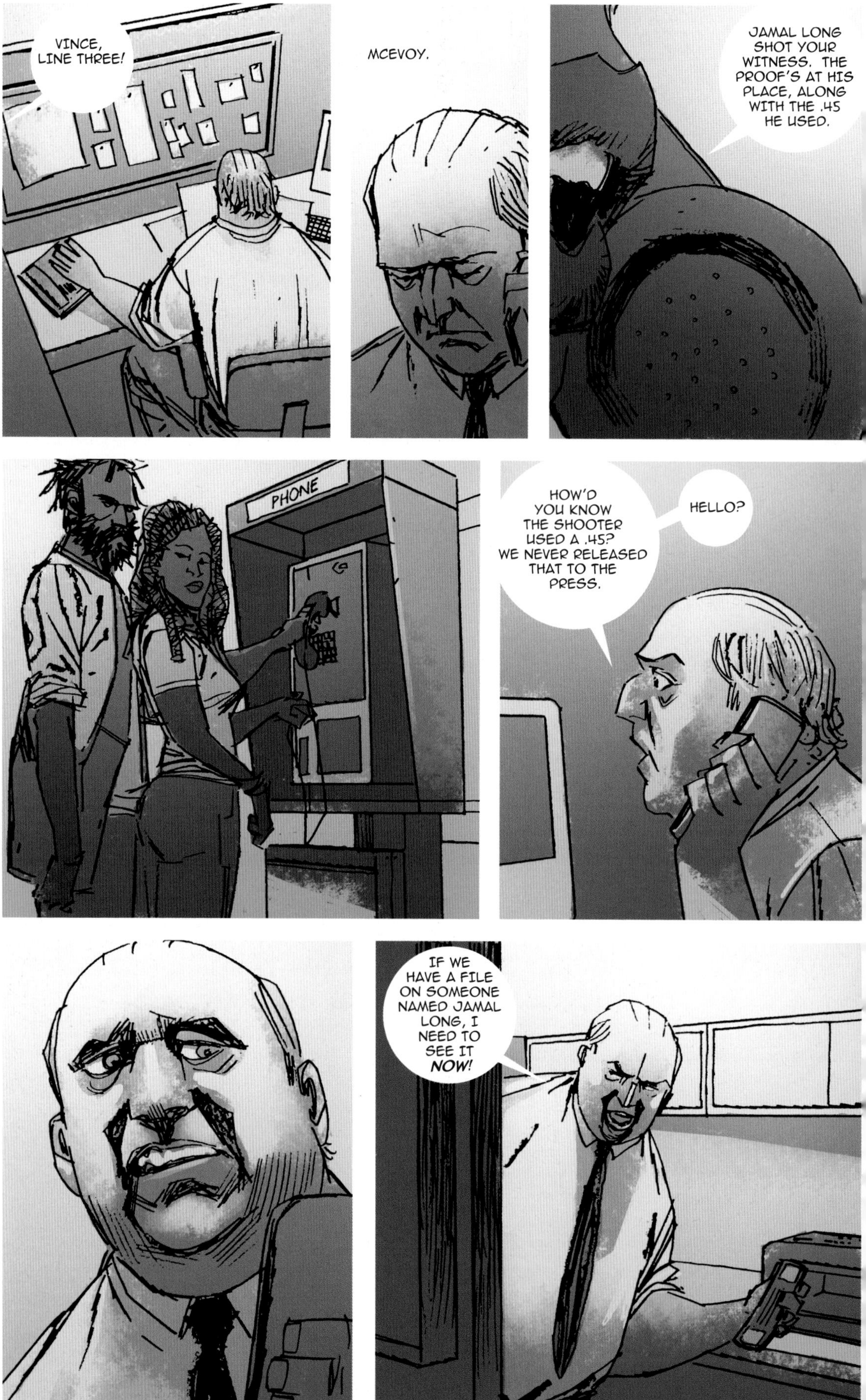
VINCE, LINE THREE!
MCEVOY.
JAMAL LONG SHOT YOUR WITNESS. THE PROOF'S AT HIS PLACE, ALONG WITH THE .45 HE USED.
HELLO?
HOW'D YOU KNOW THE SHOOTER USED A .45? WE NEVER RELEASED THAT TO THE PRESS.
PHONE
IF WE HAVE A FILE ON SOMEONE NAMED JAMAL LONG, I NEED TO SEE IT *NOW!*

FLOOR 2

235

235

BOOM

POLICE!
DON'T MOVE!

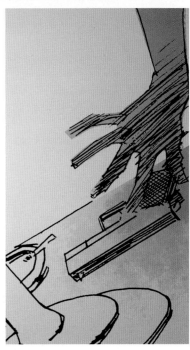

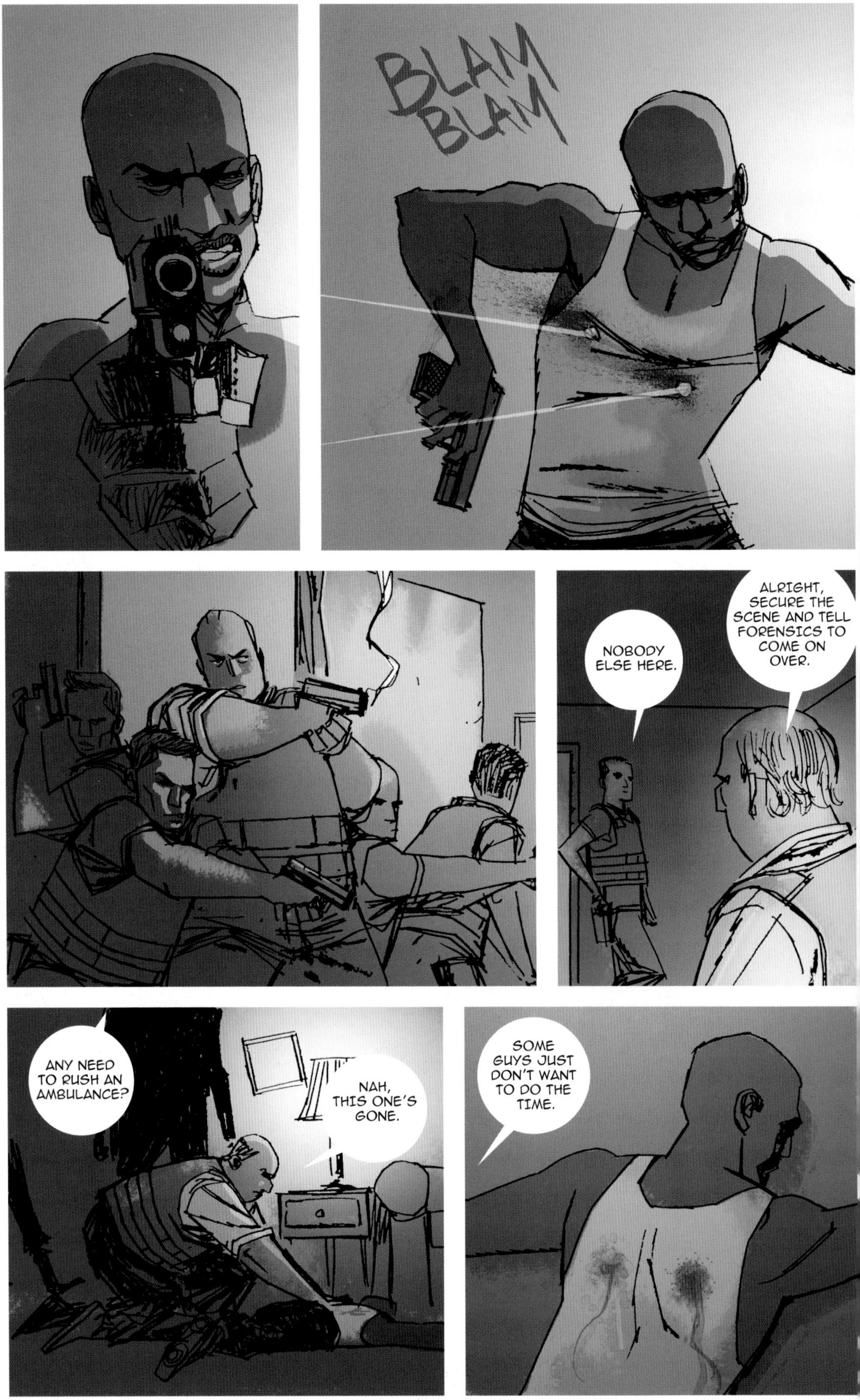
BLAM BLAM
NOBODY ELSE HERE.
ALRIGHT, SECURE THE SCENE AND TELL FORENSICS TO COME ON OVER.
ANY NEED TO RUSH AN AMBULANCE?
NAH, THIS ONE'S GONE.
SOME GUYS JUST DON'T WANT TO DO THE TIME.

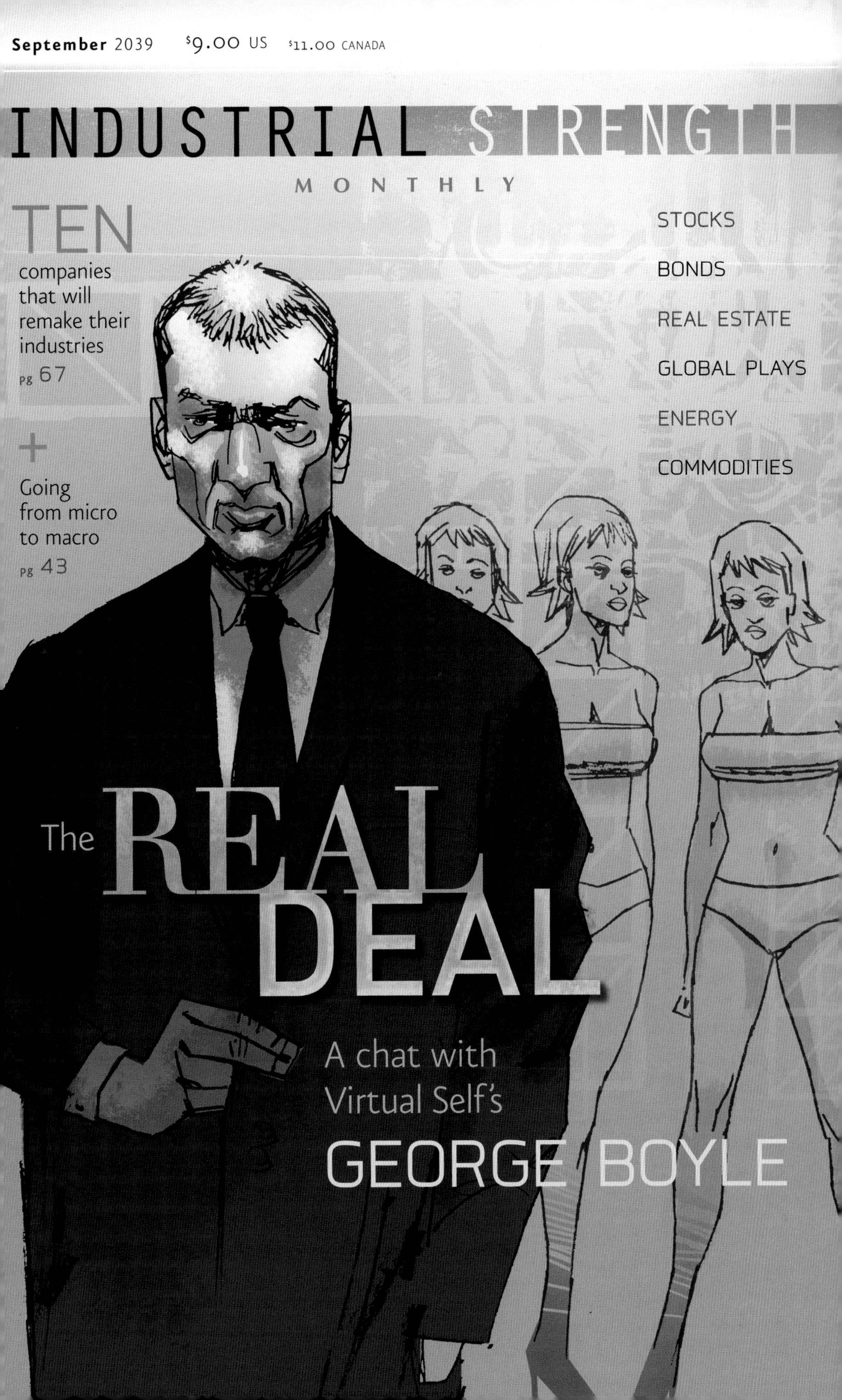
September 2039
$9.00 US
$11.00 CANADA
INDUSTRIAL STRENGTH
MONTHLY
TEN
companies that will remake their industries
pg 67
+
Going from micro to macro
pg 43
STOCKS
BONDS
REAL ESTATE
GLOBAL PLAYS
ENERGY
COMMODITIES
The REAL DEAL
A chat with Virtual Self's
GEORGE BOYLE

THE INDUSTRIAL STRENGTH INTERVIEW

George Boyle

—— BY JEFF FRANKLIN ——

In just a few years, Virtual Self, Inc. has been transformed from an obscure tech start-up specializing in virtual reality and cybernetics into one of the largest and most recognizable companies on the globe. This is largely due to their signature product, the personal surrogate, the growing popularity of which is moving it from luxury item to necessity at a rate set to outpace that of the personal computer.

VSI was poised for even more success with the release of their first youth line, a series of models that would introduce underage consumers to the experience of surrogate living. Promising parents improved lives for their children, VSI's youth line seemed like a no-brainer, that Holy Grail of scenarios where the product would sell itself. Everything changed on July 29, however, when three teens masquerading in their parents' surrogates beat a man named Zachary Hayes to death in Central Georgia Metropolis, less than five miles from VSI's corporate headquarters. The event sent shockwaves across the country, and the nation watched as Central Georgia Metropolis fell into days of civil unrest. By the time the rioting ceased, VSI's plans for a youth line had been put on hold indefinitely.

VSI's well-liked and highly respected CEO, George Boyle, has been there through it all. At a time when many executives would close their doors to the press, he graciously invited us into his office suite for a frank discussion about corporate responsibility, public opinion, and the future of VSI.

> INDUSTRIAL STRENGTH MONTHLY: *The Zachary Hayes case had far-reaching effects. Do you believe that VSI is in any way to blame for the tragedy and its fallout?*

GEORGE BOYLE: First I'd like to say that what happened to Zachary Hayes, and to the city of Central Georgia Metropolis during the aftermath, was terribly unfortunate. It's the kind of thing you just hate to see, whether it happens across the world or at your front door. As a CEO, you hate it even more when it happens as a result of someone putting your company's product to incorrect use.

As much as the hearts of everyone at VSI may go out to the victims, however, we must be careful not to place blame where it's unwarranted. When someone gets into a car accident because of reckless or illegal behavior, and injury or damage is caused to someone else's person or property, the fault lies with the individual and not the manufacturer of the car. That's not just simply the law. It's common sense.

> ISM: *Then why discontinue the youth line? Can't the move be construed as a tacit admission of culpability?*

GB: I grew up in the South, in an environment where the mom-and-pop approach to business was prevalent. Whether you owned a restaurant or a barbershop or a plumbing company, you were part of a community, and you do, a dedication that shows in the quality of our line. That personal interest makes it difficult when changes need to be made, and I'm not unsympathetic to that. In the end, though, VSI is larger than any one person or division.

had a responsibility to frame your business practices in that context. There's no reason that a corporation as large as VSI can't operate in the same fashion, even if their community is on a national or international scale, as is the case with us.

By halting the youth surrogate line, we're renewing our commitment to conduct business in the best possible way for our community. It's the same core belief that led us to provide the law enforcement officers of Central Georgia Metropolis with surrogate units at no charge to the police department, and we're very proud of the role those units played in restoring order to the city.

ISM: *It's often said that in large corporations the wheels of change turn slowly. No doubt the youth surrogate line was in development for quite some time, yet it was terminated rather abruptly. How was that decision made? Was there any opposition?*

GB: Like you said, the youth line was in the works for quite some time. We staked a considerable amount in it, and I'm not just talking about your typical expenses. Our researchers and designers put their passion into what they

> ISM: *Was the decision meant to preempt further backlash of the type that targeted VSI after Hayes's death? Were you at all surprised by the scope of that backlash?*

GB: The decision follows the best course of action for VSI in the current environment. As for the backlash, I'm not one to dismiss people's beliefs. I was raised a Baptist, and you can still find me among the pews on Sunday. I remember in late 1999, though, there was a man being interviewed on TV who was advising viewers to purchase Winnebagos and bury them in the ground, so they'd have someplace to hide when the Y2K bug knocked the planet offline. That sort of skewed perspective has no place in corporate planning.

> ISM: *There's been criticism of a different sort lately from some of VSI's proponents. How do you respond to those who say that parents and children should be allowed to decide the issue of youth surrogate use for themselves, and that your unwillingness to provide the units takes the choice out of their hands?*

GB: I'd say that, as a company, the decisions about what kind of products we make have always been, and will continue to be, made in-house. While the necessities of the business world dictate that much of what we do be determined by market forces, we must also be motivated by ethics. To put youth model surrogates in our showrooms today would be unethical.

> ISM: *It sounds like you're leaving the door open there. Are youth model surrogates something that VSI may revisit down the road?*

GB: I'm not going to say never because, after all, this is the tech industry. If tech companies planned their futures solely on the basis of what's possible in the present, we'd all still be throwing switches on our ENIACs. Having said that, youth models are not something I, as CEO, am interested in pursuing now or at any time in the foreseeable future.

> ISM: *VSI currently dominates the surrogate market- place. For all intents and purposes you have a monopoly, and I don't say that in the negative*

GB: Do you know how many patents VSI filed this year? Thirty-eight. That's thirty-eight individual hardware and software upgrades that make this year's units better than last year's. The previous year we filed thirty-two. When the terms of those patents expire, any competitor who wants to challenge us is welcome to use them. And we'll start running ads about the dozens of ways that their product is inferior to ours.

The minds we employ are the best in the world at what they do, and so long as we continue to innovate, the competition will always be playing catch-up.

> ISM: *Fair enough, but those new patents are now going to pertain solely to adult models. In terms of youth models, there is no comparison. Whoever decides to create a youth line will de facto have the best product on the market.*

GB: There are two immediate problems with that assumption. First, consumers don't want a tech product when they know that a newer version of the same technology exists. This is particularly true of

connotation of the term, but because no one has tried to challenge you. Now that you've decided against moving forward with the youth line, however, are you in any way concerned that another company may come in and establish a foothold in the marketplace with youth models of their own?

GB: Not at all.

> ISM: *But you wouldn't have pursued a youth line if you didn't believe that there was a substantial demand for the units, correct?* [**Boyle nods.**] *So then what's to prevent a more ambitious company from meeting that demand now that you've left a void?*

the under-eighteen demographic, hence the success of video game companies who release new versions of the same games year after year. So if the kids don't want it, then it's safe to assume that their parents aren't going to buy it for them.

Second, many of our patents do more than simply improve on surrogate technology. A large part of our research and design budget is spent on efforts that streamline the manufacturing process and reduce the costs of production, the benefits of which roll down to the consumer in the form of more affordable units. If someone's strategy is to compete with us by offering outdated models at higher prices, then they're going to have a tough road ahead of them. ▪

EPILOGUE

Embers

AUGUST 28, 2039.

I'VE BEEN EXPECTING THIS VISIT.

Snap

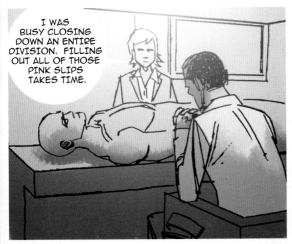

I WAS BUSY CLOSING DOWN AN ENTIRE DIVISION. FILLING OUT ALL OF THOSE PINK SLIPS TAKES TIME.

THE YOUTH LINE SHOULD NEVER HAVE BEEN APPROVED, VICTORIA. IT WAS A BAD IDEA FROM THE START, AND THE BOARD VOTED TO DO THE ONLY RATIONAL THING.

THE EVENTS OF THE LAST MONTH PROVE THAT.

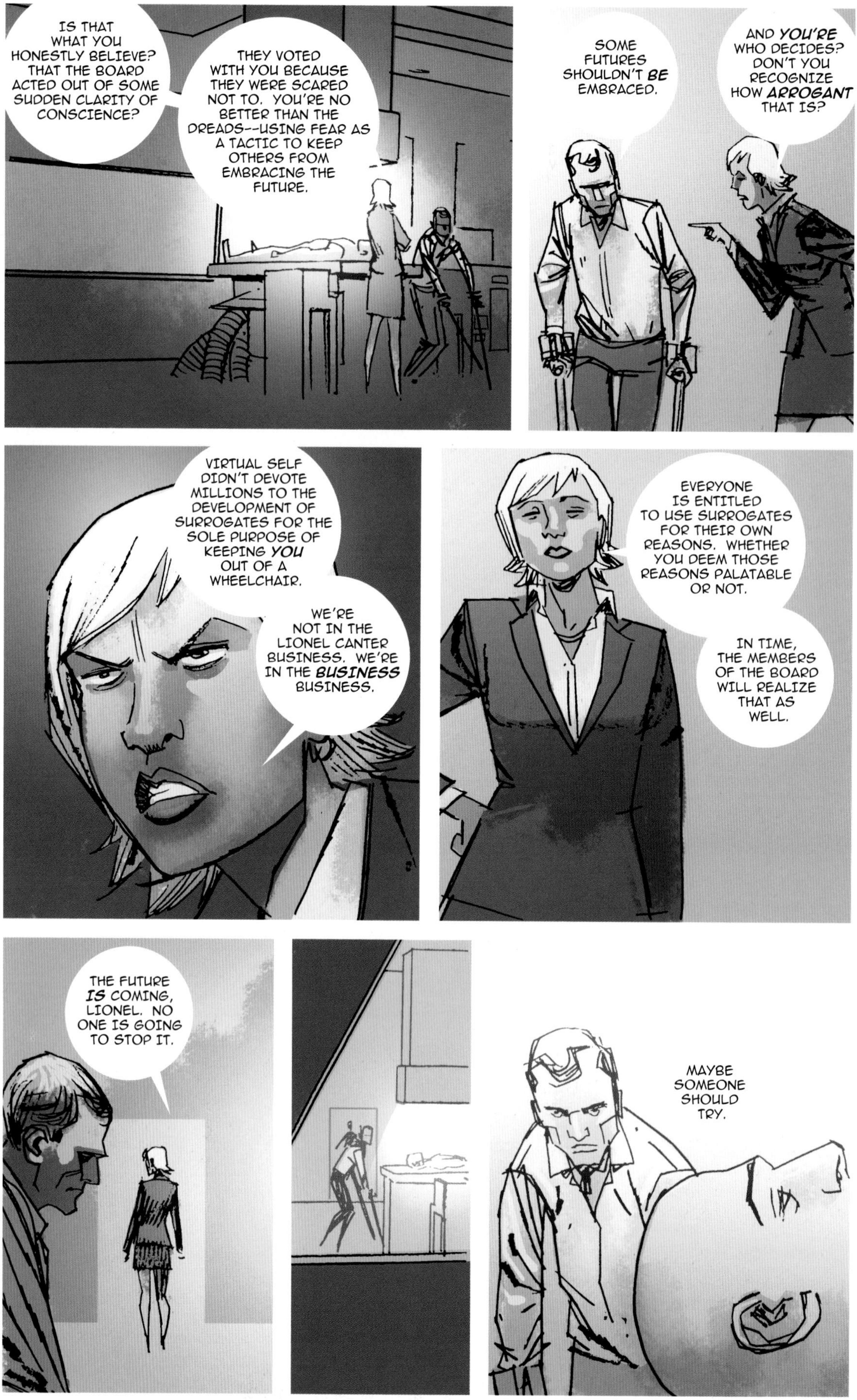
IS THAT WHAT YOU HONESTLY BELIEVE? THAT THE BOARD ACTED OUT OF SOME SUDDEN CLARITY OF CONSCIENCE?
THEY VOTED WITH YOU BECAUSE THEY WERE SCARED NOT TO. YOU'RE NO BETTER THAN THE DREADS--USING FEAR AS A TACTIC TO KEEP OTHERS FROM EMBRACING THE FUTURE.
SOME FUTURES SHOULDN'T BE EMBRACED.
AND YOU'RE WHO DECIDES? DON'T YOU RECOGNIZE HOW ARROGANT THAT IS?
VIRTUAL SELF DIDN'T DEVOTE MILLIONS TO THE DEVELOPMENT OF SURROGATES FOR THE SOLE PURPOSE OF KEEPING YOU OUT OF A WHEELCHAIR.
WE'RE NOT IN THE LIONEL CANTER BUSINESS. WE'RE IN THE BUSINESS BUSINESS.
EVERYONE IS ENTITLED TO USE SURROGATES FOR THEIR OWN REASONS. WHETHER YOU DEEM THOSE REASONS PALATABLE OR NOT.
IN TIME, THE MEMBERS OF THE BOARD WILL REALIZE THAT AS WELL.
THE FUTURE IS COMING, LIONEL. NO ONE IS GOING TO STOP IT.
MAYBE SOMEONE SHOULD TRY.

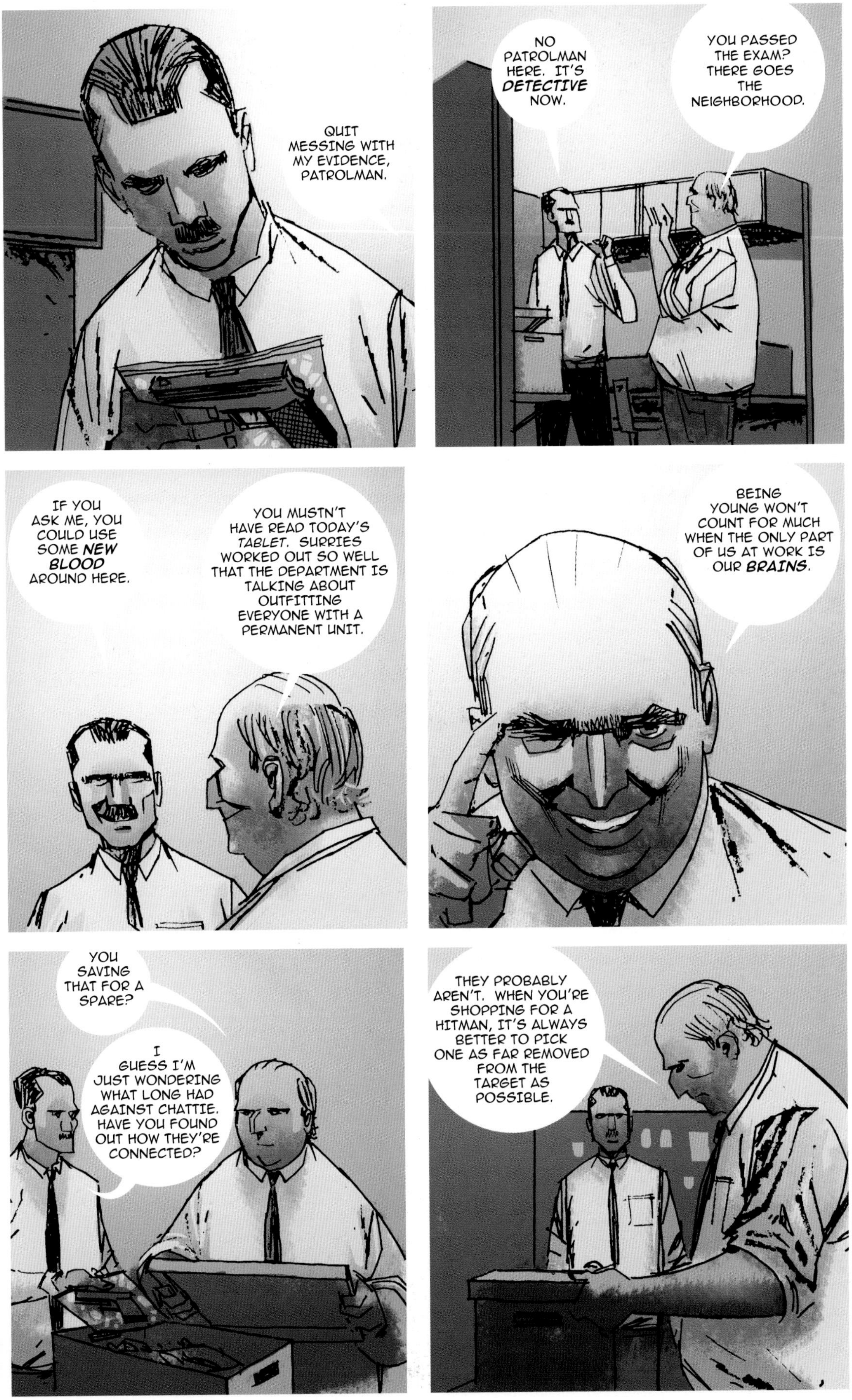
QUIT MESSING WITH MY EVIDENCE, PATROLMAN.
NO PATROLMAN HERE. IT'S *DETECTIVE* NOW.
YOU PASSED THE EXAM? THERE GOES THE NEIGHBORHOOD.
IF YOU ASK ME, YOU COULD USE SOME *NEW BLOOD* AROUND HERE.
YOU MUSTN'T HAVE READ TODAY'S *TABLET*. SURRIES WORKED OUT SO WELL THAT THE DEPARTMENT IS TALKING ABOUT OUTFITTING EVERYONE WITH A PERMANENT UNIT.
BEING YOUNG WON'T COUNT FOR MUCH WHEN THE ONLY PART OF US AT WORK IS OUR *BRAINS*.
YOU SAVING THAT FOR A SPARE?
I GUESS I'M JUST WONDERING WHAT LONG HAD AGAINST CHATTIE. HAVE YOU FOUND OUT HOW THEY'RE CONNECTED?
THEY PROBABLY AREN'T. WHEN YOU'RE SHOPPING FOR A HITMAN, IT'S ALWAYS BETTER TO PICK ONE AS FAR REMOVED FROM THE TARGET AS POSSIBLE.

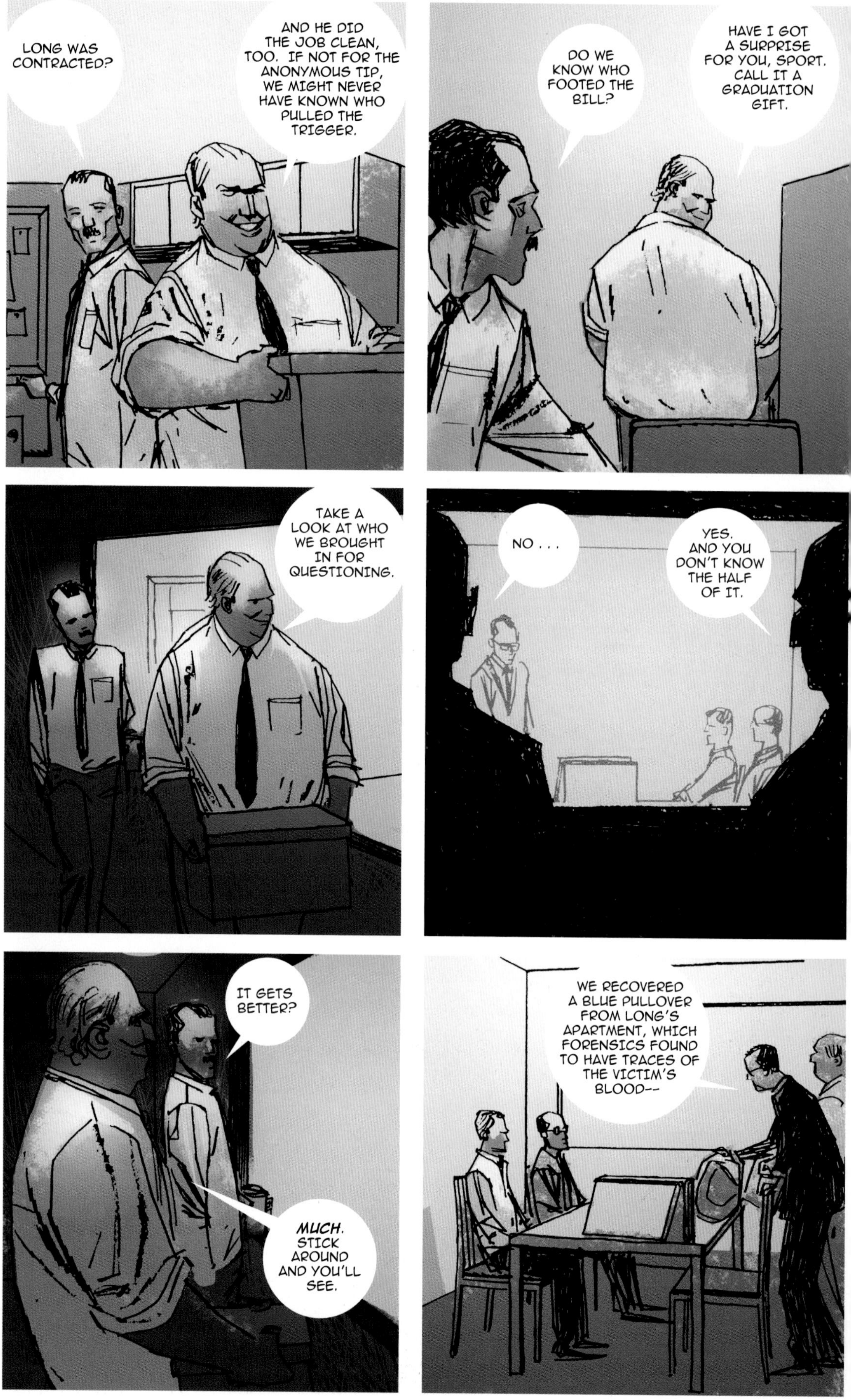
LONG WAS CONTRACTED?
AND HE DID THE JOB CLEAN, TOO. IF NOT FOR THE ANONYMOUS TIP, WE MIGHT NEVER HAVE KNOWN WHO PULLED THE TRIGGER.
DO WE KNOW WHO FOOTED THE BILL?
HAVE I GOT A SURPRISE FOR YOU, SPORT. CALL IT A GRADUATION GIFT.
TAKE A LOOK AT WHO WE BROUGHT IN FOR QUESTIONING.
NO . . .
YES. AND YOU DON'T KNOW THE HALF OF IT.
IT GETS BETTER?
MUCH. STICK AROUND AND YOU'LL SEE.
WE RECOVERED A BLUE PULLOVER FROM LONG'S APARTMENT, WHICH FORENSICS FOUND TO HAVE TRACES OF THE VICTIM'S BLOOD--

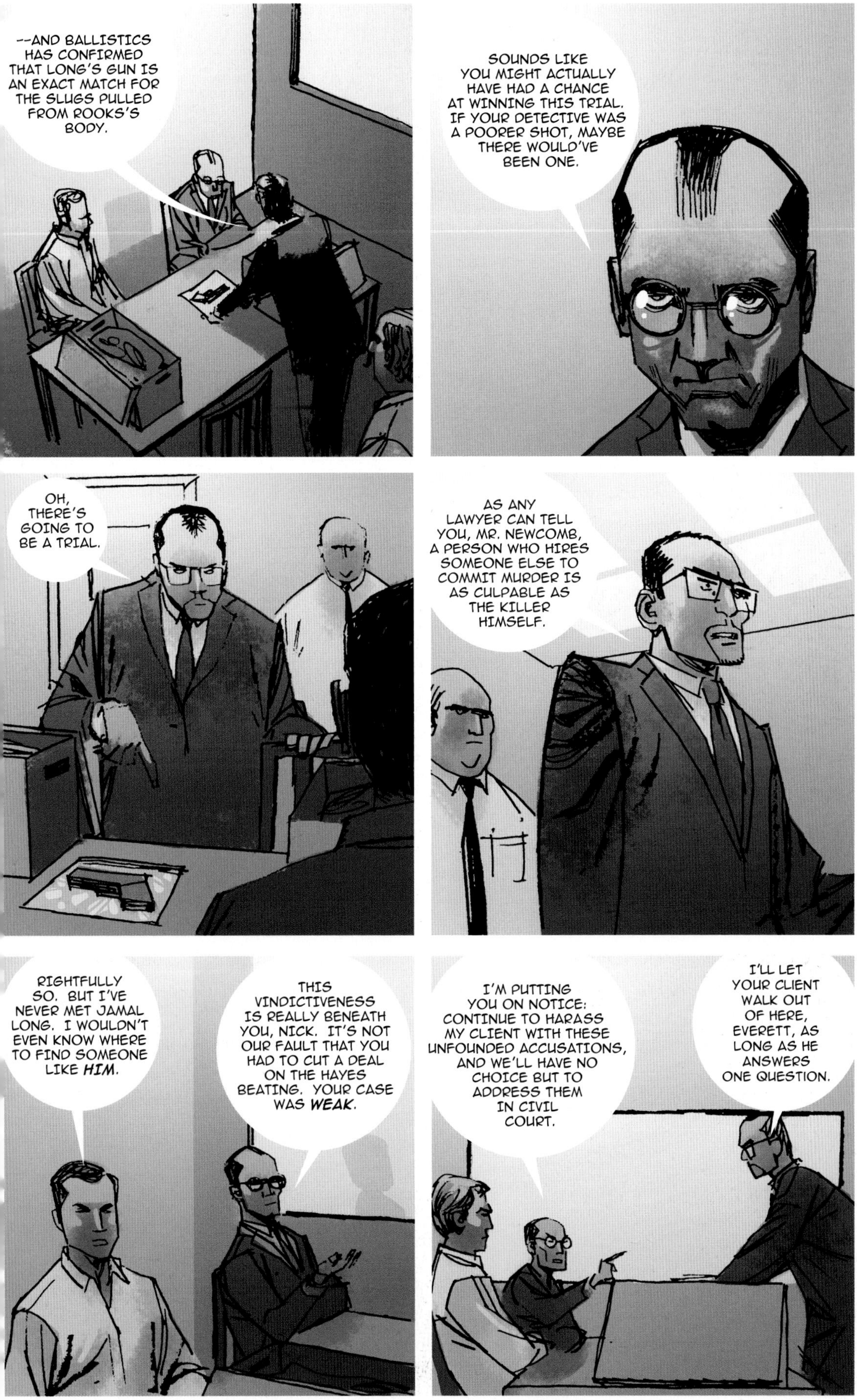
--AND BALLISTICS HAS CONFIRMED THAT LONG'S GUN IS AN EXACT MATCH FOR THE SLUGS PULLED FROM ROOKS'S BODY.
SOUNDS LIKE YOU MIGHT ACTUALLY HAVE HAD A CHANCE AT WINNING THIS TRIAL. IF YOUR DETECTIVE WAS A POORER SHOT, MAYBE THERE WOULD'VE BEEN ONE.
OH, THERE'S GOING TO BE A TRIAL.
AS ANY LAWYER CAN TELL YOU, MR. NEWCOMB, A PERSON WHO HIRES SOMEONE ELSE TO COMMIT MURDER IS AS CULPABLE AS THE KILLER HIMSELF.
RIGHTFULLY SO. BUT I'VE NEVER MET JAMAL LONG. I WOULDN'T EVEN KNOW WHERE TO FIND SOMEONE LIKE *HIM*.
THIS VINDICTIVENESS IS REALLY BENEATH YOU, NICK. IT'S NOT OUR FAULT THAT YOU HAD TO CUT A DEAL ON THE HAYES BEATING. YOUR CASE WAS *WEAK*.
I'M PUTTING YOU ON NOTICE: CONTINUE TO HARASS MY CLIENT WITH THESE UNFOUNDED ACCUSATIONS, AND WE'LL HAVE NO CHOICE BUT TO ADDRESS THEM IN CIVIL COURT.
I'LL LET YOUR CLIENT WALK OUT OF HERE, EVERETT, AS LONG AS HE ANSWERS ONE QUESTION.

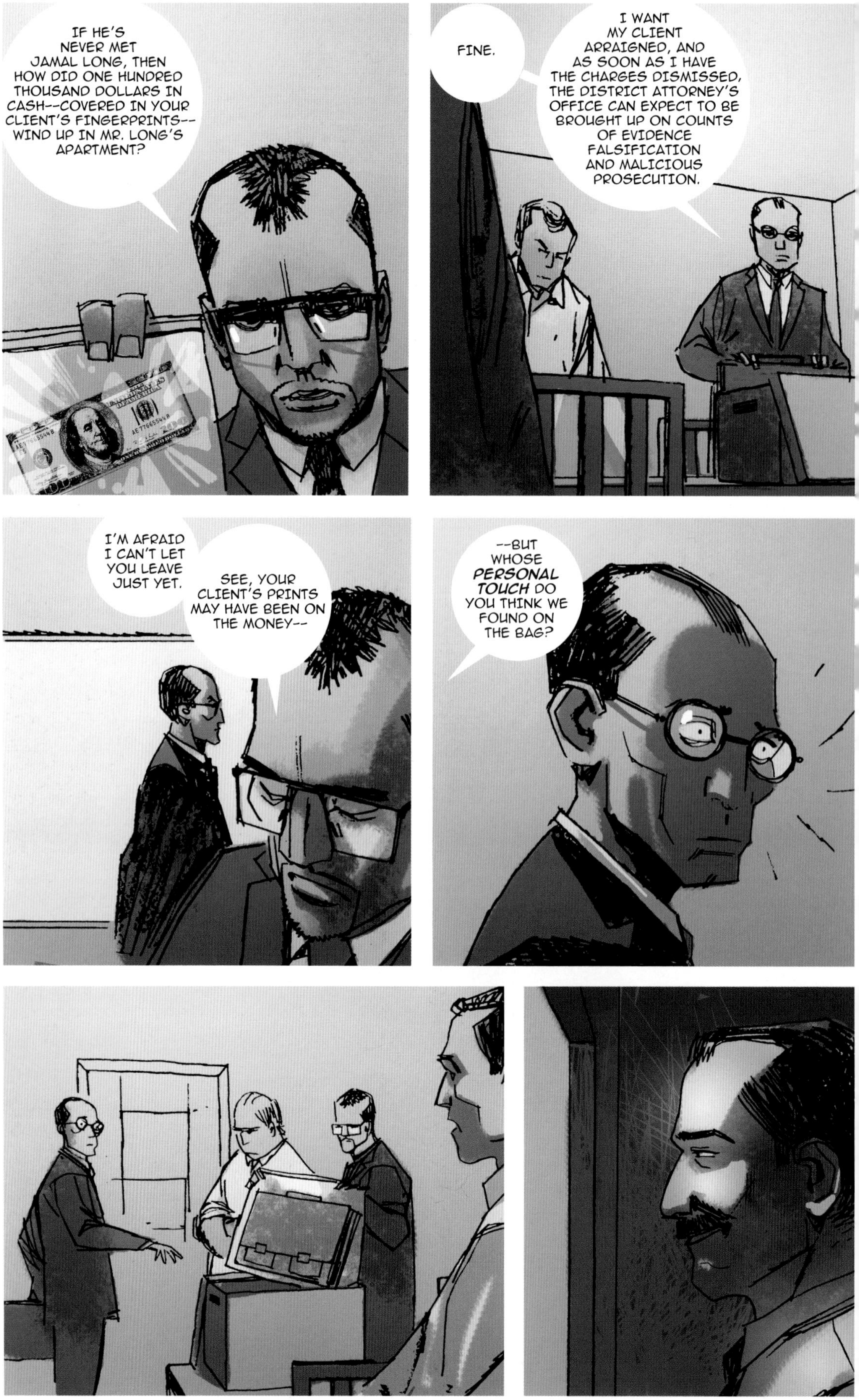
IF HE'S NEVER MET JAMAL LONG, THEN HOW DID ONE HUNDRED THOUSAND DOLLARS IN CASH--COVERED IN YOUR CLIENT'S FINGERPRINTS--WIND UP IN MR. LONG'S APARTMENT?
FINE.
I WANT MY CLIENT ARRAIGNED, AND AS SOON AS I HAVE THE CHARGES DISMISSED, THE DISTRICT ATTORNEY'S OFFICE CAN EXPECT TO BE BROUGHT UP ON COUNTS OF EVIDENCE FALSIFICATION AND MALICIOUS PROSECUTION.
I'M AFRAID I CAN'T LET YOU LEAVE JUST YET.
SEE, YOUR CLIENT'S PRINTS MAY HAVE BEEN ON THE MONEY--
--BUT WHOSE *PERSONAL TOUCH* DO YOU THINK WE FOUND ON THE BAG?

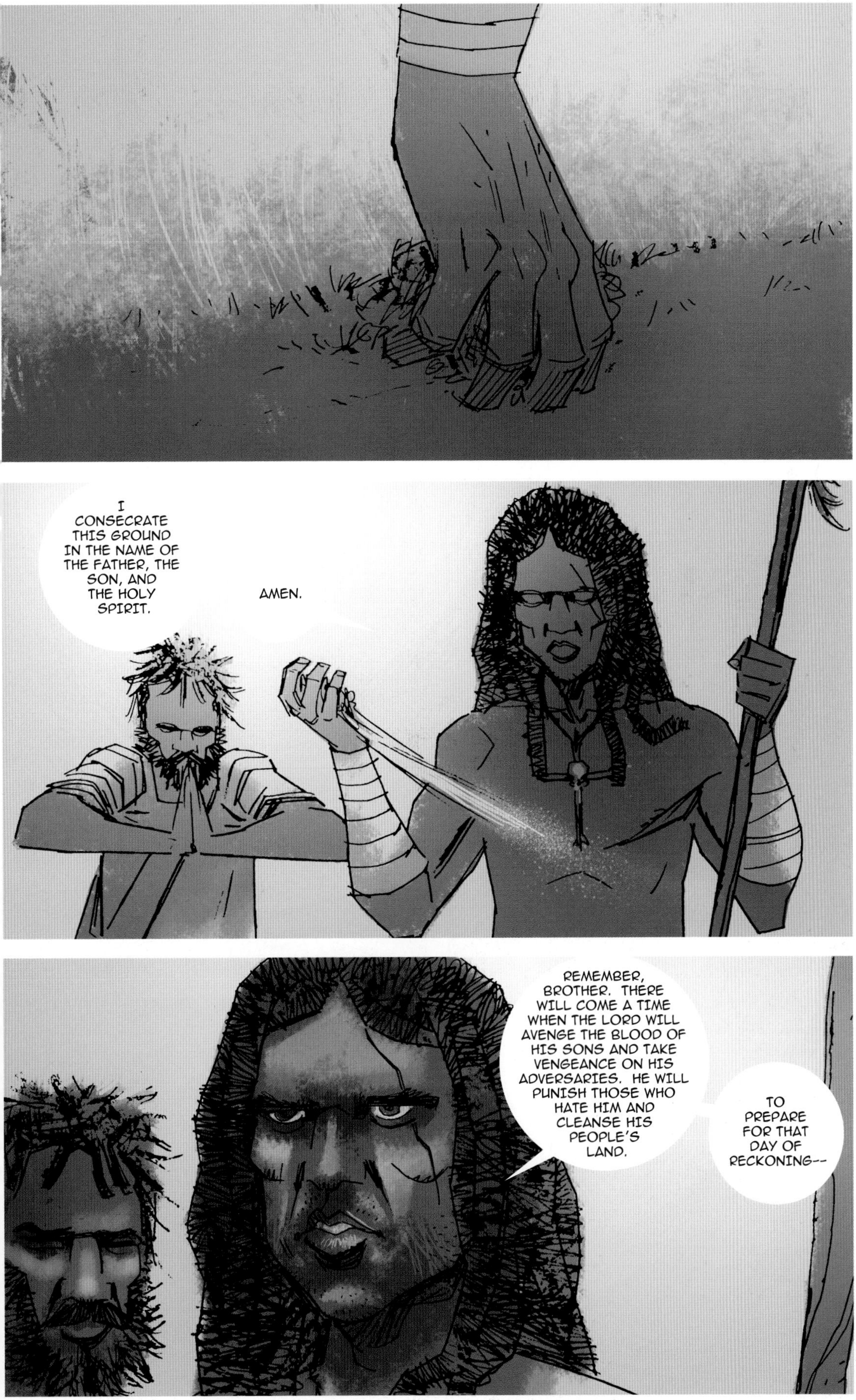
I CONSECRATE THIS GROUND IN THE NAME OF THE FATHER, THE SON, AND THE HOLY SPIRIT.
AMEN.
REMEMBER, BROTHER. THERE WILL COME A TIME WHEN THE LORD WILL AVENGE THE BLOOD OF HIS SONS AND TAKE VENGEANCE ON HIS ADVERSARIES. HE WILL PUNISH THOSE WHO HATE HIM AND CLEANSE HIS PEOPLE'S LAND.
TO PREPARE FOR THAT DAY OF RECKONING--

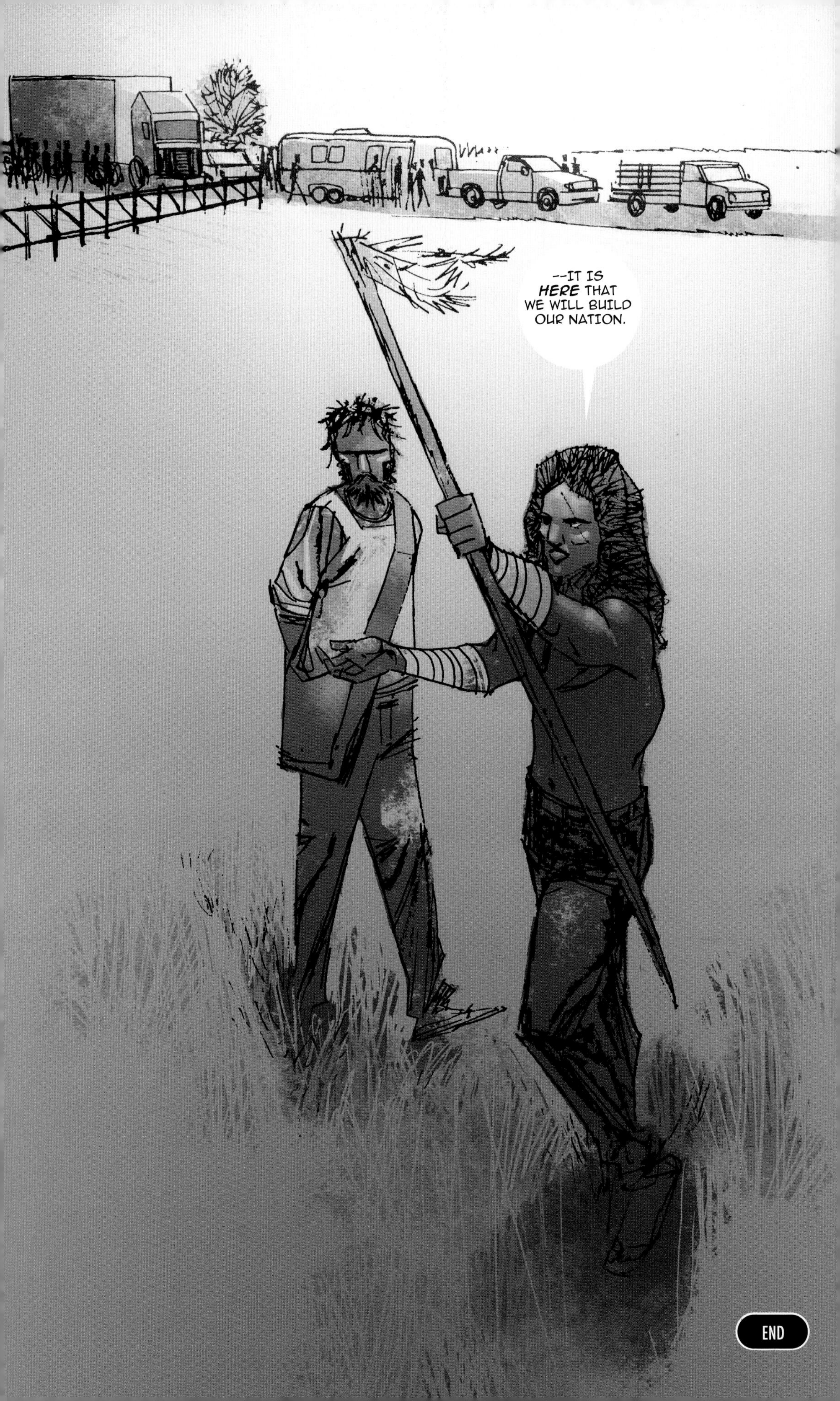
--IT IS *HERE* THAT WE WILL BUILD OUR NATION.
END

WITHDRAWN